The New Niagara

The New

Niagara

Tourism, Technology,
and the
Landscape of Niagara Falls,
1776–1917

William Irwin

The Pennsylvania State University Press
University Park, Pennsylvania

Library of Congress Cataloging-in-Publication Data

Irwin, William.
    The new Niagara : tourism, technology, and the landscape of
Niagara Falls, 1776–1917 / William Irwin.
        p.   cm.
    Includes bibliographical references (p.   ) and index.
    ISBN 0-271-01534-9 (cloth)
            0-271-01593-4 (pbk)
    1. Niagara Falls (N.Y. and Ont.)—Public opinion—History.   2. Landscape—
Niagara Falls (N.Y. and Ont.)—History.   3. Tourist trade—Niagara Falls (N.Y.
and Ont.)—History.   4. Industrialization—Niagara Falls (N.Y. and Ont.)—
History.   5. Public opinion—United States—History.   I. Title.
F127.N8I79   1996
974.7'99—dc20   95-48821
                                                                                                          CIP

It is the policy of The Pennsylvania State University Press to use acid-free paper
for the first printing of all clothbound books. Publications on uncoated stock satisfy
the minimum requirements of American National Standard for Information
Sciences—Permanence of Paper for Printed Library Materials, ANSI Z39.48-1992.

Contents

List of Illustrations

Acknowledgments

Growing up in Buffalo, I have known Niagara Falls almost my entire life. But at no time in my wildest dreams did I ever imagine myself capable of having such an intimate, committed long-term relationship with a place. Since a fateful day in graduate school when I changed dissertation topics, however, Niagara Falls has seldom been out of my thoughts. As I finish this project in South Africa, I realize that when I return home and this book is published, Niagara and I will enter a new phase of our relationship. It is a phase I am very much looking forward to.

A great many people have helped in the preparation of this book. Over the last several years I have spent countless hours at the Buffalo and Erie County Historical Society. I am forever grateful to Director of Library and Archives Mary F. Bell, and also to Pat Virgil, Yvonne Foote, and Cathy Mason. Donald Loker lent his expertise on my visits to the Local History Room of the Niagara Falls Public Library, and William P. Loos did the same at the Rare Book Room of the Buffalo and Erie County Public Library. I owe a special debt of gratitude to the staff in Special Collections at the University of Virginia Library, and thanks especially to my dear friend Heather Moore.

When my work on Niagara Falls was a dissertation, Professors Joseph F. Kett and Richard Guy Wilson helped shape my thesis. At various stages of the project, James Tice Moore, Cindy Aron, Robert Cross, Mark Mastromarino, Mike Milligan, Nancy Regan, Scott Burnet, Larry Hartzell, and Drew Vandecreek read sections of the manuscript and offered valuable criticism. I don't know how I would have carried through the project without the great insight and wise counseling of my good friend Jon Kates. Bryson Clevenger lent his superb reference skills, always on very short notice. Loren Quiring helped me overcome many a computer glitch, and Ben Philpot came to my rescue doing my legwork while I was in Africa. Special thanks also go to Pauline Page and James Klein for taking the photographs for the book. My colleagues in the History Department at the University of Natal in Durban, South Africa, generously indulged my transoceanic neuroses and taught me how to use the fax machine. And I have been extremely fortunate to have Peter Potter and Peggy Hoover at Penn State Press apply their talents to the manuscript. Lastly, I will never be able to thank Frances Irwin, Barbara Irwin, James Klein, and Dorris M. Lueth enough for all they have done to help me along. Countless times they literally ran around Buffalo and Niagara Falls for me trying to track down whatever information I needed. More important, in addition to showing remarkable patience, they have always been there to offer warm encouragement and sound advice. They are my family, and this book is dedicated to them.

Introduction

When the correspondent Rollin Lynde Hartt contemplated the Pan-American Exposition for *McClure's Magazine* in 1901, he stood astonished at the influence of Niagara Falls. "'Exhibit A' of the Pan-American Exposition" was devoted to a "new Niagara Falls"—a reference to the marvelous technological advances and magnificent commercial and industrial ventures that had swept over Niagara. Moreover, it seemed that Niagara Falls had profoundly influenced the exposition's architecture, color scheme, sculpture, and electrical lighting. Combining technology with natural sublimity, Niagara Falls promised Americans new forms of entertainment, good taste, a less burdensome everyday existence, and cultural progress.[1]

Hartt was not alone in discerning the impact of a "new" Niagara

Falls. As engineers, entrepreneurs, promoters, and tourists found new uses for the Falls, Americans in the nineteenth century referred repeatedly to Niagara's "newness." The world's first clear span railway suspension bridge established Niagara as a dramatic bridge-building site and a favorite target of industrial developers. The campaign to preserve Niagara Falls and the creation of a New York State Reservation signaled another new Niagara: New York State's use of the most advanced principles of landscape architecture to eradicate tawdry commercialism and preserve Niagara's natural splendor. Most noteworthy of all is that Niagara ushered in America's "electricity age." With the harnessing of Niagara's power, a cleaner, more efficient, productive, prosperous, and humane industrial order seemed to be ensured. "Niagarics," a term that came to be used to explain the harnessing of waterfalls everywhere, revolutionized the world, as hydroelectric power turned other American waterfalls into smaller replicas of this new Niagara.[2]

At Niagara itself, the sudden arrival of power plants and attending industries transformed a once sleepy tourist hamlet into one of the leading production centers in America. By the dawn of the twentieth century, the new Niagara Falls knew no bounds, and utopian writers and respected scientists predicted that Niagara would become the electropolis of America and the world's new metropolis. The Pan-American Exposition in Buffalo in 1901 showcased all that this new Niagara promised.

The New Niagara explores Niagara's cultural significance as an icon of progress and technology. That Niagara played an important role in American culture is not a new idea. Excellent studies examine the cataract's spur to the romantic imagination and treat the responses of artists and writers to the Falls.[3] This book goes beyond earlier work by examining how images of the Falls as sublime nature gave way to the Falls as a source of a better or even utopian future based on technology. It examines the developmental and technological achievements—what I call the "New Niagara"—that transformed Niagara and reshaped its images.

Contemporaries from the mid-nineteenth century onward read their visions of economic and cultural development into Niagara. In the New Niagara, the Falls assumed new, positive meanings that were of greater cultural importance than its sublime nature. Thanks to their faith that technology could improve on nature, advocates for the New Niagara believed they had created an ideal synthesis of the artificial and the natural, the romantic and the utilitarian. This meant that the New Niagara would not only enhance tourism but also make the city of Niagara Falls an important commercial and manufacturing center even as it transformed work and family life in the United States.[4]

Throughout the nineteenth century and into the twentieth, the New Niagara manifested itself in an astonishing array of visionary projects. Although these projects concentrate most intensely near the turn of the century, from the nation's earliest days Americans looked for ways to associate the Falls with progress. They yearned for the day when the Falls would become more than just an inspiration to poets, and they constantly lamented the wasted water tumbling over the Falls. Thus there emerges a significant dimension of continuity at Niagara Falls from American independence until the 1920s.

My strategy in coming to grips with the meaning of the New Niagara in this formative period of American history is impressionistic rather than statistical. I have organized my chapters around the signal events or themes in Niagara's technological history: bridges and bridge-building; preservation and park-building; the arrival of the electricity age and Niagara's great powerhouses; utopian schemes; the Pan-American Exposition of 1901; and the Shredded Wheat factory. In recasting the landscape of Niagara, each of these roused popular enthusiasm for Niagara Falls, but each also revealed dynamic tensions between nature and civilization, economic and social concerns, and the changing focuses of tourist interest. Consistently, these developments publicized Niagara and served to enrich its significance for the mass culture.

This work is neither a town history nor a strict chronological narrative of Niagara Falls. I am as concerned with Niagara's image as I am with Niagara as it really was. I believe that the very notion of a New Niagara arose from the interplay between romantic ideals and actual conditions, and that images propounded by tourists, tourism promoters, engineers, advertisers, architects, and artists played key roles in giving content and form to that meaning. Niagara's significance, its lure for tourists, and its appeal to visionaries abided in those images and perceptions. In the second half of the nineteenth century, the New Niagara revitalized tourist interest and gave the landmark profound national significance for a rapidly changing America.

Any study of this type must necessarily be selective in its use of evidence. Millions of people, after all, visited Niagara Falls before the 1920s, and almost everyone else knew at least something about the Falls. The themes of Niagara's relationship to culture and to technology and industry recur again and again in the almost limitless variety of the visual and written record of Niagara Falls—in the arts, in advertising, in newspaper and magazine articles, in travel accounts, in poetry, and in fiction, as well as in the engineering reports and landscape surveys that appeared in technical journals and professional forums.[5]

My cast of characters is as wide-ranging as these sources and includes European visitors, America boosters, engineers, utopians, and food-faddists. I have, for the most part, analyzed only published material that relates to the American side of Niagara Falls, although wherever pertinent I make connections and point out contrasts to developments in Canada. My study is clearly biased toward the meanings that a very literate and leisurely or professional class of travelers, experts, and com-mentators—both American and foreign—ascribed to Niagara Falls. While this narrows the perspective of the analysis considerably, that perspective largely determined the prevailing American standards of taste and established the nation's mass cultural forms up until the 1920s. Finally, despite the exclusionary nature of my source material, I have been struck by the extent to which the whole culture embraced and debated the meaning of a New Niagara.

The history of Niagara Falls parallels the history of America itself. Between 1776 and World War I, that society and culture experienced profound transformation. Propelled by the relentless industriousness of its people, the United States displaced the continent's Native American population, implemented its brand of democracy, converted from agrar-ianism to industrialism, urbanized, and emerged as a modern economic and political power.

It is not surprising that the culture-at-large imposed itself on the waterfall in myriad ways. After American independence, Niagara as-sumed nationalistic meaning as the search for cultural/national symbols fixed on nature for America's identity. Initial development at the Falls coincided with America's eager embrace of the industrial and transportation revolutions. Land use followed the nation's developmental ethos. The emergence of the region as a tourist destination bespoke the rise of an American middle class, which adopted Victorian sensibilities. Typical of those sensibilities were the Americans that ambivalently romanced Niagara Falls both as a place beyond human purview and as the American landscape most worthy of supreme human achievement. At Niagara, huge construction and engineering projects revealed and demonstrated the physical transformation of the American landscape and the increasing professionalization and corporatization of nineteenth-century American economic life. The Niagara Falls Preservation Movement and the utopian predictions for the Falls displayed America's anxieties about the industrial transformation of the nation in the Gilded Age and the Progressive Era.

By focusing primarily on the second half of the nineteenth century, this book picks up largely where the recent Niagara scholarship of Elizabeth McKinsey and of John F. Sears leaves off. As McKinsey has shown, in early-nineteenth-century American culture "the sublime" implied not only magnificent scale, grandeur, and majesty, but also an aesthetic that relished the awesome, the untrammeled, the terrifying, and the infinite force and energy of God. Sublime objects cut to the onlooker's psyche, inspiring sentiments that were both intensely embracing and repelling. Niagara Falls was frequently held up as the quintessential example of sublime nature, and it became an important national symbol for America, embodying purity, abundance, and purpose, although the real juxtaposition of the sacred and the profane in the Niagara landscape revealed complex cultural values and tensions.[6]

By mid-century, the symbolism of the technological sublime increasingly supplanted Niagara's natural sublimity. Throughout nineteenth-century America, machines and technology proliferated. As historians Perry Miller, Leo Marx, and, most recently, David E. Nye have shown, the technological sublime, which invested canals, bridges, railroads, and other human constructions with transcendent significance, played a central role in forming American social and cultural identity. The experience of the technological sublime helped bring the American people together in much the same way that a state religion or long historical tradition established common bonds among the people of other nations.[7]

No landscape reveals the impact of the technological sublime as clearly as Niagara Falls. In the period from the mid-1840s until World War I, as nature came under human domain, Niagara Falls stood on the cusps of American progress. Great structures, machines, and systems were self-consciously artificial analogs to nature at Niagara. Meanwhile, an anxious public repeatedly looked to Niagara as a crucible for the latest advances in American civilization. Alternately fearsome and wondrous technology, romantically inspired by America's supreme natural landmark and tourist attraction, continually popularized Niagara and renewed national purpose even as it energized the debate over Niagara's proper role in the culture.

Throughout this book I shall show that tourism engendered both a development and an aesthetic of its own. Travelers who were never entirely comfortable in nature marked Niagara as a spot for improvement, and as tourist facilities and transportation systems increased the number of people who traveled to Niagara Falls these improvements became attractions in themselves. Thus, the dramatic reshaping of Niagara's landscape highlighted an ever-expanding tourist experience. Nature now had a rival in technology, but each enhanced appreciation of the other. In this New Niagara, tourists confronted contradictions and tensions between progress and tradition, nature and civilization, and beauty and utility.

As the artificial supplanted the natural in the Niagara landscape, engineers, developers, and entrepreneurs, like artists, found inspiration in Niagara Falls: for every visitor who hailed the Falls as a sacred, inviolate place of nature, another marveled at its raw power and dreamed of putting it to use. American nature, and Niagara Falls in particular, inspired imaginative visions of technological heroics and magnificent development. The heroes of the New Niagara looked to adorn Niagara with monumental improvements befitting the power and grandeur of the nature in the region. At the same time, they felt (or were made to feel) a unique obligation to add to the Niagara landscape without betraying nature. This took the form of deep concern for the aesthetic and cultural consequences of development. Even as they proclaimed the superiority of the built environment, they steadfastly emphasized the preservationist qualities of their work.

Where these two themes intersect, they suggest a heightened ideal that is unprecedented in the history of American landscape. From the 1850s to the early 1900s, tourists and engineers hailed the technological additions to the Niagara landscape as the fulfillment of America's promise, the optimum integration of nature and technology. The Niagara bridges, the state reservation, the electric power plants, the Pan-American Exposition, the Shredded Wheat biscuit and factory—all came to represent this great synthesis between the natural and the civilized world, with positive benefits for both.

Of course, this new Niagara Falls always remained perilously close to outright violation of nature's Niagara. Few landscapes have ever been subject to as much criticism as Niagara Falls, both for commercialism and for industrial development. Yet, despite its flaws, Niagara Falls captured the imagination of a nation eager to see, in technology, a new golden era. Despite profound ambivalence, Americans placed their faith in the New Niagara to drown out distressing associations. Especially in the period from 1850 to World War I, Niagara Falls became a symbol of an American future in which economic and technological development and natural beauty could be reconciled and mutually promoted and preserved.

In order to understand the American romance with technology and tourism at Niagara, one must confront Niagara's meaning as the quintessential natural landscape of America, for indeed Niagara Falls was perhaps the most recognizable early national icon. After the Revolutionary War, the new nation embarked on a quest for national identity. Having cast corrupt England aside and undertaken a noble experiment in republican democracy, Americans groped for appropriate national symbols and institutions to rally behind. The newness of the continent, the diversity and geographical distance separating the thirteen states, and the colonies' former cultural dependence on England all hindered the realization of a distinct American identity.[8]

In the absence of human history or civilized attainments, nature emerged as the most obvious and unique characteristic of the new republic. The 165-foot-tall Falls of Niagara, over which passed the entire flow of the waters of the Great Lakes, was universally known as the most sublime and awe-inspiring natural landmark in North America. But

Niagara Falls was merely the most profound example of a startling array of inland seas, primeval forests, endless prairies, and mountain ranges. The nation's expansive untrammeled landscape was a stark contrast to Europe's decayed, corrupt civilization and gave Americans a claim to superiority over Europe. The promising national destiny of the new republic was thus perceived as being intertwined with nature.[9]

As a symbol of America's unique nature, Niagara Falls came to have patriotic significance. Its position on the Niagara River bordering British Canada immediately to the north made it a gateway to the nation. In fact, although the Americans actually share the Falls with Canada, and the Canadian Horseshoe Falls is unquestionably more spectacular than the American Falls, Americans appropriated the cataract as their own proud possession early in their national history. John Quincy Adams told his fellow Americans: "You have what no other nation on the earth has: at your very door there is a mighty cataract—one of the most wonderful works of God." As the chief "icon of the American sublime," Niagara represented "the type of the country": "Look at Niagara. What does it represent? What does it resemble? Does it not resemble our country—our vast, unmeasurable, unconquerable, inexplicable country?" And magazine editor and cultural critic George William Curtis noted that American pride swelled "with a proud conviction that Niagara annihilates all other scenery in the world."[10]

While unmatched natural magnificence revealed divine favor, Americans faced the immediate challenge of building a new nation out of a vast wilderness. Many ordinary Americans found no romance in pristine nature; they revered the domesticated landscape. Natural bounty thus became a great resource for a growing nation. As Tench Coxe, Alexander Hamilton's economic assistant, proclaimed in 1787:

> Providence has bestowed upon the United States of America means of happiness, as great and numerous, as are enjoyed by any country in the world. . . . Agriculture, manufactures and commerce, naturally arising from these sources, afford to our industrious citizens certain subsistence and innumerable opportunities of acquiring wealth.[11]

The new American republic was faced with the task of utilizing the mechanical genius and ingenuity of its people and harnessing the continent's unprecedented bounty. Just what shape continent-building would take was a crucial question for the new republic because the character of the nation was at stake. According to the Jeffersonian agrarian view, virtue lay in a nation of yeomen farmers. Proponents of America as "garden" idealized the frontier farmer and the agrarian future. As Americans expanded westward, benign nature would ensure a land of farms and democratic plenitude. Simple, frugal, virtuous yeomen would busily sow America's limitless fields and maintain a happy society. Abundant, fertile land guaranteed a farm for everyone, precluding a repetition of the horrors of Europe's decadent industry and over-crowded urban conditions.[12]

In the new republic, the two potentially opposing threads of nature as garden and nature as primeval wilderness were linked when artists and cultural critics historicized the sublime American landscape. Niagara's wild, savage, natural energies revealed the primal power of God and of God's original creation; the earliest artistic renderings of the waterfalls suggested a corresponding sublimity that portended Nature's raw, uncivilized power over humankind. As Americans proudly trans-formed the continent, artists and imagemakers gained a measure of con-fidence in portraying the Falls, and once America asserted its cultural nationalism, images of Niagara increasingly suggested purity, prosper-ity, and empire.[13]

Niagara's role in early-nineteenth-century prints and geographies highlights these associations by suggesting that nature united with the genius and character of republican virtue. The 1801 print "America" pairs a plump female holding a sprouting vine and George Washington's tomb in front of a Niagara Falls background. Likewise, John James Barralet's "Science Unveiling the Beauties of Nature to the Genius of America" (1814) features New World flora, fauna, and a Niagara Falls background. The frontispiece of volume two of John Howard Hinton's *History and Topography of the United States,* Thomas Cole's "A Distant View of the Falls of Niagara," used Niagara in much the same manner. The topics in that volume included physical geography, natural history, statistics, and the state of society. Cole's panoramic view of Niagara, complete with two Native Americans in the foreground and all signs of development eliminated, stood for the purity and the untold potential of the nation. Hinton's chronicle of America's progress, meanwhile,

"A Distant View of the Falls of Niagara," by Thomas Cole, reproduced in John Howard Hinton's *The History and Topography of the United States (1832)*, vol. 2. Artists frequently used Niagara Falls to symbolize the purity and potential of America. (Courtesy, Special Collections Department, University of Virginia Library)

detailed just how far the nation had advanced from this wilderness state.[14]

By the 1820s, Niagara Falls and American nature answered a clarion call to supply a missing national tradition. Led by Thomas Cole, American painters and cultural critics embraced the landscape. In *American Scenery* (1840), one of the first American gift books, the editor, Nathaniel P. Willis, announced: "Nature has wrought with a bolder hand in America" and "There is a field for the artist in this country . . .

which surpasses every other." Niagara took its place at the top of a list of favorite artists' subjects that included the Hudson River, the White Mountains, and the Catskill Mountains. In the first half of the nineteenth century, no spot equaled Niagara Falls as a gloried American subject. Paintings of Niagara supplied a visual record of homage to the cataract.[15]

From John Vanderlyn to George Catlin, John James Audubon, Thomas Cole, Jacob Cropsey, John Kensett, and Frederic Church, America's great and not-so-great artists tried their hands at representing and re-creating the wonders of Niagara. Throughout the first half of the nineteenth century, dozens of American and European lithographers reproduced Niagara scenes, and Niagara images also appeared on household items and keepsakes. Gift books such as *American Scenery* (1840), *The Rhode Island Book* (1841), *The Home Book of the Picturesque; or, American Scenery, Art, and Literature* (1852), and *Picturesque America* (1872–74) attributed patriotic importance to the American landscape and urged Americans to explore Niagara. Together with published travel accounts and moving panoramas, these images established the primacy of Niagara as a national symbol.[16]

The growing flood of artists' images and traveler's accounts affirmed Niagara's sublimity and spawned romantic longings to visit Niagara in person. Responding to this publicity, and taking advantage of travel improvements and increased leisure time, a new set of curiosity-seekers descended on Niagara. Even travelers who went west in search of fertile lands and new opportunities took time out to view Niagara. In the 1800s, American travelers on the roads leading westward could be assured of encountering fellow Americans on pilgrimages to the Falls. Visiting Niagara Falls became a primary goal of travel in North America.[17]

The more tourists frequented Niagara, the more intellectual and imaginative effort they expended on defining its meaning and significance. Visitors acknowledged the religious emotion of the sublime. Niagara both brought them closer to God and illustrated the tremendous gulf between humankind and God or nature. Travelers' accounts, guidebooks, and artistic renderings demonstrate that tourists relished the "wonder, terror, and delight in the scene." According to Thomas Cole, "in gazing on it we feel as though a great void had been filled in our mind—our conceptions expand—we become a part of what we behold." No wonder guidebooks seldom failed to describe Niagara's "splendor yet sublimity."[18]

Once Americans took greater control of their land, Niagara's visitors were as likely to romance a human analog to nature as to bow humbly before nature. This naturally led to conflict between those who appreciated Niagara Falls for its natural beauty and those who saw it as a place to be domesticated. This same conflict led to the first nascent cries for preservation when the human hand tainted Niagara's natural purity. Decrying commercial and industrial enterprises at the great waterfall in 1830, the English subaltern E. T. Coke concluded: "'Tis a pity that such a ground was not reserved as sacred in perpetuum." In 1834 two touring Scottish Methodist ministers, Andrew Reed and James Matheson, protested proposals to develop Niagara Falls: "The Universal voice ought to interfere. . . . Niagara does not belong to Canada or America. Such spots should be deemed the property of civilized mankind, and nothing should be allowed to weaken their efficacy on the tastes, the morals, and the enjoyment of all men."[19]

At Niagara, nature was neither protected nor allowed undisturbed reign. Before the Civil War, the cataract had become an all-too-familiar site for tawdry tourist shops, utilitarian mills, and irreverent crowds of visitors. To those who found Niagara's meaning in nature, human control "stripped Niagara of its meaning" and reduced it to an often embarrassing commercial tourist attraction and industrial property.[20]

If, in fact, Niagara lost its viability as a symbol of nature in the nineteenth century, what was Niagara's primary intellectual and imaginative value to the nation? Did Americans regard Niagara Falls as a failed and aesthetically bankrupt landscape in a contest between those who wanted Niagara preserved and those who exploited it? Or, once shorn of untrammeled nature, could Niagara accommodate progress and industrial development?

An examination of the interconnections between tourism and technology in the Niagara landscape suggests answers to these questions. This book shows that the new Niagara Falls of technology and development rendered Niagara more accessible, more interesting, more enjoyable, and more inspiring to a wider audience. In the late nineteenth and early twentieth centuries, tourist facilities, bridges, parks, electric power plants, factories, and utopian schemes retained Niagara's identification with the ideal American landscape, embodied America's most progressive cultural values, and enabled the Falls to become an even more appropriate symbol of America.

1

Awakening to Niagara

Early American Development and Tourism at Niagara Falls

In an 1830 farce entitled *A Trip to Niagara; or, Travellers in America* by American author William Dunlap, the character Leatherstocking, a primitive-American type, criticizes the landscape around Niagara Falls as a crowning indignity. Although the west (including Niagara) beckoned with hope for true communion with nature, Niagara had become a disconcerting tableau of tourism and technology. "That was once wild enough. Fit to look on—but it's spoilt now. What has houses and bridges to do among the wonders of heaven? They spoil all—they spoil all." But the other characters in the play are on a touring trip, and their outlook is much different: they want even more improvements and amenities at the cataract. By the end of the play a note of harmony is struck. The natural majesty of Niagara Falls is reaffirmed, and the characters, including Leatherstocking, embrace Niagara as a happy mix of wild nature, homes, and bridges.[1]

Through its focus on genteel tourism, Dunlap's farce self-consciously raises issues about the appropriate landscape at the Falls and about the role of the Falls in American culture. In this regard, *A Trip to Niagara* is but one work in a seemingly endless catalog of maps, printed images, geographies, artistic renderings, literary musings, and published travelers' accounts that confirmed Niagara's ambiguous symbolic role in the emerging American republic. Niagara Falls embodied all of American nature, but a series of cultural and developmental changes altered the real landscape around the cataract. As the frontier line moved west, bringing with it improvements in transportation, the Falls accommodated entrepreneurial initiatives, heroic visions, civilizing manners, and patriotic expectations. During the era of American nation-building, improvements at Niagara Falls mimicked development at other cataract towns in the northeast. In fact, Niagara's special scale and natural magnificence inspired grander visions: inventors, engineers, and entrepreneurs deemed Niagara Falls the site most worthy for great human achievement.

Tourism and development bolstered each other at Niagara Falls. Improvements in transportation allowed for European-style pleasure travel in the American countryside. The rise of the middle class in the nineteenth century paved the way for a more widespread and diverse tourist industry. Tourists who embarked on a journey to witness spectacular nature marveled increasingly also at new technologies and structures in the countryside. For travelers and tourists who craved an even more diverse experience, nature alone was insufficient to sustain popular interest. Improvements and entertainments at Niagara became popular attractions for visitors to Niagara and consistent with America's energetic progressive outlook. At Niagara, visitors expected an ideal aesthetic environment and a practical mingling of nature and civilization and dreamed of adding wondrous artificial attractions to rival Niagara's natural scenery. Up to 1850, only technological limitations prevented the realization of this glorious new landscape at Niagara Falls.

The centrality of Niagara Falls in American culture was intimately intertwined with travelers' experiences at the cataract. As the preeminent icon of American nature, the Falls attracted an unending stream of visitors. But leisurely travel and love of nature did not exist in the wild, remote, undeveloped American countryside. In America, as historians Hans Huth, Roderick Nash, Perry Miller, and Leo Marx found, nature was a fearsome and formidable obstacle to inhabitants before it became an object of affection. Until Niagara Falls could be brought under human control, the great cataract remained too remote, too imposing, too primitive, and too threatening to be an enjoyable place to visit.[2]

The early artists, pioneers, traders, surveyors, missionaries, and adventurers who braved the American wilderness to behold Niagara encountered a barely accessible cataract. Long-distance land travel was an excruciating ordeal in the young republic, and the trip to Niagara Falls was an epic adventure that required the traveler to "scorn all fear." The 1804 poem "The Foresters" by Scottish-born ornithologist Alexander Wilson proclaimed that the deeper the traveler penetrated into the countryside, the more gloomy, tedious, and wearying passage became. British traveler Duncan Ingraham recorded that from the Genesee River westward to Niagara he traversed "ninety miles—not one house or white man along the way," following an Indian path. When Wilson encountered girdled trees, fences, fields, cowbells, and dogs—all of which signaled relief from isolated loneliness on his wilderness trek, he rejoiced, "Hail, Rural Industry! man's sturdiest friend." Wilson finally arrived at Niagara after "three long weeks by storms and famine beat / With sore bruised backs, and lame and blistered feet."[3]

The adventurer's trials were not over when he arrived at Niagara. Catching a view of Niagara was no easy feat, because maneuvering around the cataract was nerve-racking, exhausting, and dangerous. Overgrown vegetation, the near vertical drop of the gorge, roaming Indians, wild animals (Niagara was a haunt of eagles, wolves, and rattlesnakes), and the absence of white settlers affirmed the savageness of Niagara. To get to the riverbank below the cataract, where the Falls appeared their most sublime, travelers descended the steep gorge-side on Indian ladders—old trees carved with notches for the feet, and branches and shrub vines serving as handles. Even on an "improved" ladder of 1805, one traveler noted that the swaying sent him hanging perpendicular to the cliff high above the river.[4]

"White Headed Eagle," with Niagara in the distance. This engraving by Alexander Wilson conveys the popular conception of Niagara Falls as a place where nature remains untamed. (Courtesy, Special Collections Department, University of Virginia Library)

After climbing down the ladder, the traveler still had to traverse slippery, jagged rocks to the base of the river, a descent that required great strength and endurance. Even at the riverbanks the loose shelf of slippery rocks provided such poor footing, and such dire consequences in the event of a fall, that even the most daring adventurers crawled on all fours. It is no wonder that René de Chateaubriand felt fortunate to have only broken his arm while trying to view Niagara.[5]

For certain visitors, Niagara's inaccessibility verified its sublimity. But while a traveler's code dictated that visitors experience Niagara from each of its precarious viewing stations, even the most adventurous travelers questioned the rewards, and many never risked trying to reach the best viewing spots. In the absence of tourist facilities and improvements, the words of an early missionary who encamped at Niagara still rang true: "A wilder or more frightful place is not to be seen."[6]

Despite Niagara's fame, facilities developed slowly around the cataract. Britain formally prohibited private development of its northern side of the Falls when it declared the property lining the riverbank at the Falls a Crown military reserve in 1780. Soon thereafter, a British army officer opened a clearing and erected a shanty for viewing the Falls. By the 1790s the tops of trees and bushes had been lopped off to provide more than one view of the cataract. On the American side, however, New York State, which owned a one-mile strip of land around the cataract, provided no tourist facilities. With just a few exceptions, only Indians inhabited western New York before the mid-1790s. Development and settlement emerged only after the sale of the state lands.[7]

This lack of development on both sides of the Falls increasingly surprised and disappointed travelers. European visitors, who by the end of the eighteenth century had grown accustomed to picturesque nature excursions, bemoaned the hardship of traveling in North America. Conditions at the continent's greatest attraction revealed just how remote and uncivilized Niagara remained. In 1796 the Duke de La Rochefoucauld Liancourt's tirade against Great Britain's neglect of the Canadian side of the Falls expressed the tourist's discomfort and dismay:

> It is much to be regretted, that the government of a people, which surpasses all other nations for fondness in travelling and curiosity, should not have provided convenient places for observing this celebrated phenomenon, at all possible points of view.

For a mere thirty dollars "the greatest curiosity in the known world would be rendered accessible."[8]

As bad as the tourist facilities in and around Niagara were, some artificial additions to the landscape foreshadowed the conversion of the Niagara region into a productive landscape. Native Americans had long used Niagara as a trading center and gathering place, and once they began trading with Europeans, the area around Niagara became an important portage. The French had built a small fort, a sawmill, and a mill-race canal near the portage in the early 1700s, and in the 1780s the British-Canadians enlarged the French mill and built a series of mills in the Horseshoe rapids.

These early additions to the Niagara landscape suggested commercial and manufacturing endeavors rather than conversion of the wilderness countryside into a domesticated landscape of farms. Agrarian ideal notwithstanding, foreign travelers in the American countryside foresaw a different course for America. Looking at the same natural bounty, they perceived that the industrious character of the American people could lead to a highly commercialized, developed landscape. In 1818, Frenchman Jacques Milbert claimed: "The American ambition is to rival England on the industrial plane," and during a tour of America in 1833, British actor Thomas Hamilton asserted:

> No man can contemplate the vast resources of the United States—the varied productions of their soil—the inexhaustible stores of coal and iron which are spread even on the surface— and doubt that the Americans are destined to become a great manufacturing nation.

America's most impressive natural features—its great river system, its cataracts, and its mountain ranges—all presaged internal improvements and industry more so than agriculture.[9]

America's indomitable progressive and enterprising spirit—a busy, democratic energy aimed at economic expansion—foreshadowed magnificent cities arising from the wilderness. Landscape artist Thomas Cole, in his seminal "Essay on American Scenery" (1835), looked at the American landscape and proclaimed all American associations future associations. Frederick Marryat echoed the common European refrain as he awaited the day when America's forests would become towns "with thousands of inhabitants, . . . with arts, manufacturers, machinery, all in full activity." Such anticipation reached the ridiculous when travelers looked in vain for the large towns that overeager surveyors and developers had drawn on maps.[10]

Niagara's sacral landscape, as well as its sheer magnitude and sublimity, discouraged thoughts of dedicating it to industry. But Americans had done little to reserve sacred places in nature, and Niagara Falls too was affected by the dominant themes of progress and industrious development. In fact, no tourist spot demonstrated the encroachment of development on nature more poignantly than Niagara. Niagara was fully integrated into the fabric of American society and culture.[11]

Throughout the American countryside, the real challenge of culling civilization from the wilderness precluded unqualified reverence for the pristine landscape. Americans pushed westward into the wilderness "as masters, determined to subdue it; and not as children of nature nursed and brought up in its bosom." Reflecting the prevailing ethos, the Americans who came across a pristine valley or primeval forest envisioned a magnificent landscape of fields, villages, mills, bridges, canals, and railroads. Frederika Bremer witnessed the indomitable American will to progress as a cultural trait:

> To hurl mountains out of the way; to bore through them; to form tunnels; to throw mountains into the water, as a foundation for roads in places where it is necessary for it to go over the water; all these Americans regard as nothing. They have a faith to remove mountains.

No homage to nature stood in the way of nation-building.[12]

As Americans shaped their environment, waterfalls, more than any other landform, excited ambition and prompted visions of potential development. These natural features called settlements into being and served as early meeting and trading places. River courses above and below cataracts furnished access to markets and easy communication. Moreover, before the widespread advent of steampower, waterpower represented the energy source and productive potential of the United States. The waterpower potential of a cataract promised to save labor, which was America's most scarce resource.[13]

In the eastern part of North America, where two continental shelves met, almost every river or stream had one or more waterfalls. By the first third of the nineteenth century, many of these eastern waterfalls had been put to industrial use. Because of its advantages in this regard, Oswego had numerous mills and manufactories. The mills at Glens Falls presented, for Harriet Martineau, "the busiest scene that I saw near any water-power in America." New England waterfalls at Lowell, Lawrence, Manchester, and Holyoke spawned mill towns, prompting Thomas Low Nichols to observe: "The rivers of New England cannot fall ten feet at any point in their progress to the sea without being made to propel some kind of machinery."[14]

This use of cataract waterpower was so common and predictable that Frances Trollope related the story of an American who apologized for the wilderness state of a waterfall. The American lamented that because an Englishman owned the site no factories had been built as yet and the waterfall remained idle. Were Trollope to return five years later, he assured her, either the Englishman would have become "Americanized" or he would have sold his tract. In either case, utilization of the waterpower was inevitable.[15]

As the world's greatest waterfall, Niagara suggested the developmental possibilities of other cataracts writ large. In "The Rising Glory of America" (1771), Philip Freneau and Hugh Henry Brackenridge predicted Niagara's role in the transformation of the landscape:

> Hoarse Niagara's stream now roaring on
> Thro' woods and rocks and broken mountains torn
> In days remote far from their ancient beds
> By some great monarch taught a better course
> Or cleared of cataracts shall flow beneath
> Unincumber's boats and merchandize and men.[16]

Alexander Wilson, awestruck at his first view of Niagara, proclaimed, "Lord, what a monstrous *mill-dam* that must be." DeWitt Clinton, New York State's apostle of development as well as an ardent naturalist, saw Niagara as "the best place in the world for hydraulic works." Christian Schultz, who traveled through the region in 1807–8, explained: "Nature having prepared everything, there remained little else to do but build them [mills]." Later, Spanish nobleman Diego Sarmiento wanted to consecrate his love of nature at Niagara through a "secret desire" to "stay here to live forever, to become a Yankee, and to see if I might acquire a poor factory by Niagara Falls to earn my living."[17]

Early developers recognized the potential returns not only from drawing off a portion of Niagara's waters for milling purposes, but also from making the Niagara River navigable. Because the Niagara linked Lakes Erie and Ontario, the cataract and the Niagara rapids were really the only impediment to a clear route joining the Great Lakes with the nation's inland waterway system. In one of the more outlandish schemes of the 1790s, William Tatham, an English surveyor, merchant, and engineer, envisioned erecting an inclined plane canal to overcome Niagara's inaccessibility. Believing that lock technology was slow and inefficient, Tatham devised plans for a new canal system that employed an enormous inclined plane to raise ships over obstacles. A huge masonry edifice "supported by arches and suitable columns" was to be built at the cataract, the roof of which structure would slope at 20–25 degrees to form the inclined plane that covered Niagara Falls. Waterwheels underneath this superstructure would trigger a gear system that would propel ships over the cataract.[18]

Given the strategic location of Niagara Falls as a gateway to the West, Tatham's canal promised to transform Niagara into "the grand mart for the raw and rough materials of interior American produce." Moreover, the waterwheels under the inclined plane would drive gristmills, furnaces, and forges. The result would be a great industrial village employing thousands and uniting Great Britain and the United States to enormous economic and neighborly advantage.[19]

Although Tatham's scheme fizzled, it revealed the scope of Niagara's interest to developers and entrepreneurs. The settlement and domestication of Niagara Falls coincided with the westward-moving land-rush and the opening up of the American countryside to a system of markets. By the dawn of the nineteenth century, Niagara stood squarely on the "developer's frontier." Though denied possession of a mile-wide strip of land bordering the Niagara River, the Holland Land Company opened land in western New York for settlement and development in the 1790s. Niagara was on the natural thoroughfare to the west, and westward-moving travelers found inviting farmland in the Niagara basin. Passing through the Niagara region on his way to survey the Ohio Valley, Augustus Porter coveted Niagara Falls as a magnificent milling and manufacturing center. He and other land agents, speculators, and entrepreneurs later took possession of the land around the cataract and started a settlement. Their efforts transformed the Niagara countryside from a fearsome wilderness curiosity into a growing town and popular resort in the first half of the nineteenth century.[20]

The most significant event in the early history of Niagara Falls development occurred when New York State opened the reserved lands along the Niagara River to private ownership. In 1805, New York State's land-use policy designated Niagara Falls as a site for productive exploitation. The state auctioned land tracts on the mile-long strip along the Niagara River. Whereas most lots sold for about $3.50 an acre, Peter B. Porter and Benjamin Barton jointly purchased the lots at the Falls, complete with riparian rights, for $18.00 and $13.50 an acre. That same year the state awarded exclusive trading rights to Porter, Barton & Company to transport goods by land and water around Niagara. The high price of these deals appeared to be proof that the site could be developed promptly for economic advantage. Niagara Falls was now fair game for practical improvement and entrepreneurial activity.[21]

Duplicating patterns at other scenic landmarks in the Catskills and the White Mountains, Niagara's first property owners chose sites close to the cataract or the rapids in order to profit from visitors' curiosity.

> Judge P. . . . informed me he should, as soon as possible, build a house near the best view of the falls, and appoint some proper person to keep a genteel tavern for the accommodation of the curious. He will likewise erect a stairs sufficiently safe and easy for ladies to descend to the foot of the falls.[22]

Upon purchasing the islands at the verge of the cataract from New York State in 1820, Augustus Porter erected a bridge to Goat Island, and just below the Horseshoe Falls on the Canadian side William Forsyth built Forsyth's Inn and a covered stairway down to the riverbanks. Soon bridges, paths, staircases, footbridges, taverns, and inns rendered both sides of the Falls more accessible. Pristine Niagara quickly passed into memory.

Meanwhile, the industrial transformation of the Niagara landscape proceeded apace. Niagara's owners saw no contradiction between development and romantic appreciation of the natural spectacle. Characteristic of the nation's relentless devotion to money and business, they almost immediately built mills amid the rapids. A woolen factory appeared first, in 1820, followed by a forge rolling mill and nail factory in 1822 and a paper mill in 1823. Likewise, the Porter bridge from the mainland to Bath and Goat Islands not only opened up unmatched new viewing stations but also led directly to the industrial use of the islands.

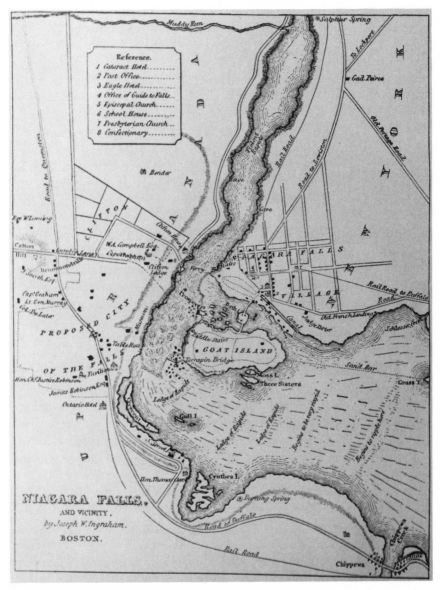

Map of "Niagara Falls and Vicinity" (1836), by Joseph W. Ingraham. Throughout the 1800s, as Niagara Falls became increasingly accessible to travelers, the area saw more and more roads, hotels, factories, and the like.

The Bath Island paper mill later became the largest paper-making facility in the United States. A section of Goat Island functioned as an iron-making site.

By 1824, "Grand Niagara," or "Manchester," was known as a mill town. Simultaneously with the completion of the Erie Canal in 1825, the Porter brothers published a call to eastern capitalists for investments. In announcing their offer to sell the islands and land adjoining the Falls, Augustus and Peter B. Porter noted that investors would assume the greatest water-privilege in the world; the many mills in the small town already suggested Niagara's potential. Half of Goat Island could be transformed into a great manufacturing center, while the other half might be left as a pleasure ground for visitors.[23]

From the time Europeans "discovered" Niagara Falls, for every nature lover who hailed the Niagara region as an eternal spectacle or an Edenic paradise another utilitarian visionary coveted its milling and manufacturing potential. Just like the nature lover, engineers and entrepreneurs found Niagara to be a romantic landscape. One ambitious scheme after another focused attention on real or imagined additions to the Niagara Falls landscape. Inventors contemplated putting waterwheels in the abyss, and waterwheel manufacturers tested their wares at the Falls; indeed, the waterwheel that withstood Niagara would work anywhere. Similarly, Francis Hall, who claimed to have assisted the heroic British bridge-builder Thomas Telford, hoped to install a tunnel directly underneath Niagara Falls. Although the idea of such a tunnel was preposterous, engineers were envisioning majestic bridges across the river. As the next chapter details, Niagara's fame and sublimity provided inspiration for nineteenth-century bridge-building science.[24]

Before such bridge-building became feasible, canal-builders sought to complete a continental waterway system by making Niagara navigable. Throughout the early nineteenth century, impetus for grand canal development at Niagara gained momentum steadily. As early as 1808, the national government considered lending financial and technical support for a ship canal around the Falls. Initial plans for the Great Western or Erie Canal called for a route around Niagara Falls. A ten-mile canal at Niagara, when joined to proposed short canals in central New York, would link Niagara and points west to New York City. This Niagara canal promised to add to the nation's military defenses as well as spur higher land values, increase trade, and effect a rapid conversion of the region's wilderness into productivity and tremendous commercial growth.[25]

When it was built between 1818 and 1825, the Erie Canal, which went from Albany to Buffalo, changed the face of New York State. For Niagara Falls, the canal held paradoxical implications. On the one hand, it bypassed Niagara and isolated the cataract from the nation's east-west commercial nexus. On the other hand, although originally conceived as a commercial avenue for produce, it popularized the trip to Niagara like nothing else before it.[26]

The Erie Canal permitted a regularized tourist procession to the Falls, instead of the unpredictable cross-state carriage or stagecoach route on primitive wilderness roads. Tourists could travel by comfortable packet boats as close to Niagara Falls as Buffalo, twenty miles away, or Lockport, twelve miles away. By reducing the journey across the state from nearly three weeks to a few days, the Erie Canal alleviated much of the hardship of travel. Indeed, the heavy traffic from canal passengers who ventured to the cataract from Buffalo created a more convenient land thoroughfare from Buffalo to Niagara Falls. For the first time, women enjoyed the tour across New York State. The American author Lydia Sigourney reported that "the facilities of travelling render it now a very different exploit from what it was in the days of our fathers," and George William Curtis conceded, "No one, I believe, not even the poets, sigh for the good old days of staging from Albany to Niagara."[27]

Easier transportation permitted genteel and middle-class travelers to enjoy the variety and contrasts of nature more comfortably. A popular guidebook author, Theodore Dwight, exulted: "Our canals often introduce us to the hearts of forests; the retreats of wild animals are almost exposed to our view."[28] The Erie Canal underscored anticipation of Niagara by offering tourists a delightful step-by-step unfurling of scenic wonders. In a tribute read at the opening of the Erie Canal, Cadwallader D. Colden gloried in the new synthesis between nature and technology: "We shall have around us the same great objects of nature: but instead of the huts of savages and . . . instead of uncultivated wilds, we shall be surrounded by a country yielding all that is necessary to the comfort of man."[29]

But the artificial additions to the landscape were often more interesting than natural landforms and vegetation in the countryside. On the way to Niagara, travelers found New York's Erie Canal to be a thrilling tourist attraction in and of itself. The Great Western Canal represented the boldest public-works project ever undertaken in the fledgling republic. Nathaniel Hawthorne overheard two traders from Michigan who noted that while Niagara was a site "worth looking at," "they would go twice as far to see the noble stone works of Lockport, where the Grand Canal is locked on a descent of sixty feet."[30]

In Canada, the Welland Canal held special interest because it "surmounted" Niagara. While the great Erie Canal effectively stymied plans for construction of a Niagara canal on the American side, its success in channeling goods through New York State led Canadian entrepreneurs to build a competing, northerly water transport route. Work on the privately funded Welland Canal, which bypassed both Niagara Falls and the Niagara River by forging a more westerly link between Lakes Erie and Ontario, commenced in 1824 and was completed in 1829. Theodore Dwight's *Northern Traveller* described the engineering accomplishment of the Welland Canal more floridly than it did the Niagara cataract. Humankind had scored a great victory over nature.

> The largest cataract in the world . . . was to be surmounted by a system of works in which the rush of the elements, so awful, resistless and destructive, was to be curbed and turned to a calm and gentle descent, and rendered useful to the objects of commerce.

Dwight's enthusiasm and rhetoric anticipated almost exactly the exaltation of the Niagara's power-harnessers seventy years later. The canal left the great Niagara "'divided and conquered,' reduced to the servitude of our race, rendered subservient to the complicated arts of civilization, and compelled to perform the most tiresome and trifling tasks in all their details."[31]

The success of the Welland Canal spurred plans for an American canal at Niagara among entrepreneurs who were jealous of losing shipping to Canada. Unlike the Erie Canal, Niagara's proposed canal was to serve the largest steamboats and schooners. Schemes calling for a deep ship canal that might also serve as a great waterpower facility showed the extent to which popular outlook on Niagara had shifted from seeing the Falls as an obstacle to seeing it as a tool. The U.S. House Committee on Roads and Canals considered two engineering surveys for a "ship canal around the Falls of Niagara" and in 1837 and 1838 pronounced the project practicable and acknowledged that Niagara's strategic and commercial location justified "this important national work."[32]

In addition to offering a military and commercial rationale for the canal, the House committee's report also stressed the intrinsic value that such an engineering feat would have for the nation as a whole. The proposed canal route would cover a section of territory acclaimed as "the most interesting on the American continent." The project merited support "if only to achieve a conquest over the mightiest of nature's works [which] involves a sentiment of sublimity." What seemed like a bastion of nature that defied human mastery would be rendered a grand and imposing "national monument of art, from its general usefulness to the country." Like the growth of Buffalo after construction of the Erie Canal, the area around Niagara would realize America's romantic vision of economic development and become "a monument to art and commerce, that eloquently speaks of extended social happiness, of fields reclaimed from the desert, of industry and talent usefully employed, and a thousand undefinable benefits to the human race."[33]

One artistic rendering of this visionary canal, "Proposed Ship Canal Around the Falls of the Niagara" (circa 1840), displayed the ordered, technological splendor that hopeful developers dreamed of. The rigid geometric lines and angles of the canal in the foreground overwhelm the background landscape of Niagara. While the Falls appear only as a misty beacon in the background, the monumental lock stands like a temple in the foreground. Square-cut marble stones form the locks and a promenade for fashionable tourists and military men. This lock system carries the vessels effortlessly through a disproportionately tall escarpment. The scale of the enterprise would equip the waterway to accommodate tall-masted ocean vessels. Human constructions provide the magnificence of the scene and silence Niagara, although the lush verdant land and the natural terracing of the forests on the cliff suggest peace and harmony in the landscape. Nature thrives all around the canal, but here Niagara is the servant of engineering endeavor.[34]

Niagara inspired engineers to dream of magnificent built additions to the natural landscape. This proposed ship canal around the Falls (1840) is as grand as Niagara itself. (Courtesy, National Museum of American History, Smithsonian Institution)

No such canal scheme ever surmounted Niagara Falls, however. Instead, Americans further domesticated Niagara Falls with the advent of the railroad. Whereas the Erie Canal carried travelers only as far as Buffalo, the railroad transported travelers to the cataract itself. Horse-drawn railroads linked Niagara Falls to Lockport and Buffalo in 1836, and in the 1840s two steam-powered daily trains connected Buffalo and Niagara Falls. To use a popular phrase of that era, steam-powered railroad lines "annihilated space." A trip from New York to Niagara Falls took as little as forty-eight hours in 1841; passengers observed that consolidating the lines and having a more efficient schedule might easily reduce the trip to thirty hours. Charles Lyell noted in 1841: "A few years ago, it was a fatiguing tour of many weeks to reach the Falls from Albany. We are now carried along at a rate of sixteen miles an hour."[35]

By the 1850s, the railroad and increased middle-class emphasis on leisure had ushered in an era of widespread tourism. Thanks to a burgeoning track network and low railroad fares, the United States became a "nation of summer migrants." America's summertime return to nature was largely a function of the desire to quit the business toil and the oppressive and frequently unhealthy climate of cities. At Niagara, the season lasted from May to October. In the mid-nineteenth century, most travelers to either side of Niagara Falls were leisure-class and middle-class Americans who came from the Buffalo vicinity or from eastern cities. According to an article in *The Crayon*, the Islamic pilgrimage to Mecca paled before the "millions of human beings . . . thus seen moving relentlessly about from New York to Niagara, from Boston to the White Mountains, from Newport to Saratoga, from Philadelphia to Cape May . . . , and so hither and thither all over the wide expanse of this vast continent."[36]

Just as significant is that traveling at "railroad speed" enabled those with limited leisure time to enjoy Niagara. Many visitors from Buffalo arrived in the morning, took a hack or a train to the Falls, stepped outside for a few minutes, and returned home to boast that they had seen Niagara. Traveler guidebooks published instructions for half-hour tours of Niagara scenery for "those who travel with rail-road speed."[37]

After the introduction of the railroad, tourist jaunts to Niagara increased steadily. The number of visitors at Niagara jumped from 20,000 in 1838 to 45,000 in 1847. According to one guidebook, more than

80,000 were expected in 1850. Once transportation improved, travelers began traveling greater distances to reach the great waterfalls. As Harriet Martineau said, "the world is fairly awakened to Niagara."[38]

The world "awakened to Niagara" only after improvements in transportation and tourist facilities remade the Niagara environment. Niagara took on more and more characteristics of a commercial town and had fewer primeval characteristics. By 1840, tourist facilities and industry became shamelessly conspicuous. Perched on either side of the cataract were Chinese pagodas, menageries, camera obscura, museums, watchtowers, tea gardens, wooden edifices, and curiosity shops. Likewise, Englishwoman Isabella Bird, upon arriving at Niagara, realized that what she had overheard about Niagara being a great water privilege was correct, "for the water is led off in several directions for the use of large saw and paper mills." And Sir Richard Bonnycastle lamented that an all pervasive "age of Materialism and Utilitarianism" had taken over Niagara.[39]

When development encroached on nature, travelers began to decry the "progress" at Niagara, contending that the rise of tourism had spoiled the more raw, adventurous, and reverent mode of experiencing the Falls. Some longed for the old days. Nathaniel Hawthorne bemoaned the diminishment of awe: "Blessed were the wanderers of old, who heard its deep river sounding through the woods, as the summon to an unknown wonder, and approached its awful brink, in all the freshness of feeling."[40]

By the 1830s a debate arose over how the land should be used and over the aesthetic appearance of the site and of the American landscape in general. While American entrepreneurialism carved out a civilization from the imposing wilderness, development was often mindless, tasteless, and ravaging. A tourist in New York State in the second quarter of the century said that some scenery lovers hesitated to publish glowing accounts of lesser-known waterfalls because "this [development] is all that water falls are good for now a days. I would describe it, but for fear of drawing the attention of some prowling villain, who would perhaps come and build a cotton mill."[41]

Critics from Alexis de Tocqueville to Thomas Cole were saddened by the loss of America's primeval wilderness. Cole pointed out an ominous trend throughout the American countryside: "The wayside is becoming shadeless, and another generation will behold spots, now rife with beauty, desecrated by what is called improvement." Tocqueville's warnings for Niagara Falls seemed real by the 1830s:

> If you wish to see this place in its grandeur, hasten. If you delay, your Niagara will have been spoiled for you. Already the forest round about is being cleared. The Romans are putting steeples on the Pantheon. I don't give the Americans ten years to establish a saw or flour mill at the base of the cataract.[42]

Despite laments over conditions at the cataract, travelers more commonly looked at Niagara's wondrous nature ambivalently. Nature's grandeur only temporarily obscured the visitor's dependence on development; travelers preferred a more familiar cultural presence. George William Curtis noted the irony of eager Niagara tourists exiting the train and lining up at the Cataract House hotel instead of at the cataract. Curtis pointed out that although Americans seemed universally eager to quit the city, "none less than the Americans know how to dispense with it." Thus, while Caroline Gilman lamented in *The Poetry of Travelling* that "this site [Niagara Falls] is ruined [by development]," she revealingly offered advice on the construction of a classical hotel at Niagara and hoped for cleared walks. Gilman's favorite nature scenes at Niagara came courtesy of engineering improvement; she believed that the view of the rapids from the Goat Island bridge "would repay nature's pilgrim, who comes to worship here." Even the view made possible by Terrapin Tower, which to many visitors signaled commercial vandalism at Niagara, "is the crown and glory of the whole."[43]

Traveler guidebooks hailed Niagara's improvements unequivocally, declaring that the new facilities rendered Niagara enchanting, pacified, and comfortable. American pride swelled at the utilitarian transformation of the landscape. Those who erected conveniences became Niagara's first heroes. Faxon's *Niagara Falls Guide* saluted George Whitney's industry for

> doing at all times all that industry and his means could afford in making improvements around the Falls and on his own premises

for the accommodation of visitors—first putting a ladder down the bank, and then a staircase; establishing a ferry and building bridges, platforms, and many other conveniences.

During her "Summer on the Lakes" in 1843, transcendentalist writer Margaret Fuller praised Judge Augustus Porter, who "heroically planted the bridge by which we cross to Goat Island." His "public spirit" further inspired him to carve walkways and carriageways through Goat Island's forests.[44]

While Niagara's natural wonders and scenic attractions lured them to Niagara Falls, many travelers recognized that conveniences and constructions added an extra appeal in the landscape. Technology became worthy of wonder and curiosity. Basil Hall described the bridge to Goat Island in greater detail than the cataract. The precarious siting of the bridge in the frightful waters near the precipice inspired Niagara's first aesthetic of construction. "One of the most singular pieces of engineering in the world, and [it] shows not only much skill and ingenuity, but boldness of thought in its projector." As a fitting paean to civilization's triumph over nature, guidebooks quoted Seneca Indian Chief Red Jacket, a vestige of Niagara's former associations with the untamed wilderness, muttering "——— Yankee, ——— Yankee" at the accomplishment.[45]

Utilitarian structures presented an arresting contrast to Niagara's sublimity and the sylvan beauty of Goat Island. Miss Caroline Spencer of New York City enjoyed the mill scenery during her outing on Bath Island in 1835. And on his first visit in 1860, William Dean Howells also found the Bath Island mills "picturesque." English author Anthony Trollope allowed that despite his distaste for Niagara's utilitarian structures, "it may be that they are not evils at all;—that they give more pleasure than pain, seeing that they tend to the enjoyment of the multitude." At a spot whose primary appeal was as a curiosity, disingenuous mills and structures were an additional fascination.[46]

No feature of the Niagara landscape manifested this ambivalence toward nature and the craving for civilization more vividly than the early resort or hotel. Hotel proprietors faced the difficult task of bringing order and organization to a place whose appearance and renown defied such constraints. Hotels played a decisive role in bringing civilization to Niagara Falls; they increased the accessibility of Niagara's scenic attractions, eased the burden on sightseers, and diversified the tourist's experience. Visitors welcomed them not only because they allowed greater communion with the environment but also because they suggested a more familiar world of convenience and social class.

An example from 1828 indicates the diverging tendencies of the resort-keepers' endeavor. During his journey through the Niagara region, Basil Hall noted how one enterprising property-owner converted his coveted wilderness tract overlooking the Niagara whirlpool into a park. He scrupulously cleared space for a house, smoothed the lawn, and installed a garden; in time, the property-owner expected his grounds to be a favorite resort among travelers.[47]

Such improvements revealed that neither property-owners nor travelers wanted primeval wilderness; they preferred a more reassuring cultural presence and a rational ordering of the land. The view overlooking the whirlpool was wild and harrowing enough for nineteenth-century tourists. By converting his land into a garden-park, the property-owner created an oasis of domestic civilization that was distinct from the sublime object of attention below. Smooth, manicured lawns and gardens reminded genteel travelers of their own homes. Social viewing stations removed the often-terrifying solitude of the Niagara experience. Indeed, William Chambers felt so at home on the grounds of the Clifton House on the Canadian side that he averred, "One could hardly believe one was out of England."[48]

Large hotels such as the Cataract House, the Eagle House, and the International Hotel on the American side, and Forsyth's Hotel (succeeded by the Clifton House) on the Canadian side, dominated the Niagara landscape and boldly bordered the brink of the cataract and the gorge. American author and editor Nathaniel P. Willis described how two travelers, arriving at Niagara on horseback and driven by anticipation and excitement about viewing the sublime cataract, finally arrived at "a vast white—hotel." On the Canadian side, there seemed to be "no village or dwellings but the hotel alone." William Dean Howells's first impression of Niagara returned again and again in his fiction: "Surely the hotels are nowhere else in the world so large!" Flanked by shoddy tourist booths, only these hotels proved to be permanent structures.

The white color of most of the hotels, and their imposing size, buttressed Niagara's conversion into a mixed environment of nature and progress. Because Americans typically conflated size with monumentality, hotels became architectural analogs to nature's achievements.[49]

Hotels gave Niagara's tourists the chance to experience nature without having to leave comfort, convenience, and luxury behind. Elaborate piazzas and verandas reached out to the surroundings. Genteel travelers enjoyed spectacular views of the Falls while resting in their hotel beds. Hotels introduced a unique indoor experience at Niagara Falls. Advertisements billed the establishments as monumental oases of healthy progress fully equipped with the latest improvements. One novel feature of the Cataract House was a privy-flushing system employing the waters of the Niagara rapids. A three-page description of the Cataract House lauded its new sanitary plumbing facilities. The addition of a colossal mirror to the Clifton House dining room enabled the visitor to "dine and gaze upon the greatest of Nature's wonders simultaneously." The mirror became a symbol of the hotel's—and Niagara's—place in the modern genteel world.[50]

Visitors' experiences revolved around the daily rhythms, social life, and recreational activities of the hotels. Indeed, the usual routines of tourist life prevailed at Niagara. As early as 1835, Horatio Parsons's guidebook beamed: "The fashionable, the opulent and the learned congregate here."[51] Niagara was part of what was called the "fashionable tour," the "Northern Tour," or the "American Grand Tour." Other stops included the White Mountains, Saratoga Springs, Trenton Falls, the Hudson River, the Catskill Mountains, and the Erie Canal. This "tour" reflected a broader attempt by antebellum Americans to emulate European-style elegance, comfort, and improvements. American gentility typically vacated the nation's cities in summer to retreat to spas or mountain and cataract resorts. According to Theodore Dwight, "the attractions of . . . scenery are redoubled by the presence of agreeable and refined society." Contemplation of nature was not enough; even at Niagara, travelers satisfied their curiosity about the Falls quickly and scenery-watching became subordinate to social entertainment.[52]

Niagara's burgeoning popularity as a courtship and honeymooning site further revealed the cataract's integration into America's antebellum culture of manners and amusement. Isabella Bird called Niagara "an abode of almost unparalleled gaiety," full of parties, picnics, dances, and flirtations. Nathaniel P. Willis's *Inklings of Adventure* depicted the flirtatious expectations of Niagara's visitors; bachelors found alluring women more captivating than the Falls, and newlyweds toasted each other rather than the cataract. A popular song of 1841 lampooned the newlyweds' choice of travel to Niagara: "Oh the lovers come a thousand miles / They leave their home and mother / Yet when they reach Niagara Falls / They only see each other." The song continues that when on the steamboat *Maid of the Mist,* "She forgot the Falls she was so busy / being hugged and kissed." Love conquered all, including Niagara Falls, as the impact of the cataract as a natural icon diminished.[53]

The era of mass tourism, with its contrived, sensational, and decidedly commercial entertainments, arrived at Niagara before mid-century. Tourists donned oilskin jackets and bonnets and received a certificate authenticating their venture behind the sheet of the falls. They viewed nature—including local flora, fauna, and geological specimens—in museums adjoining the cataract.[54] They boarded the *Maid of the Mist* for a steamboat ride up to the base of the cataract. The *Maid of the Mist,* as well as the Devil's Hole, the Buttery Elevator, and the Cave of the Winds, became distinct tourist attractions that stretched the bounds of the Niagara tourist region and demanded separate fees from guests. Adventurous spirits could not say they had "done Niagara" until they experienced those other attractions too.

Hotels and entrepreneurial ventures added to the popular appeal of Niagara Falls by crossing the fine line from enhancing nature appreciation to exploiting it. Tourist promoters recognized that travelers craved staged attractions to vary the monotony of natural scenery. In 1829, Sam Patch achieved national renown as the first conquering hero of Niagara when he jumped 85 feet into the Niagara abyss from a platform that extended from the Biddle Staircase on Goat Island. "Some things are done as well as others," said Patch. Thereafter, it became as easy to promote Niagara as a place for stunting as a place of nature.

Patch's jump pitted human beings against cataract; it inaugurated a craze of quirky challenges against nature that culminated in barrel trips over the falls before the end of the century. Patch's jump actually followed on the heels of a more publicized and organized spectacle that set nature against machine. In 1827, promoters filled a condemned Great

Lakes steamer, *The Michigan,* with dogs, cats, and wild animals (including a caged eagle) and released it to sail over the cataract. Broadsides asked whether the ship and its living cargo could survive the tumultuous plunge over the cataract. Even though the ship broke up in the rapids before it reached the cataract, onlookers enjoyed the carnival-like spectacle, and even scoured the riverbanks for souvenirs of the wreck.[55]

This cruel stunt, which ostensibly dramatized the duel at the Falls between technology and nature, revealed the excesses of the age of the common man at Niagara. Artificial contests and spectacles, rather than the lure of natural scenery, captivated the public consciousness. From Sam Patch's jump, to the later tightrope exhibitions in front of the Falls by the renowned Frenchman Blondin, staged events and daredevil shows lured thousands of visitors, especially nongenteel visitors, to Niagara. After the spectacle of *The Michigan,* landowners tried to attract big crowds again by blowing up overhanging rock platforms. William Leete Stone stood amid several thousand onlookers, "many of whom probably had never before had curiosity enough to see the falls themselves—even if they saw them now." No wonder a "distinguished English Traveller" lampooned both the relentlessly enterprising American character and the American enthusiasm for contests against nature in *The Crayon,* with his sarcastic report that a company had been incorporated to build a steamer to ascend the great Niagara cataract.[56]

Because travelers conferred so much significance on Niagara's artificial attractions and the built environment, it is not surprising that a rivalry arose between the tourist hamlets on each side of the cataract. Visitors who focused on the natural splendor of the cataract gave their plaudits to the Canadian Falls. The view from the Canadian side presented visitors with a full frontal panorama of the Horseshoe Falls. William Dean Howells, for instance, admitted:

> My patriotism has always felt the hurt of the fact that our great national cataract is best viewed from a foreign shore. There can be no denying, at least in a confidence like the present, that the Canadian Falls, if not more majestic is certainly more massive, than the American. I used to watch its mighty wall of waters with a jealousy almost as green as themselves, and then try to believe that the knotted tumble of our Fall was finer.[57]

When visitors considered enterprise and development, however, the American side outshone the Canadian side in economic development. Jacksonian America embraced the industrial revolution without the reservations of England. Americans rushed to build internal improvements and domesticate the landscape. They showed an unbridled enthusiasm for laborsaving machines, and revered signs of control over nature. Anthony Trollope said he felt as if he were going from a richer country to a poorer one when he crossed into Canada at Niagara. According to British author Amelia Murray, who visited North America in 1852, Canada had been misgoverned and was now "twenty years behind other American shores—[in] hotels, conveyance, cultivation and habits." English travelers bemoaned that the Canadians lacked the "go-ahead" spirit of Americans.[58]

The very name that residents of Niagara Falls, New York, chose for their town—"Manchester"—evoked associations of industrial magnificence. The fame of Manchester, England, had spread quickly to North America in the late eighteenth and early nineteenth centuries. Because the city's productive capabilities and fantastic growth provided a glimpse into the industrial future, Manchester became a popular stop on the elite Grand Tour of Europe. From a population of 17,000 in 1770, Manchester's population skyrocketed to 70,000 in 1801 and to 142,000 in 1832. Equally important, the wondrous machinery, the new architecture of industry, the artificial and organized processes, the furnaces, and the smells and tints of the industrial city all stunned the traveler. The city of Manchester embodied both the attraction and the repulsion of the technological sublime. Benjamin Silliman, America's preeminent scientist, called it "the wonder of the world, and the pride of England."[59]

By the early part of the nineteenth century, "Manchester" was a common name for any American township that showed promise for industrial development. Although some commentators noted the opposing associations of Manchester, Americans believed that the abundant farmland and sparse population of the countryside precluded a repeat of the evils of English industrialism, which had taken form in dense population centers. James Silk Buckingham acknowledged:

> The village that has sprung up on the American side of Niagara is called Manchester, because it was hoped by its founders that the great extent of water-power which could here be brought

"Signorina Maria Spelterina Crossing the Niagara Rapids on a Rope" (1876). One of the most popular of all Niagara stunts was crossing the gorge on a tightrope. Notice the crowd of spectators on the bridge. (Courtesy, Local History Room, Niagara Falls Public Library)

into operation from mills and manufactories would make it the Manchester of the West.

John M. Duncan's early expectations for Niagara evoked ambivalent associations with Manchester's smoke and congestion; he foresaw "wondrous changes" when factory machines would drown out the roar of the cataract and the smoke of industry would obscure Niagara's fabled mist. Parsons's guidebook of 1834 proclaimed enthusiastically: "This village is destined without doubt, to become one of the great manufacturing places."[60]

Not to be outdone, entrepreneurs on the Canadian side planned an equally bold venture called the "City of the Falls." Surveying and land allocation for this project commenced in 1831, and E. T. Coke noted that the British anticipated putting up utilitarian "grist-mills, storehouses, saw-mills, and all other kinds of unornamental buildings" and hoped to witness the growth of a "very populous city." Anna Jameson was sure that

> were a city to arise here, it would necessarily become a manufacturing place, because of the waterpower and privileges below and above the cataract which would be turned to account. Fancy if you can, a range of cotton factories, iron foundries, grist mills, saw mills, where now the mighty waters rush . . . in glee and liberty.[61]

Proposals of new developers rebuked the modesty of the settlements at Niagara. *Silliman's American Journal of Science* proclaimed that Niagara Falls offered the inestimable power of 4.5 million horsepower. Yankee enterprise promised to overcome the obstacles of the Falls and harness a power in excess of all the steampower used in England at mid-century.[62] Spanish nobleman Diego Sarmiento quoted a Yankee traveler who exclaimed that Niagara would fulfill America's industrial promise:

> Can you imagine that we will have at our disposition waterpower motors of forty thousand horsepower if necessary? Then the Niagara will be a street flanked for seven miles on both sides by turbines, each one with its own waterfall tailored to the need of

the motor. Ships will come to tie up at the port and carry merchandise to Europe and New York by way of the St. Lawrence. BEAUTIFUL! BEAUTIFUL![63]

In western New York, the man heralded as the inevitable torchbearer of Niagara's greatness was Benjamin Rathbun. A builder and entrepreneur, by the 1830s Rathbun had become the hero of Buffalo:

> The growing town needed a master hand to give it shape, and he became engineer and contractor on an immense scale. He brought land, built streets and squares, and carried out public improvements with Napoleonic and Hausemanic energy.

Rathbun's steamship and wharf construction at Buffalo secured that town's victory in its competition with Black Rock for the Great Lakes terminus of the Erie Canal. He built Buffalo's branch of the Bank of the United States and its first magnificent hotel, the American Hotel. This five-story, domed caravansary "was for years quoted by all American travelers as the *ne plus ultra* of hostelries."[64]

Rathbun's status demonstrated how the builder-architect became an early hero in American culture. While seeking to enhance his fortune and his reputation, Rathbun looked to nearby Niagara Falls as the proper site for his talents.

> His cool judgment perceived at a glance the pecuniary advantage that must result from the possession of a hotel sufficiently large and magnificent to attract and accommodate all the principal visiters to the Falls, of whom so many thousands annually arrive, and he at once set about its construction.

J. W. Orr's *Pictorial Guide to the Falls of Niagara* for 1842–45 detailed Rathbun's plans for building a grand hotel at Niagara. Sited just a few yards from the cataract, his hotel was to be a dome-topped, enormous 170 by 190 by 120 foot structure that would accommodate 600 guests.[65]

With the proposed hotel as a spur, Orr's guide predicted, Rathbun would do for Niagara what he had done for Buffalo. Now, however, he had a far more worthy and magnificent setting for his genius. The hotel-builder would enshrine God's plenty with irrepressible growth, progress, and greatness, fulfilling the promise of the American landscape.

> The prescient genius and active enterprise of Rathbun, stimulated and inspired by the grandeur of those incomparable cascades, and the glorious scenery around, would have reared a city there in a few years time, that would rival the creeping aggregations of a century and that too, by merely developing the wonderful resources of the place. It would have been no hot-bed growth, but a natural and vigorous shooting up from a rich and unhacknied soil.[66]

For all the talk about the encroaching city at "the Western Manchester" and its boundless industrial potential, Niagara Falls remained a mere tourist hamlet into the 1830s and 1840s. Deprived of a place on the Erie Canal route, Niagara's industries proved to be small and localized. Only a miniscule amount of Niagara's great waterpower was utilized, and recurrent plans for a Niagara canal fizzled. Until the 1840s, plans for erecting a span across the gorge remained only pipedreams. Benjamin Rathbun wound up disgraced and in jail for fraud and embezzlement. Meanwhile, the town at Niagara Falls retained its seasonal rhythms; by mid-October of each year, Niagara's hotels were boarded up for the winter.

Manchester also proved to be a fortunate exaggeration for many travelers. Anna Jameson sighed with relief upon realizing that typical New World exaggeration characterized the "City of the Falls" on the Canadian side. Since the City of the Falls was listed on her maps, Jameson "had no doubt of its existence till I arrived here for the first time last winter. But here it is not—Grazie a Dio!—likely to be, as far as I can judge, for a century to come."[67] Boomtowns on the Erie Canal, such as Rochester, Lockport, and Buffalo, brought home Niagara's isolation. Population statistics also told a striking story. The North American countryside had become a maze of fast-growing towns. In 1860, Toronto claimed 55,000 people, Buffalo 80,000, Detroit 70,000, and Montreal 85,000, but at mid-century Niagara's population remained under 3,000.

No wonder a Niagara guidebook of 1850 conceded that, at Niagara, "Nature has done everything, but as to the village of the falls, man has done but little." James Silk Buckingham judged by the roughness of the route to Niagara and the shoddy facilities that "this wonder of nature does not appear to have attracted such early attention from voyagers and travellers as might have been expected." The vision of Manchester was not fulfilled, "nor does it appear probable that it ever will." Even George William Curtis, who found the tourist bustle at Niagara poignant, admitted: "It is very thinly populated; civilization seems to have made small inroad upon the primeval grandeur of the spot."[68]

Many nineteenth-century travelers and commentators believed that nature continued to overmatch civilization at Niagara. The puny development at the Falls seemed merely to reveal the bad taste of Americans while affirming the magnificence of nature. Margaret Fuller said that while "people complain of the buildings at Niagara, and fear to see it further deformed, I cannot sympathize with such an apprehension: the spectacle is capable of swallowing up all such objects." Compared with the cataract, these human works remained as noticeable as "an earthworm in a wide field." Indeed, visitors proclaimed that nature merely tolerated human constructions, that at any moment the power of Niagara Falls might vanquish decades of development.[69]

Because of the cataract, Niagara continued to be the most recognizable landscape in America. Tourism, American aesthetics, even American self-identity institutionalized the natural appeal of Niagara Falls. But a tradition that glorified nature and the pristine American landscape abutted and even fused with a tradition that lionized development. In the first half of the nineteenth century, Niagara remained a natural landscape sprinkled with human constructions. The next half-century would show the triumph of the developmental strain at Niagara Falls. Cutting-edge development and technology would transform Niagara, and that transformation supplanted old Niagara's natural sublimity with a New Niagara of unprecedented technological sublimity and progress. For its proponents, the New Niagara entailed nothing short of humankind rising to nature's level at Niagara. In the mid-nineteenth century, Americans believed that the realization of this ideal became more likely with each passing day.

2

Bridge to a New Niagara

In the mid-nineteenth century, few human accomplishments earned more distinction for American civilization or proved to be a more appropriate paradigm for America's cultural promise than John A. Roebling's Niagara Railway Suspension Bridge. Although Niagara Falls was America's most famous and revered natural wonder, nothing aroused as much interest in the Niagara landscape at mid-century as bridges. Beginning at this time, Niagara Falls became a great bridge-building site. Roebling's bridge (1852–55) was immediately acclaimed one of the preeminent engineering achievements in the United States, and by the end of the nineteenth century seven different bridges had spanned the Niagara gorge in view of the waterfalls.[1]

The way in which the public experienced and interpreted the Roebling bridge defined the cultural significance of the Niagara landscape. In the national consciousness, bridge-building at Niagara paradoxically suggested not only an organic relationship with nature but also the supreme triumph of humankind over nature. John Roebling's bridge spurred bolder bridge-building and engineering projects at Niagara Falls and throughout America. The Roebling suspension bridge ushered in the railroad age at Niagara Falls and paved the way for mass tourism and the industrial transformation of the region. Bridge-building installed Niagara Falls at the cutting edge of American progress and technology. Thanks first to bridges and railroads, Niagara Falls gained a new, technological cultural significance commensurate with its intrinsic natural wonders.

It is easy to see why a bridge in front of Niagara Falls would attract attention to American engineering. Just as the Falls symbolized America's nearly boundless and unadorned nature, so bridges embodied Americans' eager extension of progress and civilization over the wild landscape. For a young nation still trying to overcome a sense of inferiority from its lack of accomplishment in the arts and sciences, bridges were conspicuous and spectacular additions to the landscape. Thomas Pope, who wrote the first American bridge treatise in 1811, envisioned bridges as sublime works of science and as strong and elegant representations of American utilitarian art that could make up for the absence in America of traditional cultural signposts such as great public buildings, ancient ruins, or achievements in the fine arts. John Roebling, who today is best remembered as the builder of the Brooklyn Bridge, looked on his bridges as timeless monuments on their sites. By spanning America's greatest waterways, bridge-builders could achieve personal and national glory. It is not surprising that engineers devised inspiring plans to span the great Niagara, Ohio, Mississippi, Hudson, and East Rivers before levels of commerce made such bridges necessary.[2]

Because the Niagara River narrowed in the spectacular Niagara gorge just below the cataract, visionaries recognized that a bridge at Niagara Falls would crown the landscape with a magnificent human response to nature. In 1824, Francis Hall, who worked with Thomas Telford on the Menai Strait (Wales) Bridge (1826), proposed erecting a similar span at Niagara Falls. Since his youth, American engineer Charles Ellet Jr., who would build the first bridge across the Niagara gorge, had dreamed of spanning Niagara, and in 1843 he claimed that a suspension span would provide "an appearance [that] would be unrivalled by any structure in the country, and perhaps, in the world." Ellet believed that such a project was the most gratifying his profession offered.[3]

Although a bridge could have been erected more easily a few miles downriver, the cataract's fame led engineers and investors to select a bridge site nearer the Falls. A committee appointed by the Legislative Assembly of Upper Canada concluded in 1836 that plans to erect a bridge at the Falls were "the least in consequence in a commercial view, but the greatest in a national one, as the magnificence of the scenery and the grandeur of such a conception evince." The first bridge built across Niagara's gorge joined the cliffbanks at the narrowest spot on the river that still allowed a view of the Falls from the east bank.[4]

In 1845, Canadian entrepreneur William Hamilton Merritt, one of the builders of the Welland Canal, and American engineer Charles Beebe Stuart led Canadian and American railroad ventures that formed bridge companies for constructing a bridge across the Niagara gorge at the Falls. In addition to its symbolic implications, this bridge project signaled both the zeal for economic development at Niagara and the emergence of the railroad in antebellum America. The profitability of the Erie Canal, the rapid settlement of the Great Lakes region and the West, and the failure of Niagara to be included in water trade—all combined to spur the desire for an east-west market connection at the site. At mid-century, railroad traffic increasingly replaced canal and steamboat traffic due to the rapid multiplication of railroad lines, added load-carrying capacities, greater flexibility, and year-round use. In the absence of an avenue over the Niagara River, goods and passengers traveled by ferry, which was slow, inefficient, seasonal, and expensive.

A bridge that linked railroads in New York to the western waterways and railroads would provide a transportation line from Boston to Detroit and ultimately to Chicago and St. Louis. Merritt looked forward to reaping the profits from the thoroughfare's freight-carrying trade as well as from the expanding summer passenger travel to Niagara Falls. Promoters of the project predicted that investment in such a railroad venture would prove "more profitable than that of any railroad line now in use on this continent."[5]

The Canadian-based Niagara Falls Suspension Bridge Company and its American counterpart, the Niagara Falls International Bridge Company, secured a joint charter from New York State and Canada to construct a railway bridge across the Niagara gorge, linking the Canadian and American sides. The project was faced with one of the chief engineering challenges of the day: to build a span capable of supporting enormously heavy loads over wide rivers and deep ravines. Anyone bridging the Niagara River had to design a clear span of 800 feet across the mean river. When the bridge companies solicited proposals from leading American and European engineers, "various replies were received, some in open condemnation of the project, others expressive of grave doubts of its practicality." Only Charles Ellet Jr., John A. Roebling, Samuel Keefer, and Edward W. Serrell submitted entries in competition for the commission. Each advocated a suspension bridge.[6]

Suspension bridges revolutionized the art of bridge-building in the nineteenth century. Because the strains on a suspension bridge diminished toward the center, such bridges could extend over great distances. Well-publicized suspension bridges, such as Telford's Menai Strait Bridge and the Fribourg Bridge (1834) in Switzerland, had brought distinction to suspension construction. In an era when spans of 300 feet were rare, wire suspension bridges would safely cross distances more than two and three times longer. Ellet and Roebling were America's pioneering scientific suspension-bridge builders. Ellet's Fairmount Bridge (1842) over the Schuylkill River at Philadelphia was America's first successful wire suspension bridge; Roebling achieved even greater renown by building the Pittsburgh Aqueduct (1844–45) over the Allegheny River and the Monongahela Suspension Bridge (1845–46). With their simplicity of line, potential for great length of expanse, and economy of construction, suspension bridges quickly became the most attention-grabbing style among scientific bridge-builders who contemplated spanning the nation's vast inland waterways.[7]

Nonetheless, the idea of a *railway* suspension bridge provoked controversy throughout the nineteenth century. In the 1840s no railway suspension bridges existed. Stuart recounted that, in response to the solicitation of proposals, many leading American and European engineers simply dismissed the possibility that such a light and flexible type of bridge could be made rigid enough to endure the strain of a moving train. Because so many American bridges, including suspension bridges, had collapsed *without* the burden of railroad traffic, the likelihood of disaster seemed excessive. In fact, in the early stages of the Niagara bridge project, the bridge companies entertained proposals for a bridge with cars pulled by horses rather than heavier locomotives.[8]

Compounding the case against railroad suspension bridges, famous British engineer Robert Stephenson introduced a new type of railway bridge just as Niagara awaited its bridge. In stark contrast to the grace and lightness of a suspension bridge, Stephenson's Britannia Bridge (1847) across the Menai Strait in Wales consisted of two iron tubes placed side by side and supported by piers at the ends and at third points. Great masonry entrance towers heralded the tubular bridge, which stood as an imposing, stolid structure in the landscape. Its rigid massiveness implicitly called into question the seeming insubstantiality of suspension bridges.[9]

The viability of a railway suspension bridge was to be proved at Niagara Falls. Publicizing this "exceedingly important project," the *American Railroad Journal* said: "A spirited competition will of course take place between the able and experienced engineers—*Mr. Ellet* and *Mr. John A. Roebling*—who have earned enduring laurels in the construction of wire suspension structures."[10] These two engineers represented markedly different temperaments and approaches to engineering problems. In November 1847 the Canadian and American bridge companies awarded the commission to Ellet, who promised to erect, at a cost of $190,000, a "secure, substantial and beautiful edifice—not one, however, equal to the claim of the locality—for nothing can match that—but a noble work of art, which will form a safe and sufficient connection between the great Canadian and the New York Railways, and stand firm for ages."[11]

In the words of Charles Stuart, "The engineering profession in this country has never had a more industrious worker, or intelligent or original thinker" than Charles Ellet. Ellet was a bold and charismatic promoter of engineering projects, although many of his plans seemed better in theory than in practice. His Niagara proposal called for a single-deck 800-foot-long bridge with stone towers, two carriageways, two footways, and a railroad track in the center. The bridge would be built for trains not to exceed 24 tons, which would be drawn by six-ton locomotives.

The bridge that Ellet erected at Niagara in 1848 lacked a substantial appearance and never served railroad traffic. Initially, two narrow footways spanned 800 feet across the gorge and linked opposite, 25-foot-high towers. Ellet planned on joining these footways to form a pedestrian/service bridge that would function as a scaffold for the principal, railroad bridge. Ellet's design called for a railroad platform suspended from 70-foot stone towers to be built directly above the service bridge.[12]

But Ellet never saw the latter bridge to completion. He quit the project because of a financial dispute with the bridge companies, leaving behind a fragile nine-foot-wide bridge. The addition of three-inch heavy flooring strengthened the structure to withstand a load of 250 tons. Although a far cry from a railway bridge, "the structure is now a thoroughfare perfectly safe for all business, . . . and has been adopted as the point of crossing for the line of stages to Detroit, Sandwich, &c."[13]

Ellet's bridge marked the affinity between engineering marvels and tourism at Niagara. Although some visitors decried any artificial alteration of Niagara's landscape as an outrage against nature and God,[14] most travelers deemed the bridge fit to span the chasm in front of the sublime waterfalls. *Burke's Descriptive Guide* asked, "What visitor could say, he saw the Falls of Niagara, but not THE SUSPENSION BRIDGE?" Guidebooks christened Ellet a hero and celebrated the bridge's features and utility. Well-traveled tourists compared it to the world's greatest bridges. According to Susanna Moodie, the first Niagara suspension bridge was "a grand and successful effort of mechanical genius over obstacles that appeared insurmountable." Alexander Marjoribanks was even more effusive: "Next to that wonder of nature, the Niagara Falls," he wrote, "may be placed that wonder of art, the Suspension bridge. This bridge, . . . though not above ten feet in width, is perhaps the most sublime work of art in the world."[15]

Ellet's work altered the Niagara tourist experience forever. Visitors immediately hailed the view from the bridge. Although the bridge was nearly one and a half miles from the cataract, no other viewing station offered a more uneasy and yet entrancing sensation of immersion in the Niagara environment. Emboldened tourists crossed the bridge giddily, braving the flimsy platform high above the rushing river. Marjoribanks called this "aerial excursion . . . thrillingly exciting" and attempted to convey a similar sense of wonder. The bridge, he observed,

> looks like a strip of paper suspended by a cobweb—being made of wires. When the wind is strong, the frail gossamer looking structure sways to and fro as if ready to start from its fastenings, and it shakes from extremity to center under the tread of the pedestrian.

The bird's-eye perspective from this artificial threadlike span reintroduced the sublime to the everyday tourist experience at Niagara. Majoribanks considered the bridge itself worthy of a trip to the Falls, "although numbers of people have not the nerve to cross it."[16]

Two years after Ellet resigned his commission, the anticipated railway suspension bridge remained a tenuous wooden carriageway. One view of a carriage "rolling just as like a ship" while crossing the bridge on a windy day was enough to dismiss the possibility that such a structure would ever support railroad traffic.[17] Moreover, the reputation of Stephenson's Britannia Bridge added to the anxieties about the feasibility of railway suspension bridges. In their search for a successor to Ellet, the two bridge companies even asked Stephenson, who had commenced work on another tubular bridge for the Grand Trunk Railway in Quebec, to submit a bid for the project. Finally, the companies granted John A. Roebling the contract for completing a railway suspension bridge at Niagara.[18]

Picking up where Ellet left off, Roebling endeavored to build a practical, secure, and aesthetically appealing structure. German-born and educated at the Royal Polytechnic School in Berlin, Roebling worked on several public works projects in Westphalia before emigrating to Pittsburgh in 1831. After an unfulfilling stint as a farmer, he returned to engineering and to his specialty—suspension bridges. His Allegheny suspension aqueduct and his wire suspension bridge over the Monongahela won renown for Pittsburgh as a place of beauty and massive public works. At the time he was selected for the Niagara commission, Roebling had the most impressive professional qualifications of any engineer in America.

Approaching this new project, Roebling was determined to build a structure that would be in harmony with Niagara's sublime site and befitting its importance. If he had been free to follow his aesthetic sense, Roebling would have erected a single platform bridge with graceful pendant lines that would have harmonized better with the Niagara landscape. Without budgetary constraints, Roebling might have indulged the impulse to ornament his bridge with a huge Gothic portal or "in massive Egyptian style and joined by massive wings; the cables watched by sphinxes, with parapets and all the rest of the approaches put up of appropriate dimensions."[19]

This preference for the Egyptian style betokened an Egyptian revival in monumental architecture in the United States during the middle third of the nineteenth century, as well as Roebling's conscious search for the most appropriate symbolism in his engineering. Egyptian motifs evoked sublime associations and, after Isambard Kingdom Brunel's Clifton Bridge (1831) in England, became specifically associated with suspension bridges. The upward tapering of Egyptian pylons and piers from thick, massive bases proved functionally adapted to the needs of suspension bridges and was cheaper than a Gothic portal scheme. Egyptian towers suggested learning, engineering, permanence, and harmony with their sites, and engineers hoped these associations would reassure a dubious public of the security of suspension bridges. Finally, at Niagara Falls, associations with the world's oldest civilization were fitting for a site whose gorge sides revealed America's timeless geologic antiquity.[20]

Although he did erect less-elaborate Egyptian towers, Roebling addressed financial and safety considerations by devising a double platform structure at Niagara. He conceded that a narrower, less expensive, double-deck bridge lacked the beauty of a single platform structure. Nonetheless,

> the double-floor bridge . . . will, however, present a very graceful, simple, but at the same time, substantial appearance. The four massive cables, supported on isolated columns, of a very substantial make, will form the characteristic of the work; and this will be unique and striking in its effect and quite in keeping with the surrounding scenery.[21]

Roebling's aesthetic considerations aside, the stickiest question about the pioneering Niagara bridge was not whether it was fit to stand but whether it *would* stand. Could it support a moving train? As late as June 1852, a correspondent for *Scientific American,* one of America's leading scientific and engineering journals, dismissed the possibility of a railway addition to the suspension bridge at Niagara.[22] American engineering was clearly on trial. In the face of doubts from the international engineering community, the Roebling bridge seemed to be another reckless American project. Roebling even halted construction and reassessed his bridge in 1854 when he heard the shocking news that Ellet's suspension bridge at Wheeling, West Virginia, had collapsed. The Wheeling disaster was especially distressing because of Ellet's ties to the Niagara bridge and his eminent reputation in engineering circles. Roebling acknowledged the dire implications of the tragedy for all suspension bridges: "One of the scientific journals remarked at the time, that the failure of this bridge would appear to be conclusive evidence against the practicability of *large* spans."[23]

To counteract misgivings about the railroad suspension bridge, the *Niagara Falls Gazette* pointed out that Roebling's superior engineering skill belied the frail appearance of the span. "His numerous iron structures are yet standing and have stood for many years as evidence of his ability and are monuments to his fame." During an era of loose professionalization in American engineering, when "any man (in the United States) who has carried a rod or chain is called an engineer" and when bridge-building commissions were frequently entrusted to carpenters and blacksmiths, Roebling's professional training in Germany further legitimized his project.[24]

Roebling took every possible precaution to ensure the construction of a safe and permanent suspension bridge. In contrast to Ellet's bridge, Roebling's double-deck bridge design featured timber trussing that joined the two platforms and provided extra stiffness. Like other engineers, Roebling calculated his bridge to bear more than five times the strain of its maximum load. He used an integrated system of weight, stays, girders, trusses, and anchors to stabilize the bridge. Taking advantage of the Niagara limestone on the site, he embedded the bridge cables deep into the local rock, and after the Wheeling disaster he added extra stays to further minimize the risk of oscillation in the bridge platform.

Ironically, one of the aesthetic flaws of the Niagara railway bridge was its excessively redundant safety devices. Nevertheless, contemporary engineers recognized that the pressures of erecting the first railway suspension bridge in the face of substantial public and professional skepticism justified those safety measures.[25]

On March 8, 1855, the first locomotive-driven train chugged across the Niagara Railway Suspension Bridge. Spanning more than 800 feet, Roebling's bridge nearly doubled the length of the world's next longest railway bridge. Its railway platform was directly above the carriage platform, making it the only railway suspension bridge in the world. The two decks hung from four cables, which were manufactured from wires spun on the site. Heavy timber trussing joined the two decks in the manner of a continuous hollow girder and gave the bridge an almost cagelike aspect. The Egyptian masonry towers stood between 75 and 90 feet high on each side of the gorge.

Despite the bridge's successful opening and years of reliable service, Roebling's structure remained a focus of engineering debate. Funding limitations forced Roebling to use lumber in the bridge's truss and platforms, but iron would have been a stronger and perhaps more permanent material. Roebling himself conceded that spending a few (but at the time unavailable) thousand dollars for an entirely iron structure would have alleviated his bridge's frequent maintenance woes.[26]

Observation added to the solicitude over Roebling's bridge. Trains crossing the bridge at the conspicuously slow walking speed of four miles an hour encouraged fears of the bridge's instability. Excessive stays, which exaggerated the spider-web look of the bridge, suggested the bridge-builder's own anxieties. The stodgy Robert Stephenson, upon building another massive and prohibitively expensive tubular bridge at Montreal, Quebec, supposedly said to Roebling, "If your bridge succeeds, mine [the Victoria Bridge, 1859] is a magnificent blunder."[27]

By 1860 debate over the Niagara Railway Suspension Bridge had become so heated that the renowned British engineer Peter Barlow inspected the Niagara bridge for the British Society of Civil Engineers. Barlow sided with Roebling. He lauded the bridge as much for its strength and stability as for its economy. Concluding that the stays

The first locomotive crosses John Roebling's Railway Suspension Bridge on March 8, 1855. Note the Egyptian revival towers. (Courtesy, Buffalo and Erie County Historical Society)

extending from below the platform to the rocks of the riverbanks were "an excellent precaution," Barlow insisted that the Niagara bridge was very secure and expected it to stand for "hundreds of years." "The Niagara Bridge . . . is the safest and most durable railway bridge of long-span which has been constructed."[28]

Roebling was frustrated by the engineering community's lingering skepticism. Despite verifiable scientific calculations, conservative building techniques, and the obvious utility of the bridge, the Niagara bridge faced prejudicial criticism simply because it was a suspension structure. "Vibrations which pass unnoticed in a bell or tubular bridge, boom up like distant earthquakes and threaten to destroy bridge and all, when the bridge happens to be suspended." A defiant Roebling compared his bridge to the world's other great bridges. "Where is the Railway bridge in this country or in Europe, which in point of economy and strength, will favorably compare with the Niagara bridge. That bridge does not exist." Roebling pleaded with engineers to judge his bridge in action: "One single observation of the passage of a train will convince the most skeptical that the practicality of suspended railway bridges, so much doubted, has been successfully demonstrated."[29]

Roebling enjoyed one great advantage in the ongoing debate with his critics. Because of the location of his bridge at Niagara Falls, public attention of tourists, artists, and even commercial promoters focused on the span. Souvenirs, photographs, and other widely disseminated images helped spread the bridge's fame worldwide. According to Roebling, popular prints (accompanied by publication of bridge specifications and construction techniques) helped to popularize and legitimize the structure even as they served as guidelines for other engineering endeavors.[30]

More important, everyone wanted to see the great new addition to the Niagara landscape. Like other sublime objects, the bridge had to be seen to be fully appreciated. William Chambers said the view from the bridge "is probably the most sublime of all." Although the cataract was in sight, some visitors were disappointed that it was so distant; the clarity of the day and strength of vision determined how distinctly a traveler could see the Falls. Much more inspiring and exhilarating was the sensation of looking downward into the gorge. Positioned on the

Roebling's suspension bridge became an immediate tourist attraction in the Niagara landscape. For some it even rivaled the cataract itself. (Courtesy, Local History Room, Niagara Falls Public Library)

gorge span, Niagara's tourists were approximately 250 feet above the river's surface. At this extraordinary height a heavy train might rattle over the heads of visitors, as gulls and other birds, sometimes even a bald eagle, flew below them. For Walt Whitman, who otherwise found Niagara disappointing, this scene from the bridge represented an epiphany of "some lucky five minutes of a man's life."[31]

Roebling's bridge did not convey instant assurance. One tourist who lauded the beauty of the bridge hoped it would "last for ever, though it does not look like it." Crossing over the bridge evoked the same feelings of terror and rapture that travelers experienced from dangerous vantage points in the days before Niagara was domesticated. Mark Twain recalled:

> You drive over to Suspension Bridge and divide your misery between the chances of smashing down two hundred feet into the river below, and the chances of having a railway train overhead smashing down onto you. Either possibility is discomforting taken by itself, mixed together, they amount in the aggregate to positive unhappiness.[32]

While it had been built primarily to carry passengers and freight, Roebling's bridge achieved a significance beyond its utilitarian purpose. Tourists gaped at it with a sense of awe, pride, and fear heretofore reserved for the cataract itself. Some felt exultation and wonder at the architectural grace of its structure. Its beauty "one cannot praise too much." The bridge, then, embodied the very qualities that Thomas Pope called for in his treatise. Roebling accomplished what Ellet had promised but failed to do. The bridge was both a noble work of art and one of the world's greatest engineering accomplishments. British visitor Charles Mackay quoted the proud American reaction: "Niagara is a handsome thing, but what is it to the bridge! The bridge! why, I hold *that* to be the finest thing in all God's universe."[33]

Thanks to its pioneering boldness and its siting at Niagara Falls, Roebling's Niagara Railway Suspension Bridge became one of the most recognizable structures in America and an instant symbol of modern America. Commentators soon began to analyze its form, significance, and meaning. Guidebooks proclaimed it "one of the few structures that not only harmonizes with the grand scenery of the vicinity, but even augments its impressiveness." For advocates of American engineering and promoters of Niagara Falls tourism, Roebling's bridge stood as a safe and appropriate addition to the landscape. Although the idea of a railroad bridge at Niagara Falls seemed to contradict natural laws— onlookers openly considered "it beyond the power of humanity to pass . . . over the chasm of Niagara"—no other bridge type matched the bridge's harmony with nature.[34]

Roebling himself thought deeply about the aesthetics of his bridge. His writings reveal a belief in the union of human works with God's divine plan for nature. According to Roebling, the engineer need only look to nature for the most economic models of strength and elegance—by mimicking nature in his creations, the engineer could reach his goal of bringing order and harmony to the world. Thus, Roebling denied that there was any novelty of invention in his bridge-building. From vegetation to spider webs, suspension bridges occurred in nature. Even the most primitive civilizations had spanned rivers with suspended vines.[35]

The lore of the Niagara Railway Suspension Bridge echoed this consonance with nature. The most famous story about the Niagara bridge described how Ellet's original bridge owed its genesis to a child's kite. A young boy flew the first wire across the riverbanks and made all subsequent construction possible. Set apart from other more cumbersome and unnaturalistic engineering feats, such as the tubular bridges, the new Niagara suspension bridge was in peaceful harmony with its environment.[36]

Although allusions to naturally occurring "suspension bridges" suggested the fitness of the design for a great bridge at Niagara Falls, contemporary visual representations of the suspension bridge suggest that Americans valued human achievement over its natural setting. At the same time that the landscape painter Frederic Church paid tribute to the majesty and sublimity of nature in "Niagara Falls" (1857), a new series of lithographs, gift cards, souvenir books, photographs, and advertising brought the Niagara suspension bridge into the popular consciousness. Prints with such titles as "Niagara and Its Wonders: Niagara Suspension Bridge" (1856), "The Niagara Suspension Bridge" (1855), "The Great International Railway Suspension Bridge, over the Niagara River Connecting the United States & Canada, the New York Central and the Great Western Railways" (1859), and Charles Parsons's "The Railroad Suspension Bridge, Near Niagara Falls" (1856), which later became a Currier and Ives scene, featured heroic representations of Roebling's bridge. Indeed, the bridge, as much as rapids and cataracts, became an instantly recognizable feature of the Niagara landscape.[37]

Just as these lithographic depictions of the bridge presented the public with an alternative to scenes of the cataract, the bridge itself rivaled the cataract for prominence in the Niagara landscape. Once again the prints mentioned above are illustrative, for the suspension bridge occupies the visual center in each. The bridge grandly links the two sides of the gorge, but Niagara Falls appears merely as a feature of the background. Perhaps more significant is that the cataract is visible only *under* the bridge. No wonder the *Journal of the Franklin Institute* referred to Roebling's bridge as "the Suspension Bridge over the Falls of Niagara," even though the bridge stood one and a half miles from the cataract.[38]

Prints such as "Niagara and Its Wonders: Niagara Suspension Bridge" were in striking contrast to Church's master painting. According to contemporaries, no single account or rendering came as close to capturing Niagara's essence as Church's.[39] The enormous size of Church's canvas, and its grand idealization of the sweeping curve of the Falls, pay tribute to the magnificent expansiveness of Niagara and America. The perspective of the painting creates an intimate communion with nature by eliminating any attenuating border and thrusting the viewer on top of the water at the verge of the precipice. Only in the background of the painting does Church subtly detail the human world at Niagara, yet so small are those artificial elements that they confirm Niagara as the province of nature.[40]

While Church's painting accentuates the majesty of nature, "Niagara and Its Wonders" gives Niagara Falls another essence. The print leaves the viewer wondering where the cataract is. Several of the smaller outlining scenes depict the Falls, but the eye focuses on the larger rectangle that encloses the bridge. Images in this rectangular center convey the pride in this triumphant conquest over nature. The solidity of the bridge and the disproportionately large, boldly colored American and British flags dominate the spectacle. The crossing train and carriage suggest the democratic productivity of the structure. Underneath the bridge, the Falls is relegated to obscurity by mists and distance. The Niagara Railway Suspension Bridge thus symbolized technology, progress, and patriotism in the national consciousness. The stately structure attracted onlookers who marveled at a new utilitarian monument. Beauty, science, and service made the bridge a glorious addition to the Niagara landscape and an appropriate subject for artists.[41]

From lithographs to photographs, from guidebooks to advertisements and travelers' accounts, a strong cultural nationalism pervaded the mean-

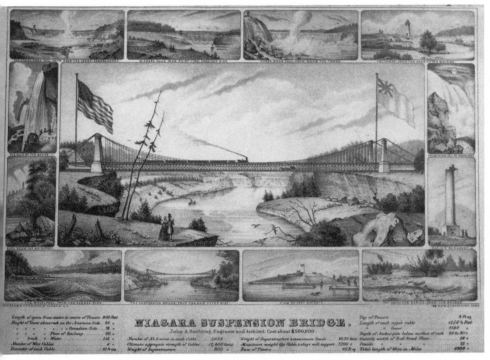

"Niagara and Its Wonders" (1856) shows Roebling's bridge as a wondrous and patriotic accomplishment of technology, nearly overshadowing the Falls in the background. (Courtesy, Buffalo Bookstore Collection, Buffalo Bookstore, Buffalo, N.Y.)

ing of the Niagara Railway Suspension Bridge. Throughout the nation, engineers were spurring technological growth, bringing fundamental improvements to everyday life. Americans who might have felt culturally inferior to Europeans (especially in the fine arts) reveled in the great engineering accomplishments in the American landscape. In assessing American railroad engineering in 1858, the *Atlantic Monthly* asserted:

> If America does not show a Thames Tunnel, a Conway or Menai Tubular Bridge, or a monster steamer, yet she has a railroad bridge of 800 foot clear span, hung two hundred and fifty feet above one of the wildest Rivers in the world.[42]

Bridge to a New Niagara　　　47

Widely published statistics on the Niagara bridge reinforced the magnitude of the engineering feat. Yet, American commentators who tried to define the nation's unique contributions to engineering immediately recognized that Roebling had built his bridge "in a manner peculiarly adapted to our country." Compared with the other great bridges of the world, the very *economy* of the Roebling bridge stood out as its most impressive characteristic. According to the *Atlantic Monthly,*

> Mr. Roebling's Niagara Railroad Suspension-Bridge cost four hundred thousand dollars, while a boiler-plate iron bridge upon the tubular system would cost for the same span about four million dollars, even if it were practicable to raise a tubular bridge in one piece over the Niagara River at the site of the Suspension Bridge.[43]

In America, the definition of civil engineering stressed economy. The American Society of Civil Engineers claimed: "That is the best engineering, not which makes the most splendid, or even the most perfect work, but that which makes a work that answers the purpose well, at the least cost." Recognizing the limits of financial resources in America and critiquing English engineering extravagance as well, Roebling insisted that the fittest bridge provided the maximum strength at the least cost. When compared with Robert Stephenson's costly tubular bridges, the economy of the Niagara bridge was a testament to the ability of American engineers to make more out of less than any other great engineer.[44]

Beyond economy, the Niagara Railway Suspension Bridge showed bold American enterprise in the face of doubt from the rest of the world. As the Niagara bridge served ever-expanding train schedules and carried heavier loads with no disruption of service, it verified the progressive vision of the American engineer. Without entirely silencing critics who continued to doubt whether the bridge was safe, proponents of Roebling's bridge applauded its utilitarian service. Ultimately, utility conferred success: from its opening until its replacement by the Lower Steel Arch Bridge in 1897, the Roebling bridge functioned safely.[45]

Today, the Brooklyn Bridge still stands as a monument to John Roebling, but the Niagara Railway Suspension Bridge was what made Roebling's reputation in his own day. Charles Stuart used Roebling's bridge as the frontispiece for his 1871 history of American engineering, *Lives and Works of Civil and Military Engineering in America.* In his posthumously published treatise, *Long and Short Span Railway Bridges,* Roebling asserted that the success of the Niagara bridge guaranteed the future of long-span railway bridges. Even before the Niagara bridge was complete, he was at work on bridge commissions on the Kentucky and Ohio Rivers. In 1857, two years after his work at Niagara, Roebling announced his proposal to link the cities of New York and Brooklyn by suspension bridge.[46]

Thus, although the Niagara Railway Suspension Bridge long remained the only bridge of its kind, it made a great symbolic contribution to American engineering. Americans who were just then awakening to a growing spirit of cultural nationalism acknowledged that engineering gave the nation a claim to greatness. As architectural critic Montgomery Schuyler said, bridges were monuments of the power of humankind to change nature, and no more formidable natural obstacle existed than Niagara Falls. The "Bridge over the Falls of Niagara" demonstrated to visionary American engineers the possibility of scores of other great or unlikely engineering projects.

Here the American continent offered chances for cultural distinction. The peculiar American landscape—an expansive countryside of spectacular chasms, canyons, mountain ranges, and rivers—inspired engineers to great accomplishments and tested the engineers' ingenuity in taming the most formidable obstacles nature could offer.[47]

Following Roebling's Niagara bridge, forward-looking Americans took the challenge as a matter of course. In 1865, Charles Woodman invoked the triumph of the Niagara Railway Suspension Bridge during his pleas before the U.S. Senate for approval to construct a marine railway on an enormous inclined plane around Niagara Falls:

> Every locomotive that thunders over the Suspension Bridge, rushing through space, over the seething torrent, bids us to beware of imitating the examples of those who, by utter disbelief, expressed by contemptuous sneers, have attempted to stop the world's progress and arrest the onward march of civilization.[48]

A *Scribner's* article entitled the "Feats of Railway Engineering" likewise proclaimed: "No heights seem too great to-day, no valleys too deep, no cañons too forbidding, no streams too wide. If commerce demands, the engineer will respond and the railway will be built."[49]

In the post–Civil War era of "technological enthusiasm,"[50] as the nation developed a comprehensive transportation system, bridge-building and railroad-building proceeded at an astounding rate. By 1888 more than 3,000 miles of bridges—enough to span the whole continent—had been built in America. While the railroad itself was commonplace (indeed, by 1870 it was almost inconceivable to build a significant bridge without making provision for rail traffic), spectacular bridges stood as obvious wonders. Contemporary commentators recognized that these utilitarian monuments were America's most characteristic cultural accomplishments. Although suspension bridges accounted for few of these structures, the most magnificent spans crossed great symbolic venues. In the nineteenth century, Colonel James Eads' triple-arch steel bridge (1874) over the Mississippi at St. Louis, and John and Washington Roebling's Brooklyn Bridge (1883), became national symbols.[51]

In the second half of the nineteenth century this real and symbolic human transformation of the landscape and conquering of nature occurred most strikingly at Niagara Falls. Before the opening of the railway bridge, Niagara had both the look and the outlook of a small town. During the 1850 summer season, only two daily trains linked Buffalo and Niagara. Roebling's bridge immediately fixed Niagara as a conspicuous crossroads on America's east-west travel nexus. Only a year after the bridge opened, nineteen trains served the area daily in season over four different tracks, and Niagara enjoyed its most profitable season to date.[52]

Lithographs and photographic images of Roebling's span indicate that both ends of the bridge became focal points for commercial development. The bridge actually shifted the locus of activity away from the settlements and nearest the Falls. The new town of Suspension Bridge rivaled the town of Niagara Falls for tourism and commerce, and in 1855 a five-story hotel, the Monteagle House resort, opened near the bridge. Disturnell's guidebook even referred to the settlement at Suspension Bridge as "Niagara City." While many visitors criticized this emerging town for its tawdry shops, tree stumps, imperfect roads, and decrepit factories, its appearance reflected the growth generated by the railroad and the bridge.[53]

Along with this heightened commercial activity came renewed interest in building more bridges. In the 1850s, Theodore D. Judah, who later achieved fame as chief engineer for the Central Pacific Railway, proclaimed that his Niagara Falls office was prepared to "build Suspension bridges of all kinds." Robert Stephenson even designed a plan for a tubular bridge across the Niagara gorge; a chromolithograph showed Stephenson's bridge adjacent to Roebling's.[54]

Roebling's bridge and the competition for tourism spurred calls for a bridge located nearer to the Falls to provide easier mobility in and around Niagara's main attractions. As long as the Railway Suspension Bridge provided the only gorge crossing, travelers who wanted to move between the Canadian and American hamlets at Niagara Falls had to travel nearly three miles to make the passage. Visitors paid twenty-five cents to cross the suspension bridge on foot and seventy-five cents for a round-trip carriage crossing.[55] Promoters and tourists also realized that a bridge situated closer to the Falls would present a far more impressive scenic view than the Roebling bridge. Even though the surroundings of the suspension bridge offered varied scenery, the Falls remained a distant blur to many visitors.

The Clifton Suspension Bridge, designed by Samuel Keefer,[56] opened just one-eighth of a mile below the American Falls on January 4, 1869. Originally only 10 feet wide, the wooden span that joined Niagara Falls and Clifton was the world's longest suspension bridge. More important, the narrow structure at Niagara was truly a tourist's bridge, providing an ideal vantage point from which to view the Falls. A carriage ride across the Clifton Bridge provided one of the world's most spectacular drives. And the span's intimacy with the cataract, as well as its narrowness, immense length, and airy, graceful lightness, led newlyweds to claim this bridge for their own. Unlike the Roebling structure, the single-platform Clifton Bridge came close to realizing the aesthetic purity of pendant suspended cables. In William Dean Howells's novella *Their Wedding Journey*, the newlywed couple agrees that "of all the bridges made with hands it seems the lightest, most ethereal."[57]

The Niagara Railway Suspension Bridge, and then the Clifton Suspension Bridge, established Niagara Falls as the world's preeminent bridge-building site. But no succeeding Niagara bridge received as much attention as the Niagara Cantilever Bridge of 1883. By 1899, *Scientific American* conceded: "It is not necessary to give any lengthy description of the cantilever railroad bridge, . . . so well is it known to the public." Upon construction, the Cantilever Bridge at Niagara assumed immediate national and international significance. Built for the Michigan Central Railroad by civil engineer Charles C. Schneider, the Niagara Cantilever Bridge was "one of the earliest successful applications of the cantilever construction" and became the exemplary cantilever structure.[58]

Ironically, Roebling's Railway Suspension Bridge at Niagara hastened implementation of this new cantilever style, because railroad companies had been seeking less expensive and more secure load-bearing alternatives to suspension bridges. "The object of the cantilever bridge," explained Charles Jameson in 1890, "is to make possible the economical construction of long, clear spans of a rigid truss, and thus do away to a great extent with the necessity of suspension bridges." In cantilever "erection by overhang," bracket-like arms extend from the piers piece by piece toward each other, and as the two arms approach each other they are united by an independent middle span. The cantilever principle reduces the amount of material in use and produces a lighter, stiffer, and less costly bridge, as compared with a suspension bridge.[59]

Schneider's bridge thrust another engineering marvel onto the Niagara landscape. Whereas the Roebling bridge essentially left the treacherous gorge side and riverbank unchallenged, the Cantilever Bridge tamed that terrain. Immense piers anchored in a concrete foundation over the irregular limestone boulders at the edge of the water rose up 132 feet on each side of the river. Two 325-foot cantilever arms extended bracket-like from each pier, and a fixed center span of 125 feet united these arms. Built of steel and wrought iron, the Cantilever Bridge stood 293 feet above the river and just 300 feet closer to the cataract than the Roebling suspension bridge.[60]

More awe-inspiring still was the speed with which the Niagara Cantilever Bridge was erected. The bridge contract was signed on April 11, 1883, ground was broken on April 15, and the bridge opened on December 23. Each day crowds lined the cliffbanks to watch the "thrilling spectacle" of the construction. The arms of the cantilever extended before their eyes as a traveling derrick put piece after piece into place. The pieces were then fastened with pins by workers suspended from platforms high over the river.[61]

Unlike the reception of Roebling's bridge, the engineering reaction to the Niagara Cantilever Bridge was favorable immediately. "The Niagara bridge is undoubtedly the boldest and best in existence, both in danger and execution, and it has in this respect, well-deserved the world-wide reputation which it has gained." The bridge was sturdier and built on a grander scale than Roebling's bridge, and heavier trains could cross the double-track structure at higher speeds. All these advantages came at a cost comparable to the amount spent to construct the railway suspension bridge thirty years earlier.[62]

The Niagara cantilever structure, like the Roebling span before it, stood for the progress of American scientific bridge-building. Side by side in the Niagara landscape, the two bridges vivified the continual triumph of the new over the old at Niagara Falls. Whereas the suspension bridge ambivalently harkened back to associations of nature and venerable civilizations, the Niagara Cantilever Bridge commanded the landscape with neither ornament nor allusions to Egyptian and classical antiquity. Widely distributed images of the Cantilever Bridge highlighted the structure's spindly trussing and vertical standards. Like other wrought iron and steel bridges, the Niagara Cantilever Bridge showed the lines of strain. It gloried its modern materials with machine construction in a modern motif. For the first time, a great engineering structure at Niagara proclaimed unequivocally the aesthetic appeal of the technological sublime.[63]

By the turn of the century America's best progressive bridges were built of steel. Following the invention of the Bessemer steel process, steel represented the future of American bridge-building; the strength and economy of steel was capable of bearing the greatly increased weight of American locomotives and rolling train loads. So it is not surprising that massive steel arch structures replaced the great suspension forms at Niagara. Articles on Niagara Falls in popular magazines labeled this change the most vivid example of "the New Niagara [that] lies at your feet." These new and modern structures, products of a richer and more

The sight of bridge workers dangling precariously above Niagara was a "thrilling spectacle" for the tourists who lined the cliffbanks. This drawing is from *McClure's Magazine*, 1901.

complex technological order, reaffirmed Niagara's central significance as the site of America's most impressive bridge-building.[64]

Two steel arch bridges, each built by Leffert L. Buck, replaced the Roebling bridge and the Clifton Bridge. Although steel towers and a new metal truss converted the Roebling bridge to a completely iron-and-steel structure, the Grand Trunk Railroad decided to erect a new type of bridge that could more adequately accommodate the heavier loads of modern trains. By the late 1890s the weight of locomotives approached 170 tons, whereas the first locomotive to cross the Roebling bridge weighed only 23 tons. As a link to the Railway Suspension Bridge, the Lower Steel Arch Bridge occupied the very same site; the old bridge was taken down while a completely new structure took its place, with no delay to train traffic.[65]

Despite this homage to the forerunning Roebling suspension bridge, the aesthetics of this new bridge, along with that of the longer and more spectacular Upper Steel Arch Bridge, bespoke progressive values in structural design. Simple efficiency and sparseness of lines characterized the new bridges. The steel arch bridges implemented graceful arches and presented an open, airy balance. Compared with the suspension bridges, or the straight truss of the Cantilever Bridge, the streamlined, unornamented steel structures were more efficient and more beautiful according to modern standards.[66]

Thanks to its geographic location and its bridges, Niagara Falls (in 1892 the town of Suspension Bridge merged into Niagara Falls) gained unprecedented railroad service for a town its size. Almost every freight and passenger line sought to run its east-west route through or past Niagara Falls. In the late nineteenth century the railroad turned Niagara tourism into a big business. Great trunk lines, such as the New York Central and the Hudson River Railroads and the Western Shore, Michigan Central, Grand Trunk, Lehigh Valley, Erie, Lake Shore, Baltimore & Ohio, Canadian Pacific, and Wabash Railroads, as well as electric railways, all vied for a share of the Niagara passenger trade. By the 1890s, during each day of the summer season ninety-two regular trains stopped at Niagara; on busy days, an equally high number of special excursion trains brought hundreds of extra carloads of visitors. Between May and August of 1897, excursion trains alone brought 276,900 visitors to Niagara Falls. While a large majority of excursionists—usually church groups, school outings, or trade groups—came from nearby Buffalo, a growing percentage originated from cities in the Midwest, from Canada, and from the East Coast.[67]

In addition, the Upper Steel Arch Bridge (1898) accommodated the electric railroad. The electric railroad was a perfect match for electricity-rich Niagara Falls, although builders faced an almost insurmountable obstacle in laying this tourist line. On the American gorge, an army of one thousand men blasted through rock and built the line out into the river wherever the cliff was too steep or the danger from rock slides was too severe. Thus, the most modern form of transportation of the 1890s extended for miles over terrain that, eighty years earlier, few humans were brave or strong enough to traverse. Now the finished tracks took tourists on a thrilling joyride through the gorge and along the banks of the raging river.

This "Great Gorge Route" and its Canadian counterpart (the Niagara Falls Park & River Railway) further democratized the tourist trade at Niagara. Thousands of pleasure-riders from Buffalo and other towns visited Niagara on lines that charged "Half a Dollar, and in Half a Day." Soon the new bridge served an electric rail belt line that joined the Canadian and American scenic attractions.[68]

Given the growing popularity of pleasure travel in late-nineteenth-century America, it is not surprising that each railroad line helped establish a new identity for the landscape of Niagara Falls. Each promoted the spectacular natural scenery available on its own right-of-way. Railroads considered their lines to be "attractions" and took pride in their ability to immerse travelers in an ever-changing panorama of scenic wonders. The New York Central Railroad billed itself as "the magnificent tourist line in the U.S." Its New York City to Niagara Falls connection was "the finest one day ride in the world."[69]

In the competition for passenger traffic, railroads topped each other claiming to be the true "Niagara Falls Line"; each stressed the "infinite variety" of the scenic natural marvels that its right-of-way showcased. Train routes hugged the gorge side and slowly crossed over one of Niagara's bridges. The New York Central's observation train presented a route that permitted a broad view of the Niagara River and gorge scenery. Michigan Central trains stopped for five or ten minutes at the "Falls

By electric railroad that ran almost at the water's edge, tourists took an exciting ride on the "Great Gorge Route." The experience revealed the wonders of the natural and the technological sublime. (Courtesy, Buffalo and Erie County Historical Society)

View Platform" on the Canadian side. The 300-foot platform was "on the brink of the Horseshoe Falls," and the *Niagara Falls Gazette* praised it as "really one of the finest views of the Falls anywhere to be had." Similarly, the Canadian Southern Railway, which ran trains between Buffalo and Toronto, boasted that "Passengers Have a Full View of Falls" from the same platform and that "all trains stop long enough to give a full view."[70]

While touting the natural attractions along the right-of-way, each railroad claimed distinction for the wondrous and sublime *artificial* attractions along the Niagara route. The very trains on which passengers rode became tourist marvels. Special touring booklets, such as the New York

Turn-of-the-century brochure for the Niagara Gorge Railroad. (Courtesy, Buffalo and Erie County Historical Society)

Central's *Two Days at Niagara,* from its "Four Track Series," artfully emphasized the luxury, comfort, safety, and technological wonders the railroad passenger could enjoy. *Scribner's Monthly* offered its readers a peek into the proud railroad mind-set when it published "Traveling by Telegraphy—Northward to Niagara," which described a special railroad company excursion. The excursionists feasted their eyes on a dramatically altered landscape. All along the right-of-way, tunnels, bridges,

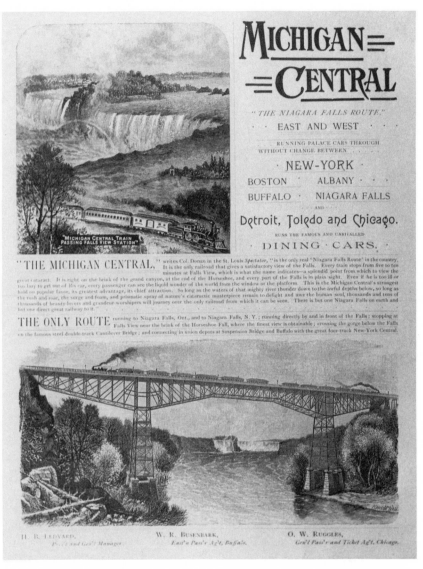

Several railroad companies had passenger routes that passed by the Falls. In this advertisement from 1885, the Michigan Central trumpets its "Niagara Falls Route" as "the only route." (Courtesy, Buffalo and Erie County Historical Society)

crossways, and even railroad workshops exhibited elegant design and engineering skill to overcome an imposing and adversarial landscape. Above all, "to a genuine railroad man there is nothing so pleasant to look upon as a new bridge—the newer and straighter the better."[71]

A great railroad bridge at Niagara Falls conferred credit on the line that used or owned it. Roebling's Railway Suspension Bridge confirmed the Great Western Railway as one of the world's great railroads. Tourist notices for the Niagara Cantilever Bridge announced it was the property of the Michigan Central Railroad; the line's advertisements invariably proclaimed that the bridge was "built and owned by the Michigan Central Railroad."

In a similar fashion, the Grand Trunk Line gained notoriety for its Lower Steel Arch Bridge, especially because the span was the successor to Roebling's historic suspension bridge. When the Lower Steel Arch Bridge was completed in 1897, the Grand Trunk Railroad staged a three-day festival to officially open the new structure. Since the opening of the Erie Canal, public parades and celebrations marked America's great technological achievements. For the opening of the Lower Steel Arch Bridge, a lineup of heavy locomotives on the bridge provided a powerful visible test of the bridge's sturdiness. County-fair amusements and fireworks brought the community together to honor the bridge-builder and the Grand Trunk Railroad. The ritual helped humanize the new bridge and diminish regret for the passing of the older, simpler era of the suspension bridge. Ultimately, the Niagara bridge celebration was a paean to progress. As a Grand Trunk Line souvenir booklet put it:

> Second in wonder and sublimity only to the great cataract itself, it [the bridge] lends an added interest to a visit to Niagara by its beauty and grace as a feature of the landscape, and as a triumph of engineering skill—a worthy companion piece of man's handiwork to be associated with the great works of nature among which it is placed.[72]

Throughout the second half of the nineteenth century, Niagara Falls remained a crucible for revolutionizing tendencies in bridge-building, and its bridges became models for the world. In 1901, Gebhard Napier wrote:

> The Niagara River presents a succession of examples of the methods by which the engineer of each generation overcame difficulties which opposed him by means best known in his time. It affords, indeed, something of an epitome of the history of bridge building.[73]

As the pace of this history and of engineering accomplishment quickened, Niagara Falls itself underwent a transformation from a sleepy tourist hamlet to a busy railroad center. John Roebling's bridge catalyzed this transformation and gave rise to an ethos of human mastery and control over nature that replaced the old Niagara of nature in the second half of the nineteenth century. The evolution of bridge-building itself revealed this transformation. Whereas suspension bridges embraced their natural setting, the later bridges and railroads appropriated the landscape; natural materials gave way to artificial materials. A similar transformation altered tourist habits at the waterfalls: artificial attractions increasingly supplanted natural scenery in the public consciousness.

What united the New Niagara to the old Niagara, ultimately, was place. Tremendous spans might be built and then overhauled or replaced by more modern structures, but the site remained the same. The Niagara bridges demonstrated special inspiration as well as creative and constructive genius. They stood majestically in front of nature's most formidable landmark and brought unmatched attention and acclaim to American engineering. With irony to be repeated, the timeless Niagara gorge and cataract had served as the chosen site for prototypical advances in one of the world's dynamic technological fields.

3

Preserving Niagara and Creating the State Reservation

In the American countryside, many waterfalls command admiration, but there is only one Niagara Falls. In the latter half of the nineteenth century, that often-uttered sentiment would have been both a tribute to the cataract's unparalleled sublimity and a plea for its preservation. Notwithstanding Niagara's continued busy popularity as a tourist attraction, it was both the excesses of the tourist trade and industrial growth in the area that eroded the cataract's identification as the emblem of American nature. Since the 1820s, landowners and entrepreneurs had developed ever more striking or tawdry amusements, facilities, and improvements, and by the 1870s, large mills and manufactories infringed upon the gorge-sides and riverbanks at the Falls. Not even Niagara's most hallowed viewing points were spared from the contest between nature and commercial enterprise.

While outraged tourists began bypassing Niagara for more pristine or peaceful holiday resorts, socially conservative, highly cultured reformers, led by Frederick Law Olmsted, came to Niagara's aid beginning in the 1870s. As they strove to create a Niagara reservation, these reformers imposed a Victorian moral order on the cataract and its surroundings and made the Niagara landscape a rallying cry for national enlightenment. By 1887 the broad-based Niagara Preservation Movement led by Olmsted eventually succeeded in securing government parks on the lands adjacent to the Falls on both the American and Canadian sides. Guided by a commitment to restore the scenic beauty of Niagara Falls, the supporters of the New York State Reservation at Niagara Falls, created in 1885, hailed the "new" Niagara that would be free from vandalism and secure from disconcerting commercial and industrial exploitation.[1]

The struggle to preserve Niagara often seemed to be a conflict of values between those seeking to use Niagara and those seeking to preserve it, but the reality is much more complex. The Niagara Preservation Movement of the early 1880s succeeded by uniting scenic preservationists and reformers with businessmen, tourist promoters, power developers, politicians, the traveling public, and even the general populace, although each of these groups had different visions of Niagara's future.

Once the state reservation had been created in 1885, the leading spokesman for preservation, Frederick Law Olmsted, applied the highest principles of landscape architecture to the Niagara landscape. The return of nature at Niagara was accomplished by a thorough overhaul of the image of the cataract and was in fact integrated with technology, tourism, professionalization, and modernity. The New Niagara of nature preserved was constructed—literally—and resembled Olmsted's urban parks. Ironically, the implications of Olmsted's vision for Niagara Falls were foreseen best by the enlightened businessmen who supported the preservation movement and yet were most eager to put the cataract to use.

From 1873 to 1885, the favorite destination of railroad excursion travel to Niagara had been Prospect Park. Guidebooks also directed tourists who had little time to spare at Niagara Falls to Prospect Park first, for that was the best vantage point on the American mainland from which to view the Falls. The park, which abutted the American cataract, included Hennepin Point and the riverbank above the Falls. Newspaper advertisements noted that the park contained "11 acres of original forest" on the American side and boasted the "best views of American and Canadian falls." For the fifty-cent admission fee, visitors were entitled to a day-long visit; for an extra fifty cents, they could make unlimited return visits during the entire season. Benches, walks, and retaining walls accommodated greater numbers of tourists with safe, convenient, and spectacular views. During its years of operation, Prospect Park attracted 862,753 visitors.[2]

Notwithstanding its ideal siting beside Niagara Falls, Prospect Park was *not* about nature. Rather, "its proprietors have taken notice into consideration that there are a number of visitors who do not, during their short stay, fully appreciate the beauties of old Niagara." A white picket fence that enclosed the park, along with the restraining wall at the edge of the precipice, separated the park from the nature beyond. An inclined railway, a ferryhouse, two pavilions, an art gallery, an electric lighthouse, and two or three open lunch houses provided abundant evidence of the human presence within the grounds. As gardens supplanted indigenous vegetation, nature itself was displaced. At the foot of the Falls, the Prospect Park Company eliminated the full view of the Falls from below by erecting an enormous, brightly painted "tunnel" for visitors entering the "Cave of the Winds."[3]

Evening proved to be the most popular time to visit the park. The pavilion served as a commercial pleasure garden complete with dance hall and bar. For an extra fee of twenty-five cents, visitors were entitled to see Prospect Park's spectacular nighttime electric light exhibition. A Brush dynamo and Brush illuminating machines and arc lights lit the park grounds and the Falls. Electric fountains shot colored jets of water high into the air. In language reminiscent of earlier tourist accounts of the cataract itself, advertisements touted the sublime effects of reflected light on the water. One review of Prospect Park proclaimed: "Although mainly the result of artificial aids to the natural scenery of the Falls it is a most enjoyable park, and as such well worth the visit." Financial success hinged on the novelty of artificial improvements and contrivances.[4]

Tourist buildings at Prospect Park, 1870s. The brightly painted tunnel led up to the "Cave of the Winds," but it obscured the view of the Falls from below. (Courtesy, Local History Room, Niagara Falls Public Library)

While Prospect Park came to be a favorite destination for most tourists, reformers and nature lovers deplored it as a "foolish waste of time and money." Frederick Law Olmsted bluntly concluded that the park's purpose "was to draw visitors by any means to a particular piece of ground where money could be made out of them." Henry Norman, an English journalist who campaigned to bring Niagara's landscape outrages to an end, accused entrepreneurs of trying to dignify a series of hokey attractions by calling them a "park."[5]

Critics singled out the electric illumination as the park's greatest affront to the Niagara landscape. J. B. Harrison, who wrote and lectured for the Niagara Falls Preservation Movement, likened the spectacle to a "poor circus with a cheap celebration of the Fourth of July." Norman saw Prospect Park's initial lighting effects as an omen of the future: "If this thing continues there will doubtless soon be people putting indigo or cochineal into the water to improve its tone, and arranging with Edison to furnish artificial sunsets every day at three o'clock." In his view, electric-light shows replaced uplifting nature with vulgarity and ugliness.[6]

As tawdry as this tourist landscape at Niagara was, its ramifications paled before the more ominous threat of industry. Improvements in transportation and technology heightened expectations that Niagara could be a site for waterpower production. When the Niagara Falls Hydraulic Power & Manufacturing Company began producing electricity in 1881, the toll this development took on the landscape pained even callow observers. Ramshackle mills adjacent to the company shamelessly dumped refuse over the cliff and piled other materials beside the mills. Harrison acknowledged:

> Now it is difficult to imagine, if one has not seen it, so much ugliness, untidiness in places, squalor, as one sees on parts of this small belt of land. There are spots that recall the dismal, hopelessly littered and neglected look of the suburbs of some towns in Arkansas.

The state's generous policy of encouraging industry and development by granting charters to companies that sought to use Niagara's waterpower threatened the Falls even more. Without any protection for the land

"Niagara Seen with Different Eyes," *Harpers Weekly,* 1873. Niagara accommodated all sorts of visions in the nineteenth century, although

popularity led some nature lovers to abandon Niagara for more peaceful resorts. (Courtesy, Special Collections Department, University of Virginia Library)

around Niagara, "manufacturers and capitalists can wholly destroy the beauty of the Falls, and they are likely to do so."[7]

People came to Niagara Falls looking for a wide variety of pleasures, but for many middle- and upper-class visitors, ugliness, poor taste, vandalism against nature, and industrialism rendered the trip to Niagara more distressing than enjoyable.[8] Until 1885, every viewing station on the American side was private property. Indian curiosity shops, bazaars, photographer's booths, fences, and advertising boards gave Niagara the appearance of a county fair. With no defense against Niagara's hackmen, showmen, and resort owners, viewers simply went from paying one toll to paying another as they "did" Niagara. What made matters worse was Niagara's disproportionate share of gougers. *Picturesque America* (1872) reported: "In no quarter of the world is the traveller fleeced as at these falls"; Niagara became "a byword for extortion and annoyance."[9]

It is not surprising that travelers who sought a retreat into natural scenery increasingly spurned Niagara. In "Niagara Revisited, Twelve Years After Their Wedding Journey" (1883), William Dean Howells's disillusioned couple, Basil and Isabel, suddenly realized that Niagara seemed different because all the honeymooners were missing; Niagara was eerily empty. A New York State survey of 1880 concluded that Niagara Falls had no summer-long guests. Hoteliers were dismayed that the summer season had been given over to a nonleisured class of excursionists who visited for the day and departed without spending the night. Harrison attributed the lack of the more leisured and cultured tourists to landscape disfigurement at Niagara. According to the *Niagara Falls Gazette*, if a reservation to protect scenery were not created, "the number of visitors would have gone on diminishing with each season, until something approaching the present condition of Cohoes or Trenton Falls was reached."[10]

Niagara's shame translated to boom time for other resorts. Gift books like *Picturesque America* suggested abundant alternatives of less expensive or less commercial resorts. Innumerable streams and vales offered peaceful, undisturbed picturesque scenery. Whether visited on a free afternoon, a camping holiday, or a summer vacation, these less famous getaway spots promised healthier communion with nature without the disturbing distractions now ingrained in the Niagara experience. *Picturesque America* specifically urged cataract-seekers to escape Niagara's extortions for the polished hospitality of Trenton Falls and the Trenton Falls Hotel.[11]

As tourists found summertime replacements for Niagara Falls, Niagara was also eclipsed as America's foremost symbol of nature. From Albert Bierstadt to Thomas Moran, William Henry Jackson, and John Muir, champions of the American sublime romanticized the fresher, purer, and more spectacular landscapes of the West. National magazines chronicled adventurous journeys to Yellowstone Falls, the Yosemite Valley, and the Grand Canyon. Military, geological, and artistic surveys in the western regions proved that "the eastern half of America offers no suggestion of its western half."[12]

Paeans to these western attractions echoed earlier tributes to Niagara. Adventurous or nature-loving travelers reveled in the chance to explore more-remote nature. Travel accounts, sublime paintings, and spectacular photographs vivified the unspoiled magnificence of the nation's great western landforms. Samuel Bowles, editor of the *Springfield Republican*, marveled at western scenery "to pique the curiosity and challenge the admiration of the world." *Picturesque America* contended that no spot in nature grouped such a variety of attractions as Yellowstone. The Lower Falls "is a site far more beautiful than Niagara." Meanwhile, compared with the beauties of Yosemite, "Niagara has nothing." No wonder Niagara's day had passed: "Thirty years ago the attraction of America to the foreign mind was Niagara Falls. Now we have attractions which diminish Niagara into an ordinary exhibition."[13]

Mounting outrage over the condition of Niagara, in fact, had impelled early efforts to reserve magnificent natural scenery in the West. Although Niagara was permanently scarred and given over to commercial endeavors, there was still hope for the wilderness wonderlands of Yellowstone and Yosemite, where the preservation impulse emerged before the area had become privatized. But the travesty of Niagara loomed in every nature advocate's consciousness. In 1872, *New York Times* correspondent Grace Greenwood protested plans to commercialize the Yosemite Valley by pleading, "Let it not be said by any visitor that [Yosemite Valley] is a new Niagara for extortion and impositions." The head of the U.S. Survey of Yellowstone warned Congress:

> Persons are now waiting for the spring to enter in and take possession of these remarkable curiosities, to make merchandise of these beautiful specimens, to fence in these rare wonders, so as to charge visitors a fee, as is now done at Niagara Falls, for the sight of that which ought to be free as the air or water.[14]

As nature advocates pressured government to prevent future "Niagaras," diffuse cries to stop the outrage at Niagara Falls coalesced into a full-fledged preservation movement. The successful creation of national parks at Yellowstone and Yosemite in the 1860s and 1870s had drawn attention to America's sublime nature and had given new hope for remedial action at Niagara Falls. Owing to Central Park's success in New York City, a New York state park boom swelled interest in creating an Adirondack forest reserve, a comprehensive New York City park system, and a Niagara reservation. As parks became ever more popular retreats for the middle class, worsening conditions at Niagara strengthened the case of those who urged state or national action to preserve Niagara.[15]

By the 1870s and early 1880s, Frederic Edwin Church, landscape architects Frederick Law Olmsted and Calvert Vaux, architect Henry Hobson Richardson, and literary men such as Charles Eliot Norton and Robert Underwood emerged as the champions of preservation at Niagara. Cherishing Niagara Falls as a great national symbol of nature, they called for a publicly owned reservation to safeguard the Niagara landscape. Nothing short of public ownership could restore Niagara's pristine, natural wilderness aspect, they believed.[16]

By 1879, Niagara activists began to have reason for optimism. In a message to the state legislature, New York Governor Lucius Robinson assailed the tawdry conditions of Niagara Falls and spoke of New York's responsibility to protect such a sacred spot for visitors from all over the world. Following Robinson's proposal, the New York state legislature established a state survey "to determine the character of such defacements [at Niagara]; to estimate the tendency to greater injury; and lastly, to consider whether the proposed action by the state is necessary to arrest the process of disfiguration and restore to the scenery its original character."[17]

The survey, performed by James T. Gardner and Frederick Law Olmsted, began at once and reached the anticipated conclusion that the private parceling of land around the cataract led to the unsightly and distasteful conditions at the Falls. Gardner and Olmsted's more nettlesome task was to devise a plan of action. The majestic charms of Niagara Falls could be saved only if the state became caretaker of a reserved landscape. Because the land surrounding Niagara was all privately owned, the survey addressed the crucial question of what land should be included in the reservation. The surveyors realized that although an extensive reservation encompassing the scenic magnificence of the Niagara gorge and the whirlpool rapids was merited, the governor and the state legislature would probably dismiss such a romantic (and potentially expensive) plan. Gardner and Olmsted therefore recommended that a small reservation around the cataract be formed immediately.[18]

Even this pragmatic proposal lacked state legislative and gubernatorial mandates until 1883. State action to remove such an extensive tract of productive private property for sentimental reasons contradicted New York State's overall land-use policy and history. Governor Alonzo B. Cornell opposed the measure strongly, as did the state's grange associations and farming population. Opponents trivialized the sacralization of a mere waterfall, resented the special favor accorded to one specific place, bemoaned the tax burden the reservation would put on the entire state in a financially depressed time, and feared the likelihood of jobbery and corruption in the scheme. Given Niagara's reputation for gouging visitors individually, opponents were wary of a Niagara preservation scheme that might bilk them collectively.[19]

Meanwhile, with every passing day the cause took on new urgency for the promoters of preservation. If the state did not buy the desired Niagara lands, reformers insisted, manufacturing and tourist interests stood ready to exploit Niagara's most scenic sites on a magnitude previously unheard of. Investors especially coveted Goat Island, where a single real-estate deal could seal the doom of Niagara's lone remaining realm of unspoiled nature. According to one rumor that illustrated the precarious hold of nature on the island, Commodore Cornelius Vanderbilt had planned to purchase Goat Island from the Porter family in the

1870s for $200,000 and to invest up to $1,000,000 in a palatial hotel to rival Saratoga's best summer resorts. As part of this venture, P. T. Barnum "was to establish a zoological garden on one end of the island and maintain a permanent show there during the summer months." Only when the Porters raised the price to more than $500,000 did a disgusted Commodore Vanderbilt order his agent home.[20]

The year 1883 was pivotal for Niagara's preservation. Grover Cleveland's election as governor in November 1882 had put a staunch friend of preservation at the head of the state government. More important, Olmsted's efforts to stir up interest in Niagara preservation among socially prominent gentlemen and businessmen in New York City's elite Century Club, as well as in Boston, led directly to the formation of the Niagara Falls Association. Counting George William Curtis, J. P. Morgan, Robert Lennox Belknap, Charles Lanier, Edward Dean Adams, and Theodore Vanderbilt on its roster, this preservation society numbered more than 300 members, including about 50 women.[21]

The Niagara Falls Association proved to be an invaluable lobbying group. Membership in the association became almost a badge of enlightenment for elite businessmen who favored a scheme of such "intelligence and public spirit." "Gentlemen mentioned the enterprise to their acquaintances at the clubs, at social assemblies, and in their offices and places of business." Along with another organization of prominent citizens of Niagara Falls, the association launched letter-writing campaigns, used a concerted strategy of press releases, and relied on the personal influence members carried in their local communities and among the state legislators. The relentless pressure by the Niagara Falls Association overcame the opposition of local manufacturers at Niagara Falls and those who remained doubtful in view of the initial and future maintenance costs of a reserved Niagara.[22]

After winning preliminary passage of the reservation bill in 1883, the state legislature appointed appraisers to set values on the lands to be taken under the state's right of eminent domain. Although the appraisers set property awards at substantially less than the property holders wanted, creation of the reservation was delayed by the legislature's reluctance to release funds to pay for the condemned land. The reservation bill allowed the state only two years to fund the project.

In 1884 the Niagara Falls Association began pressuring the legislature and the governor for disbursement of the extra funds. Under the direction of Olmsted and Norton, J. B. Harrison traveled throughout the state on a lecture tour that effectively exploited every tawdry threat to the scenic wonder. When the state legislature passed the measure, only Governor David B. Hill's signature was needed. Hill visited Niagara Falls personally in late April 1885, although he appeared unmoved by the disfigurement of the Falls region and questioned why the productive paper mill on Bath Island was included in the reservation. Finally, moments before the bill was to expire, and only after the intervention of Governor Hill's former mentor, Samuel Tilden, the governor signed the bill to appropriate $1.4 million to reclaim Niagara Falls.[23]

The "Free Niagara Movement," as the Niagara preservation impulse was known, succeeded by conquering Gilded Age suspicions of government jobbery, new taxes, and the honored American tradition of upholding property rights and favoring private, market-driven initiatives. Olmsted, Harrison, and Norton believed their best chance for success was in a high-minded exposure of the gross affronts to good taste at Niagara. The state survey declared: "Niagara is not simply the crowning glory of the great resources of the State . . . , but the highest distinction of the nation and the continent." In trying to shame the state, the nation, and the people, Free Niagara advocates employed each new outrage on the scene as another opportunity to publicize their campaign for Niagara. According to this view, privatism ensured the defacement and debasement of natural scenery; it spawned tawdry, sensational attractions at best, and hideous, degrading desecration at worst.[24]

Preservation advocates challenged New York State and the nation to do right by Niagara; they argued that the polluting mills on Bath Island and the petty businesses and shops, the shoddy shacks, and the gaudy advertising in the area—all of which manifested indifference to natural scenery—signified baseness, greed, and cultural inferiority. They claimed that if a Niagara-like cataract were discovered in the wilds of Africa, Americans would demand its preservation. As long as Niagara remained a "shrine of pilgrimage from every country," lack of preservation only brought shame on the area. New York State risked the ire of the world in its treatment of Niagara.[25]

Conversely, because only bold public action could save Niagara from doom, the creation of a Niagara park became analogous to New York State's other great revolutionary public project—the Erie Canal. As a public work, a Niagara reservation could take its place beside noble bridges, expansive railroads, great machines, public libraries, and museums. As a measure to preserve scenery, the reservation would establish New York State's primacy in recognizing the value of nature. It would show American patriotism, progress, sophistication, and advanced culture. No other New York State action could earn comparable praise and respect.[26]

Fortunately for Free Niagara boosters, sentiment and practicality conjoined in the Niagara reservation scheme. The businessmen and elites who first heard of the movement to preserve Niagara Falls at the Century Club prided themselves on their patronage of the arts and their allegiance to motives higher than financial gain. Such so-called enlightened businessmen feared the instability of the nation's business cycles, the social chaos of America's heterogeneous democracy, rising labor tensions, and the blight of America's urban-industrial landscape. Thanks to the mid-century propagandizing efforts of Andrew Jackson Downing and the success of Frederick Law Olmsted's Central Park, middle-class Americans believed in the instructional and harmonizing recreational virtues of nature and parks. Nature and natural scenery eased the strain of modern life, captivated the imagination, inspired feeling and thinking, and ultimately made better, more efficient, contented, and peaceful citizens.[27]

No nature spot promised to bring home these elevating benefits more thoroughly than Niagara Falls.[28] Consequently, while the preservation of Niagara improved conditions at Niagara Falls, it also served as a blueprint for using nature in social reform. Olmsted, Charles Eliot Norton, and others believed that Niagara Falls represented an antidote to runaway social change and the nation's ever-increasing urban problems. To them a reserved Niagara symbolized timeless, pure, and pristine nature in a late-century sea of artifice, anarchy, and flux. It offered a breathing place of health-giving nature for people who suffered from the nervousness, exhaustion, and alienation of city confinement. If New York State created a Niagara reservation, "the people of the United States would derive more benefit from this central park situated on the great railroad thoroughfare of the United States and the dominion of Canada than will ever be engaged on 100 Yellowstone Parks or a dozen islands of Mackinaws."[29]

Olmsted and Norton believed that parks and nature retreats relieved the festering distress of the poor and working classes, who could not escape to suburban residences, summer villas, or lengthy vacations. At Niagara, where formerly the visitor was gouged by fees, a reservation would open the world's most uplifting scenery to everyone free of charge. Conservative commentators argued that whereas typical working-class recreation centered around such sensuous pleasures as eating, drinking, strenuous exercise, boisterous music, and ethnic festivals, Niagara, thanks to its renown and popularity, could play a sobering role in modern life. Olmsted and his disciples disdained Niagara's older sublime and sensational associations as too unsettling and terrifying. Instead, they hoped a Niagara reservation would subtly imbibe the conservative, ennobling, and quieting qualities of nature.

While on the one hand preservationists appealed to the high, uplifting ideals of nature, they also addressed the pecuniary realities of American life. J. B. Harrison reassured skeptics that nature lovers were not anti-capitalist radicals—that the preservation and restoration of Niagara would not preclude manufacturing. Harrison insisted that no private interest was to be wronged:

> It is a wonderful thing that owing to the conformation of the ground here, and the peculiar grouping of the various objects or places of chief interest, the beauty of the scenery can be restored, and its value retained forever unimpaired, by the appropriation of so small a region . . . for the purposes of a reservation.[30]

The proposed Niagara reservation consisted of a one-mile stretch of territory that ranged only between 100 and 800 feet in width along the river at the cataract. Little industrial real-estate need be lost.

In fact, the Niagara reservation actually promised to spur the region's developmental impulse. Railroads would have renewed reason to promote Niagara as a hub of east-west travel. Larger crowds at a hassle-free Niagara would boost the earnings of anyone who made a living from the tourist-related procession across the state to Niagara. It is not surprising that railroad lines and hoteliers became insistent backers of the Niagara reservation plan; only the paper manufacturers and the hackmen remained vociferous local opponents.[31]

Finally, Free Niagara boosters told of new prosperity and productivity that would accompany the state reservation at Niagara itself. Throughout the nineteenth century, as they tried to convince an often wary public of the benefits of nature, nature advocates insisted that beauty and utility were mutually rewarding. Using New York City's Central Park as an example, preservationists showed that the urban park created real-estate value. Far from wasting the choicest mill locales in the world, preservation of the cataract would immediately cause bordering lands to rise in value. Harrison, Free Niagara's most prolific spokesperson, anticipated that Niagara would become a power and manufacturing center. Likewise, guidebooks insisted that the Niagara reservation would still allow industry to "draw all the power required from the river above the Falls, without in any way marring the scenery of the latter, and that while in the years to come, this village may grow to be a city, teeming with life and activity, its value as a health resort will be in no wise abated." A reserved Niagara would follow the Central Park model of shutting out the city within the specific reserved grounds.[32]

The Free Niagara issue, insisted Harrison, "is not whether Niagara is more valuable as factory power or as beauty and sublimity, but how it shall best serve both use and beauty." Taking his cue from Olmsted, Harrison addressed the conflict of values between those seeking to use nature and those seeking to preserve it; he proclaimed a new, emerging ethos that nature becomes more profitable when well preserved. Thus, wise businessmen perceived that tourism declined when scenery was ruined. While tourists would shun a mill-lined cataract, preservation of the Falls would allow Niagara to remain the continent's greatest landmark even as it stimulated bigger business. In a new golden age, railroads would continue to feature Niagara Falls as a great tourist mecca; thousands might be employed in the tourist trade, while thousands more would be employed in the industry that developed beyond the preserved areas.[33]

On July 15, 1885, a great civic celebration attended by tens of thousands marked the opening of the New York State Reservation at Niagara Falls.

In nineteenth-century America, such public pageantry typically heralded the opening of public works projects and denoted significant cultural accomplishment. Military brass bands and fireworks suggested the patriotic significance of the event. Orators read paeans to Niagara and chronicled the epic struggle leading up to the creation of the reservation. A lavishly published program featured expressions of gratitude from railroad companies and manufacturers alike. Most significant of all, however, was that the celebrants gathered to enter the free, reserved areas. Lured by the throng and the pageantry, most were unaware of the sort of space they entered. All that was certain was that the New York State Reservation at Niagara launched the Falls into a new era.[34]

The avowed purpose of the Niagara reservation was to return the area to a pure and primeval wilderness condition. Lord Dufferin, the governor-general of Canada who suggested an international Niagara park in 1878, originally envisioned a new Niagara "carefully preserved in the picturesque and unvulgarized condition in which it was originally laid out by the hand of nature." Niagara advocates attached extraordinary significance to the motto "to preserve and restore the natural scenery of Niagara." As the *Niagara Falls Gazette* reported on the reservation's inaugural day, "the spirit of the wilderness has come back to Niagara."[35]

Because the creation of the Niagara reservation set aside a unique landscape not only for preservation but also for tourism, decisions about the practical management of the reacquired lands and how best to restore Niagara's scenery raised prickly issues. To those who pictured Niagara in its natural state, the idea of a park was anathema. In the speech that introduced the reservation bill to the New York State Assembly, Niagara Falls Assemblyman Thomas Welch insisted that "nothing like a park, in the ordinary acceptance of the word, is contemplated or desired at Niagara."[36]

Nineteenth-century Americans understood that a park might designate everything from aristocratic or European manicured gardens to "fair grounds, race tracks, play grounds, city squares, groups of adjacent private residences, and many other things equally incongruous" to America's great nature spots. Free Niagara boosters designated Niagara's protected lands a "reservation" rather than a "park" or "pleasure ground" because they wanted to rid Niagara of all artificial associations, not the least of which was the meddling of overeager landscape architects. Because Niagara embodied the ideal of pure American nature, preservationists insisted that it "presents a spectacle of more beauty and grandeur than all the artificial parks of the world combined."[37]

Given the novelty of the scheme, and the faith in Niagara's natural fecundity, the reservation commissioners initially tried to run the reservation in a laissez-faire manner and without any professional guidance whatsoever. They realized, however, that even if the Niagara reservation was not actually a park, it required parklike administration. The traveling public had little taste for the austere primitivism of an unimproved Niagara landscape. Tourists anticipated a varied reservation that integrated tourist conveniences with nature.

Many reservation supporters saw no harm in enhancing the landscape around the cataract. Most nineteenth-century Americans believed natural beauty could be made more attractive through artificial aids. Frederick Law Olmsted, a virulent opponent of any artificial feature that detracted from nature contemplation at Niagara, feared that the American passion for statuary and monuments might overrun the reservation. *Garden and Forest*, a journal Olmsted founded, admitted that "good people" deemed the reservation ideally suited for monuments, museums, and educational institutions. Letters of support for the reservation from scientists joined in the call for a museum of geology to house indigenous rocks, fossils, flora, fauna, as well as local maps and surveys. The secretary of the History and Forestry Society of Rockland County believed that

> an international museum should be built and an effort made to
> gather articles of history's value pertaining to the neighborhood
> it would add much to the interest of the spot. A call might be
> published to our citizens generally to return articles that have
> been taken away during the years gone by, many curious relics
> of the Falls might then be gathered and preserved.[38]

When setting everyday policy for the state reservation, the commissioners at first emphasized the smooth transition between the old Prospect Park and Goat Island resorts and the new reservation. The *Niagara Falls Gazette* claimed that "but little change has taken place here save the usual entry fee." Drawing on the public's familiarity with Prospect Park, reservation notices initially boasted that "the grounds are kept in the same neat condition by the state as when it was private property"; by implication, the familiar pleasure-garden sorts of social entertainment also remained available at the reservation.[39]

When State Reservation Superintendent Thomas V. Welch actually took a step toward restoring Niagara to more natural conditions by implementing a ban on electric lights and closing the reservation at dusk, he incurred the wrath of Niagara businessmen as well as ordinary tourists. These policy changes seemed to type Niagara as a rarified reserve rather than a pleasure ground for the people. Angry critics denounced the new landscape purity at Niagara as the whim of reactionary aesthetes. As hoteliers cried foul, the early closing of the state reservation gave tourists little incentive to spend the night at Niagara. Niagara boosters who had favored the reservation hoping that it would spur business now questioned policies that disdained convenience and technological marvels. The *Niagara Falls Gazette* continued to urge that the reservation accommodate the commercial needs of the New Niagara:

> Many people who would stay over night for the lights leave town and go to some city. As it is a matter of interest to every person doing business here to have people remain as long as possible, we are pleased to note that an effort is being made to have the lights restored.[40]

Welch's ban on electric lights and his curious plans to develop the reservation with new elevators, roadways, and walkways quickly alienated both the strict preservationist faction and the entrepreneurial faction in the dispute. His suggestions followed an inconsistent, piecemeal plan. An article in the *New York Tribune,* "How to Preserve Niagara," objected to the reservation commissioners working without a master plan. The *New York Sun* boiled that the park commissioners would not have attempted to build a cathedral or a railroad or a bridge yet presumed to "build" the reservation at Niagara.[41]

According to middle-class critics, what Niagara needed most, distrust for landscape architects aside, was expert management. The perceived need for a managerial ethos at Niagara Falls represented the ascendancy of professionalization in the late nineteenth century, when Americans increasingly believed specific knowledge and training were necessary to address pressing problems. Indeed, the call to passively "preserve" Niagara was misleading; Gardner and Olmsted concluded in their original survey that the American shore had lost its natural character. George Barker's haunting photographs accompanying the 1880 survey depicted the starkly disfigured environs of Niagara. Barker's images of the entrance to Goat Island, the enormous Bath Island paper mill, and the hotels and shops on the river's edge verified that Niagara was far too disfigured to simply remove the structures and let nature take its course. Olmsted admitted that the extent of development forever precluded a return to Niagara's former majesty; the landscape architect would use all his skills just to avoid the appearance of blight once the buildings were removed.[42]

Only trained experts and good taste would allow Niagara to become "more Niagara-like." Niagara preservationists clearly envisioned an idealized natural landscape. The landscape architect at Niagara had to disguise his professional manipulation of the landscape to look like a wilderness ideal. Nonetheless, any successful reservation required hard decisions regarding land use and reclamation.

> There are wounds to be healed upon the banks of the rapids and they demand the most skillful treatment. . . . There will be constant importunity to introduce incongruous and distracting objects, to build or plant something on the place that will be useful or pretty, to construct a wheelway here or a footpath there, and the only security against certain disfigurement is to entrust the work to men who are trained in making adequate provision for the convenience of visitors and where taste can be trusted to nurture a comprehensive plan where no detail of planting or construction will violate the spirit of the scenery.[43]

The more skillfully park designers and managers applied engineering and artistic principles, the more natural Niagara would appear. Even where nature remained predominant, it could not be left alone; tourists trampled vegetation, trees became craggy and decayed, and unpruned vegetation overran scenic outlooks. Time altered the idyllic splendor of

Photographs of Niagara's disfigured banks by George Barker, 1880. Barker's striking images of the desecrated Niagara landscape helped intensify the movement for a state reservation. Above: Approach to Goat Island. Below: Bath Island. (Courtesy, Buffalo and Erie County Historical Society)

picturesque nature. Landscape architects only improved on nature; they interceded to maintain the idyllic illusion of pristine nature through inconspicuous gardening.

When Commissioner Andrew H. Green, who had administered Central Park with Olmsted in the 1850s, took over the chief administrative post of the New York State Reservation at Niagara in 1886, he immediately sought to bring in an expert to restore the reservation grounds. The *New York Sun* insisted that the work demanded a skillful landscape architect. "A more difficult, delicate, and responsible task has never been given to a master of landscape construction, and none but a mature hand will ever accomplish anything worthy of Niagara." Olmsted also viewed Niagara as the landscape architect's greatest professional challenge. "I feel . . . that if not the most difficult problem in landscape to do justice to, it is the most serious,—the farthest one shot work—that the world has yet had." In 1887, no other job matched the Niagara reservation for professional prestige.[44]

Although he had a contempt for Green dating back to Green's high-handed and parsimonious administration of New York's Central Park, Olmsted dearly wanted the Niagara job, and when Green nominated Vaux as sole landscape architect for the reservation, Olmsted exerted his influence to secure a joint appointment. In a letter to Governor Hill, Olmsted outlined his own unique qualifications for the post and pointed out that he had helped initiate the call for the Niagara reservation. Moreover, despite his collaboration with Vaux on Central Park and Brooklyn's Prospect Park, Olmsted claimed to have greater practical experience in superintending park grounds than Vaux. Professional rivalry with Vaux aside, Olmsted's impassioned defense of his practical skills and qualifications revealed the attractiveness of the Niagara reservation appointment and the degree of professional expertise required.[45]

The agenda of Frederick Law Olmsted and Calvert Vaux for the Niagara reservation was to restore the primacy of nature at Niagara Falls. They pledged to "reestablish a permanently agreeable national character, harmonious with that of the undisturbed parts," while making adequate and safe accommodations for visitors. This posed an inherently contradictory challenge. On the one hand, the landscape architects tried to re-create Niagara's original pristine natural condition; on the other hand, they had to accommodate the needs of thousands of tourists.[46]

Olmsted and Vaux attacked this contradiction by insisting that the tourist's experience itself needed reformation at Niagara. Whereas most visitors anticipated a quick, astonishing "show" not only from the sublime waterfalls but also from Niagara's myriad bridges, elevators, electric lights, and fountains, the reservation emphasized quiet relaxation: "People will in the future be expected to come to Niagara to look at Niagara, not to picnic or play, and not to gaze at mountebanks, or peep shows, or 'galleries of art' or collections of natural curiosities."[47]

Unlike Prospect Park, the New York State Reservation would tolerate no attractions that diverted attention from nature. Olmsted argued that neither monuments nor otherwise noble or educational institutions would be allowed to enter this reserve of nature. Niagara's unique and supreme value to humankind was as a school of nature. Even if the Statue of Liberty were offered to the reservation, the commissioners must decline it. Nothing artificial should be allowed on the site.[48]

This said, Olmsted and Vaux adopted a practical, pragmatic approach. The New York State Reservation forever sublimated nature at Niagara; it "reserved" nature conveniently for visitors in a limited, boundary-specific, and organized space. Idle curiosities and sideshows would be banned, but thousands of tourists who had little serious love for nature would experience an educational landscape, not in a raw wilderness setting but in comfort and safety.

The Niagara reservation ultimately differed little from Olmsted's and Vaux's other parks. Olmsted pointed out that although visitors believed that Central Park remained in its original state of nature, it required a bold scheme of blasting, excavation, digging, and development to transform a swampy Manhattan wasteland into a picturesque recreational greenbelt for New York's urban masses. At Niagara, Olmsted advised anyone who wanted a preview of what to expect from the reservation to examine his work at Buffalo's Delaware Park. It is no wonder that Vaux, in a moment of candor about Niagara, wrote to Olmsted: "The word park has no bogey in it for me and should not have for you."[49]

Tourism necessitated that the Niagara reservation function as a park rather than a realm of wild nature. In fact, attendance at the Falls skyrocketed once Niagara became free. Thomas Welch announced in his first "Annual Report of the Superintendent" that 1,000 to 6,000 visitors frequented the reservation daily in 1885, more than quadrupling the previous season's figures. Welch especially noted an increase in the number of visitors of limited means. Renewed railroad interest in a "Free Niagara"—made manifest by special promotions and railroad advertisements for the reforms at the Falls—lowered fares enough to put the journey to Niagara Falls within reach of most Americans. A typical railroad excursion from the Midwest cost five dollars round-trip, about one-fifth the regular train fare two decades earlier. During the initial 1885 season, 188,000 excursionists, and a like number of travelers coming by regularly scheduled trains, visited Niagara. The "General Plan" of Olmsted and Vaux accounted for up to 10,000 daily visitors.[50]

To accommodate these crowds, the Niagara reservation needed roads, shelters, seats, and bridges. Yet, unlike other parks, Niagara's sacred scenery and attractions were now considered inviolate; homage to nature permitted only improvements that promoted communion with nature. Indeed, if Olmsted's toughest task at Central Park was to reconcile seclusion and festivity, Niagara posed the additional challenge of re-creating a primeval landscape amid city-like crowds.

Curiously, Olmsted's re-creation of the Niagara landscape summoned the same ideal of nature that he had used in his urban parks. Olmsted always preferred the picturesque in nature to the sublime. He welcomed the refreshing, restorative, and calming aspects of nature and believed there was as much to contemplate in ordinary woodland or an open field as in great mountain peaks or cataracts. Olmsted's most cherished aspect of Niagara's scenic splendor was the view of the rapids. No other spot in the world presented a view of "nature more majestic."[51]

America's greatest landscape architect rejected Niagara's meaning as an "icon of the American sublime." The sublimity of the cataract, according to Olmsted, merely excited sensuous passions in the average visitor. As long as visitors came to Niagara to indulge their curiosity, Niagara would remain susceptible to tawdry sensationalism. Ironically, Olmsted believed that the cataract detracted from true nature appreciation at Niagara. A too terrifying or freakish curiosity, which is how much of the public regarded Niagara, would never realize the restorative, contemplative, and uplifting benefits of nature.[52]

Olmsted's picturesque ideal led him to diminish the role of the cataract in the Niagara reservation, and the configuration of the riverbank aided his cause because no full frontal view of the cataract was visible from the reservation. In addition, the prevailing but soon-to-be-outdated belief that the waters and "the Falls themselves man cannot touch" justified more scrupulous devotion to Niagara's immediately threatened landscapes. As Olmsted and Gardner reported, the cataract was only one of four major features (the others being the rapids, the islands, and the deep gorge) that together comprised the wonder of Niagara Falls. According to the New York State Survey of 1880, "within certain limits at Niagara there are probably a larger number of distinct and rare qualities of beauty in combinations of rock, foliage, mist, sky and water, than in any other equal space of the earth's surface."[53]

Olmsted, Vaux, and their backers carefully structured the tourist experience in the Niagara reservation in a way that emphasized Niagara's quieter virtues. Their vision for the reservation focused most adoringly on Goat Island and its remaining primeval vegetation. Reservation boosters frequently echoed claims by such eminent authorities as botanists Sir Joseph Hooker and Asa Gray that Goat Island possessed the greatest vegetative variety of any place on earth. Similarly, J. B. Harrison recognized that verdant green foliage gave Niagara its more distinct beauty:

> If the trees should be destroyed, and the shores and islands denuded of their green and living beauty, the waters might rush and leap in the rapids, and roll over the cliff into the gulf below, as now; but our sense of their sparkling gladness and gayety, and of the tenderness and passionate, eager youthfulness in the life of the scene would be gone.

Without its lush setting, the great cataract would be of interest only to manufacturers.[54]

Having conceived of the state reservation less as a paean to the world's greatest cataract than a picturesque retreat from city pressures and influences, Olmsted confronted two immediate problems that threatened the entire vision. First, the hustle and bustle of Niagara's industry and development was visible not only from the mainland but also from most points on the reservation islands. How could the encroaching city be walled out of the reservation? Second, because it encompassed a very narrow tract of land, how could the reservation be a true breathing-place rather than a bounded tract that reinforced city confinement and constraint?

The solution to the first problem necessitated not only landscape construction but also reservation superintendence and regulation. Tree plantings blocked out the city behind the reservation grounds and muffled the sounds of the passing trains. Vaux directed that new trees be arrayed so as to prevent visitors on Goat Island from seeing crowds on the mainland. Additional plantings filled in the barren eyesores created by the dismantling of Prospect Park. Finally, the reservation carriage-way and footpaths took visitors through progressively more verdant vegetation and symbolically insulated them from the city.[55]

Reservation regulations further eliminated social and commercial distractions, banning all advertising signs and also picnicking beyond the Upper Grove. Because only licensed reservation phaetons were allowed on the reservation islands, predatory hackmen no longer annoyed visitors at Niagara's most majestic viewing stations.

The more difficult problem was how to create the impression of grandeur and expanse. After all, the entire reservation comprised only about 100 acres of land. The group of islands and the narrow tract of land on the mainland varied in width from 100 to 800 feet.

As a start, Olmsted and Vaux laid out a parklike introduction along Buffalo Avenue. The large open "Upper Grove" served as the reception area for Niagara's largest crowds, where arriving travelers could acclimate themselves to the reservation. Olmsted wanted tired, anxious, and otherwise ill-prepared visitors to use the grove as an intermediary space between the city and nature. A pavilion provided checkroom and toilet facilities. The landscape of the Upper Grove was "not inconveniently wild or rugged, nor densely wooded, but of a large and simple natural topography and in a degree, of a secluded sylvan aspect." The flat, open grassy grove was suitable for picnicking.[56]

From the Upper Grove through the rest of the reservation, Olmsted and Vaux utilized curved lines to maximum effect. Carriageway and footpaths took visitors on a meandering route through Niagara's lush natural vegetation. The contours of Goat Island's numerous trails isolated visitors in "forest seclusion." As at Central Park, the visitors coursed through varieties of light, shade, and shadows, allowing innumerable picturesque outlooks.[57]

The Niagara reservation continually illustrated Olmsted's efforts to accommodate crowds yet offer solitary appreciation of nature. Whenever possible, Olmsted gave the advantage to the solitary nature-lover. The reservation carriageway was a case in point. Called the "Riverway" to overcome the mean associations of a roadway, it followed the riverbank from one end of the reservation to the other. Although Vaux preferred that the distance between the river and the Riverway and the carriage path on Goat Island be shortened to enhance the enjoyment of hurried travelers, in accordance with Olmsted's vision, no point of the carriageway came within 50 feet of the riverbanks.[58]

Likewise, no carriage stops along the Riverway or on the Goat Island drive infringed pedestrians' choice views. Olmsted and Vaux concluded that the most appreciative visitors at Niagara walked the grounds. Because space on the reservation was limited and hundreds occasionally craved a vantage point that could accommodate only a handful, the landscape architects forced carriage riders to walk to viewing stations.[59]

Finally, the fact that the Niagara reservation and the preservation of Niagara hinged on a similar Canadian venture added the hope that complex landscape coordination could further enlarge the realm of nature. Although Lord Dufferin had vociferously urged restoration of a primeval Niagara without any landscape gardeners, artificial constructions, or tourist guides, the Canadian park had, from its creation in 1887, presented a distressing agenda. Because the Canadian park commissioners had to manage Queen Victoria Park without any public monies, they rented concessions to private concerns within the park grounds and cultivated a more ostentatious park. Olmsted immediately recognized that the Canadian park threatened to become "a sumptuous park and flower garden, [though] nothing could be more deplorable." He even enlisted historian Francis Parkman as a letter-writer to "prevent the Canadian side from becoming a tea-garden."[60]

Despite these fears, Olmsted admitted that the Canadian park presented unique opportunities for mass enjoyment. Unlike the American side, the Canadian terrain consisted of a large expanse of land. Two large, level areas were ideally suited for picnics. Because one of these

The New York State Reservation at Niagara Falls opened in 1885, comprising a one-mile stretch of land that ranged between 100 and 800 feet in width along the river. In 1887, Frederick Law Olmsted and Calvert Vaux were brought in to restore Niagara

groves was above the Falls, and the other below Table Rock, visitors to a Canadian park would need at least three hours to walk the estimated five-mile circuit. The distance separating the Canadian parklands from the tourist village led the Canadian park commissioners to authorize construction of tourist facilities within the grounds. Olmsted feared that this diffuse nature of the Canadian side might lead entrepreneurs to install sensational attractions throughout the site. Initial proposals to build a roadway 380 feet back from the river, where the cataract and the river rapids would have little hold on the visitor, seemed certain to foster a commercial strip. Acknowledging that Niagara's visitors wanted full-frontal views of the cataract, Olmsted urged the Canadians to build a carriage road, complete with waiting stations, along the edge of the precipice. Compared with the carnival-like alternative, at least the roadway combined healthy sociability with an inspiring view. Moreover,

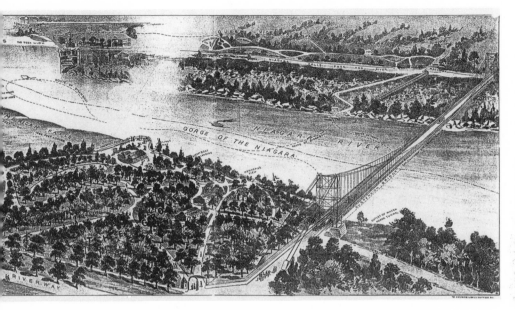

to its wilderness condition while also accommodating thousands of tourists. This map, from an 1890s guide, shows the reservation after the landscaping was complete. (Courtesy, Buffalo and Erie County Historical Society)

these diversions in the Canadian park would accentuate nature in the more picturesque American reservation.[61]

The New York State Reservation at Niagara redeemed Niagara's image. From a byword for extortion and annoyance, Niagara Falls became a leader in civic and landscape reform. "The work of reform which began this spring is still being carried on for the betterment of all concerned." New York State Governor Hill insisted that Niagara was a great philanthropic project and said: "We rejoice, not at the victories of science or the sublime efforts of mechanical genius—but over that exhibition of elevated sentiment, unselfish generosity, creditable public spirit, and genuine patriotism."[62]

So often criticized for devotion to mean, material interests, New York State residents—and indeed all Americans and Canadians—could point proudly to the new Niagara Falls. Human vandalism had been undone. Guidebooks proclaimed that "Niagara has been freed from the dominant materialism of the age." In an era of jobbing and the machine corruption of the Tweed Ring and Tammany Hall, when professed high motives only masked hidden political deals, the creation of the Niagara state reservation represented the first large-scale use of the "machinery of government for a purpose belonging so entirely to the realm of elevated sentiment and noble spiritual emotion." Thanks to judicious management and the commitment of the people of the state, the reservation upheld its pure motives and remained a great "school" for public education.[63]

The New York State Reservation at Niagara took its place among the nation's and the world's great parks. Erastus Brooks likened it to Central Park and Prospect Park in New York City, to Buffalo's Delaware Park, and to "Washington Park in the nation's capital."[64] Following the triumph of Niagara, park mania gripped the United States. "Everybody desired to see as many refreshing and interesting spots as possible dedicated to the public enjoyment of our own and future generations."[65] As the first use of eminent domain to reclaim natural scenery, the Niagara reservation set the precedent for future scenic redemption. Fifteen years after the reservation opened, Commissioner Andrew Green proclaimed: "The Niagara experiment has shown the wisdom of setting aside great natural features of forest, cataract, mountain and seashore, for the common enjoyment of the people."[66]

Even as it glorified Niagara's nature, the Niagara state reservation became one of the most significant landscapes in America precisely because it was a human creation. Local guidebooks hailed "a park of surpassing beauty embellished with a horticultural richness that represents the highest achievement of the landscape architect." The new parks dominated the Niagara landscape.

> All roads on the American side seem to merge into the direct route to the State Reservation, which, under the careful cultivation of less than ten years, has developed into a beautiful park. The high fences, shantees and cheap John shops have disappeared, together with the extortionate rates which at once pre-

vailed and the most inspiring sight in nature is, as it should be, absolutely free to all the world.[67]

Far from concluding with the removal of Niagara's tawdry buildings, reservation landscaping increased with every passing year. In their efforts to achieve organic fulfillment of the Niagara landscape, Olmsted and Vaux (and later, Samuel Parsons Jr.) planned even the minutest details. "Keep off the grass" signs were added to prevent the trampling of vegetation, and for visitors' benches Olmsted and Vaux chose rustic-looking seats made from wooden slatwork and the stone of old buildings. The landscape architects also replaced the old stone retaining wall, noting that the protective wall created its own light and shade, blocked visitors' view of the Canadian cataract, and intrusively separated the natural from the artificial. They recommended replacing it with guard railings.

Indeed, the natural beauties of the Niagara reservation required continuing construction and maintenance. Reservation maintenance entailed a complicated program of grading, drainage, water routing, mason work, planting, and transportation. An estimate for the work completed up to 1889 put the price tag of the improvements at nearly $400,000. Only funding limitations in the state legislature prevented more thorough reorganization of the landscape to both restore a natural appearance and improve the tourist's enjoyment. It is not surprising that the construction of such substantial improvements as new shelters and permanent stone bridges to the islands coincided with expectations of great tourist increases during the exposition summers of 1893 and 1901.[68]

Secure from landscape desecrators, this reserve of "beauty and joy forever" realized preservationists' cherished synthesis between development and nature at Niagara Falls. No longer would nature be overrun by greed, baseness, and deceit. Niagara boosters immediately perceived a new spirit at Niagara, and observers commented on the happy variety and newness of Niagara since the reservation was formed. By refurbishing a moribund tourist image, the state reservation rekindled activity in the region and promised "a new life for Niagara."[69]

The Niagara reservation offered something for everyone: in addition to sustaining a tourist boom, it opened up exciting opportunities for commerce and industry. Hotel proprietors optimistically awaited the crowds of twenty or thirty years earlier. The *Niagara Falls Gazette* became a morning paper in order to take advantage of the larger numbers of arriving tourists. No wonder it was reported that "the outlook for Niagara was never better than at present" and that "the establishment of the Niagara reservation last year, has so far proven a success."[70]

Although the creation of the state reservation satisfied nature lovers and set aside the landscape for preservation, it also spurred power developers. The Free Niagara Movement and the harnessing of Niagara power were not unconnected. In fact, Olmsted and the preservationists at Niagara and other sites, such as Yellowstone and Yosemite, were able to win their cause only after gaining support from railroad lines, industrial giants, and politicians. These groups promoted tourism with an eye to exploitation as well as preservation. Railroads that touted natural wonders and lobbied for the creation of parks extended their lines up to and in many cases through the attractions in their efforts to bring the public to nature.[71]

At Niagara, the same entrepreneurs and corporate financiers who urged the Niagara reservation had invested heavily in transportation systems and tourist industries, and they soon bankrolled the cataract's power development and manufacturing ventures as well. Likewise, the State of New York encouraged the divergent uses of Niagara Falls. Almost immediately after allocating funds for creating the reservation, the state's liberal charters allowed various power developers to exploit Niagara's waterpower potential.

Niagara boosters continually insisted that power development and the integrity of the Niagara reservation were compatible. During the movement to preserve Niagara, broad appeals for support emphasized that power development would not be hindered. By the 1890s, however, power developers had used the creation of the Niagara reservation to take freely from the land and waters beyond the boundaries of the reservation. For these power developers, Niagara's sacred nature seemed to be confined almost exclusively to the reservation. In this way, the role of the Niagara reservation patterned Olmsted's urban parks. No wonder E. T. Williams, a journalist and longtime industrial agent to the city of Niagara Falls, said, "Free Niagara was the forerunner of greater industrial Niagara."[72] In ways far beyond anything the scenic preservationists could have imagined, the Free Niagara Movement opened doors to a truly New Niagara.

4

Capturing the Falls

Power, Powerhouses, and the Electricity Age

Just when Niagara Falls gained cultural attention from the scenic preservation movement, the world's leading engineers stirred the scientific world by suggesting that Niagara's inexhaustible energy potential might be put to use. Awareness of the possibilities of technology in America after the Civil War suggested that this grand vision was now an attainable goal. The perfection of the turbine, which replaced waterwheels, allowed manufacturers to harness more horsepower under greater heads of water. Moreover, each advance toward a practical system of electricity—arc lighting, the light bulb, enormous dynamos, alternating current, and electric motors—brought the dream of utilizing and transmitting Niagara's waterpower closer to reality. The first central power station in Niagara's milling district began operations in 1882.

Notwithstanding the creation of the New York State Reservation at Niagara Falls, New York State continued to offer inviting terms on waterpower use in the Niagara River. In 1886, within a year after the opening of the state reservation, New York State also granted a charter to the Niagara Falls Power Company entitling it to take an unlimited quantity of water from the river at the cataract for the development of power.[1]

By 1900 the New Niagara of electricity and industrial productivity overwhelmed the older, natural Niagara. Constructions at Niagara Falls in the 1890s and early 1900s arose from the combined efforts of inventive geniuses and system-builders, financial barons, budding utility companies, opportunistic corporations, and curious consumers. The New Niagara represented a technological milieu of power plants and power lines, huge factories, electric railways, and electrified homes.

No turn-of-the-century tourist could visit Niagara without confronting the electricity age. Nighttime illumination of the Falls had long confirmed the wonders of electricity, and beginning in the mid-1890s, views of power tunnels, electrical construction sites, and manufacturing districts, as well as power-plant tours, became inescapable features of the visit to Niagara. Trolley lines along spectacular gorge-side routes, which provided quick, inexpensive joyrides through the Niagara region on electric cars, opened the New Niagara to anyone.

This electrical development led Niagara boosters, factory managers, power developers, railroad companies, and guidebook-writers, as well as the nation's scientific and popular press, to rethink Niagara's meaning. Promoters of the New Niagara popularized the harnessing of Niagara enthusiastically, if ambivalently. The New Niagara spoke to late-nineteenth-century America's romance of technology. It dramatized bold financial enterprises, daring engineering projects, powerful machines, and the wonder of electricity. In short, it extolled humankind's ability to conquer nature and displayed national pride in the wondrous handiwork of the engineer and the industrialist.

Yet, while popularizing an electrical identity for Niagara Falls, advocates of this New Niagara also welcomed the future with resolute appeals to traditional and conservative American values. Power-company spokesmen conflated Niagara's limitless development with domestic and preservationist ideals. And while opponents saw a blighted landscape, proponents of the New Niagara put a friendly face on development and stressed harmony between technology and nature. They invited visitors into power plants, control centers, and electric railcars to demystify that most mystifying and frightening of forces—electricity. For the tourist, the New Niagara was to be an improved but recognizable spectacle. Now tourists could see Niagara in all its potential—an educative, serviceable, entertaining electrical mecca, the engineering focus of the nation, and still the most impressive nature spot on earth.

Compared with other cataracts, Niagara had always seemed an unmatched waterpower site. The enormous volume of water from America's inland seas fell 336 feet in a narrow strait between Lakes Erie and Ontario. Over a one-mile span the converging waters dropped 165 feet at the cataract, 55 feet at the upper rapids, and 94 feet in the lower rapids. No wonder common usage of the word "Niagara" bespoke raw power—experts estimated Niagara's full power potential at 6 to 9 million horsepower, enough to drive the nation's entire manufacturing output in 1890.[2]

Equally important, the great cataract was situated in a developed region. Accessible to the nation's laboring and consuming population, and connected to nearby markets by ample railroad facilities, a harnessed Niagara Falls promised to be more useful than waterpower from western waterpower sites. Once engineers devised a suitable method for tapping the cataract's energy potential, Niagara's location near the nation's population centers meant that its energy awaited ready and ever-emerging markets. The Niagara region seemed to be destined to be the nation's manufacturing hub.[3]

Still, geographical coincidence alone cannot account for the reason Niagara Falls became the site of the world's most extensive hydraulic power and electrical experimentation. Over the centuries, Niagara's owners treated the cataract as a resource to be exploited rather than as a sacred throne of inviolate nature. The first French and English mills near Niagara Falls dated back to the mid-1700s. After American independence, New York State's auction of the mile-wide strip of land lining the riverbanks near Niagara Falls sanctioned the industrial development of the cataract. As was typical throughout America in the nineteenth century, New York encouraged the riparian use of waterpower sites at

Niagara. Liberal charters placed few if any restrictions on waterpower users.[4]

In tandem with the state's hospitable land- and water-use policies, visionary power developers also recognized the intrinsic value of an engineering project at Niagara Falls. At Niagara, scientists, inventors, and engineers confronted the landscape's peculiar ability to inspire noble achievement. English engineer William Siemens's charismatic pronouncement that full utilization of Niagara Falls was possible amounted to a clarion call to action. In an era when inventors and system-builders believed they could—and would—conquer all challenges, the idea of harnessing Niagara took on ennobling and even spiritual significance.[5]

In addition to the obvious challenge of harnessing nature at its most powerful, the beauty, sublimity, and tourism renown of Niagara Falls supplied power developers with a practical reason to focus their projects on the great cataract. Before large corporate research and development took over technological systems in the twentieth century, independent inventor/entrepreneurs and small corporations seized the day. To attract investment, to convince the public of the merits of the new technology, and to spur consumer acceptance and consumption, first inventor/entrepreneurs and then corporations exploited the tourism possiblities of big machines, inventions, and engineering projects. Choosing the most advantageous venue for their projects was equally important. As American bridge-building had shown earlier in the century, spectacular natural landscapes and tourist sites caught the interest of the nation's foremost technical experts.[6]

Because electrical development was still in its infancy in the late nineteenth century, effective promotion and public education proved especially vital for electrical inventors and system-builders. To ordinary Americans, electricity remained an enthralling mystery—silent, invisible, and dangerous. To overcome the public's fear of this unknown force, Thomas Edison turned his first display of the incandescent light bulb at Menlo Park in 1879 into a tourist event that attracted more than three thousand spectators. By 1882, Edison had likewise established his first central power station in New York City on Pearl Street, in the heart of the city's commercial and restaurant district. Here the conspicuous electrical lighting display piqued the curiosity of passersby who might be potential investors and consumers.[7]

A similar strategy of electrical promotion prevailed at world, state, and local expositions. Engineers and inventors regarded them as crucial opportunities to unveil and publicize the latest technological advances. Beginning with the Crystal Palace Exposition in 1851, each world's fair featured a central organizing technology or machine. In addition to the International Electrical Exhibitions in Paris in 1881 and in Frankfurt in 1891, the world's fair that best showcased electrical technology was Chicago's World Columbian Exposition of 1893.[8]

Niagara Falls served as a perpetual world's fair to power developers and electrical experimenters. Waterwheel designers, especially, tested their improved wheels under Niagara's floods. America's most image-conscious electrical geniuses—Thomas Edison and Nicola Tesla—readily dropped references to Niagara Falls to attract attention. In 1878 the *New York Sun* reported that utilizing Niagara for power was a logical next step for Edison, "the Wizard of Menlo Park," after he had perfected the light bulb. Nicola Tesla, whose breakthrough work on alternating current and a polyphase motor made him one of Edison's chief rivals, had typically secured financial backing for his experiments by cultivating a dashing aura, erecting futuristic laboratories, and staging surreal displays of artificial lighting. Tesla admitted to a lifelong dream of being the first to harness Niagara.[9]

Despite its unprecedented potential, the enormous power of Niagara was little utilized into the 1880s. Niagara's mills drew waterpower from the rapids, not from the cataract. Before the turbine was perfected, the enormous head of Niagara's waters overmatched waterwheel technology. More manageable "miniature Niagaras"—as small, power-producing cataracts everywhere were called—supplied more utilized waterpower than Niagara itself. To be sure, in the 1870s and 1880s Niagara hoteliers and tourism promoters lit the falls with arc lights and then with incandescent lamps for a public abuzz about Edison's work on electricity. Much of Prospect Park's popularity was attributable to nighttime illumination by an early Brush dynamo. Nonetheless, the only suggestion of large-scale Niagara power use came from the milling district of the Niagara Falls Hydraulic Power & Manufacturing Company below the cataract.[10]

Niagara Falls milling district, 1890s. Beneath the mills at the water's edge is the central station of the Niagara Falls Hydraulic Power & Manufacturing Company. The artificial waterfalls became a popular sight with tourists. (Courtesy, Local History Room, Niagara Falls Public Library)

First chartered in 1853, the Niagara Falls Hydraulic Power & Manufacturing Company finally completed its hydraulic canal in 1861. This 35-foot-wide, 8-foot-deep canal took water from the Niagara River above the cataract at Port Day to mill sites below the falls. Financial problems stalled the company until the mid-1870s, when new ownership attracted various manufacturers to these cliffside mill sites. Harnessing a head of water of only 25 to 75 feet, each manufactory at the top of the cliff initially used its own waterwheel and produced its own tailrace. By 1881 the power company had built a central station and began furnishing limited electricity to light the village of Niagara Falls and to power some of the mill-district manufactories.[11]

Although it offered no pathbreaking technology, the works of the Niagara Falls Hydraulic Power & Manufacturing Company immediately became Niagara's foremost industrial attraction. While many visitors and cultural custodians denounced such a utilitarian disfiguration of Niagara's cliffbanks, tourist literature hailed the runoff waterfalls as one of Niagara's most recognizable images. These tailraces inspired comparisons with the great cataract. "The tailrace discharges . . . [and] the foaming cascades . . . constitute one of the beautiful effects on the American side of the Gorge." Published photographs and postcards testified to the interest of this riveting addition to the landscape. Finally, because the cascading waters of the tailraces pointed out just how little of the drop at Niagara was being used, they provided a further spur to solving the engineering problem of how to harness Niagara Falls.[12]

A large step toward that solution was taken in 1886 when Thomas Evershed, a New York State division engineer, submitted a plan for the generation of 200,000 horsepower at Niagara Falls. Unlike previous utilization schemes, Evershed's plan called for systematic exploitation of the entire drop of the waters. A series of inlet canals would serve hundreds of mills just above Port Day, while a huge runoff tunnel would extend under the town of Niagara Falls and empty the "tailrace" back into the river near the Clifton Suspension Bridge. Using Evershed's proposal as a blueprint, a local corporation, the Niagara River Hydraulic Tunnel, Power & Sewer Company (later renamed the Niagara Falls Power Company), secured a charter from New York State in 1886 to divert water from the Niagara River just outside the Niagara reservation.[13]

The Evershed Plan marked the first serious scheme for the "application of Niagara power on a scale commensurate with the magnitude of the falls and with the demands of modern industry."[14] The proposal evoked the attention of the international engineering community, and engineers from all over the world tried to improve on this working blueprint for Niagara's mass utilization. Their efforts revealed not only the cultural implications of a huge engineering project at Niagara Falls, but also the cooperative, cosmopolitan character of the engineering profession. At the time of the St. Louis World's Fair of 1904, the American Institute of Electrical Engineers insisted that "the world-wide fame of

THE EVERSHED SCHEME INDICATING ELEVATION OF THE TUNNEL AND PLAN OF THE CANALS

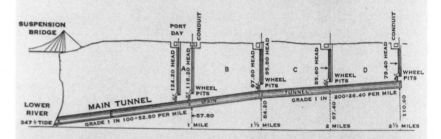

VERTICAL SECTION SHOWING SEVERAL OF THE WHEEL-PITS

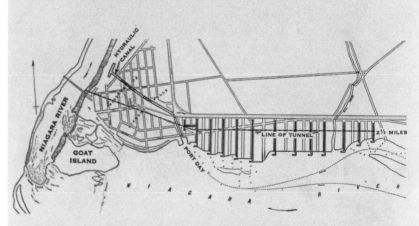

MAP INDICATING LOCATION AND SCOPE OF EVERSHED PLAN

Twelve canals supply water to 238 wheels distributed over an extended area which discharge through a common tunnel system

[1] See Chapter XVII, Volume II, for details of the Evershed proposals and of its modification by The Cataract Construction Company.

Thomas Evershed's proposal. In 1886, Evershed was the first to present a serious plan to harness the entire drop of the Falls. As a working blueprint, the proposal attracted the attention of the international engineering community.

Niagara Falls has for many years attracted the engineers of all nations, and they have been at work devising means for utilizing the great water power in these falls."[15]

Although Thomas Evershed's plan galvanized electrical development at Niagara Falls, his scheme was scarcely recognizable by the time the Niagara Falls Power Company finally harnessed the power of the falls. Between 1886 and 1890, a series of critical problems stalled construction of the great Niagara tunnel. Evershed's mill-over-wheel plan was too inefficient and costly. No suitable way to transmit the power yet existed, nor had a decision been made on a motor to put that power to work. The remaining stumbling block was the lack of indigenous industry at Niagara. Even if Niagara were harnessed, developers would be left with far more power than they could possibly use unless it could be transmitted over long distances, to Buffalo and beyond.[16]

Consequently, as engineers revised the Evershed Plan they concentrated on schemes to distribute the power from a central station; power transmission and distribution would obviate the need for separate canals and wheels and even riverfront factory locales. At the time, however, this approach was highly dubious. Power plants typically served an adjoining factory or lit a neighborhood, converting limited amounts of energy for a very limited locale.[17]

If efficient power transmission and distribution proved the viability of the Niagara project, a more fundamental problem concerned the enormous head of the Niagara waters. Niagara's waters broke even iron waterwheels. Although stronger turbines replaced the old wheels, Edward Dean Adams pointed out that "no American experience could be depended upon to design turbine units to develop 5000 horse-power." Both in turbine design and in electrical transmission, American engineering lagged behind the state of the art in Europe. Few American machines had a capacity for more than 100 horsepower, and the Niagara Falls Power Company plans called for the development and use of 200,000 horsepower, but such a technological leap was beyond the limited financial means of the company's local owners. According to Edward Dean Adams, "it was believed that the familiarity of the great public with the name Niagara and what it represented in water-power going to waste, might be utilized to secure the necessary capital." But when the company presented its plans to potential backers in several cities, not even the renown of Niagara could attract sufficient investment.[18]

Only in 1889—when a company subsidiary, the Cataract Construction Corporation, was incorporated in New Jersey—did the Niagara venture attain the requisite financial support. "Money subscribers" such as J. P. Morgan, Francis Lynde Stetson, Morris K. Jesup, John Jacob Astor, Edward Dean Adams, William K. Vanderbilt, and several other Vanderbilts had formed the corporation, which was "the representative of the Niagara company, charged with the design, financing, and construction" of the plant and power operations. The prestige of these money subscribers immediately guaranteed the credibility of the Niagara power venture and gave it national import. Most of the money subscribers were already involved in financial sponsorship of the Edison Electric Light Company and the Westinghouse Company and, not surprisingly, several of these socially prominent New York City capitalists had previous ties to Niagara as members of the preservation-minded Niagara Falls Association.[19]

Backed with enormous capital, the Cataract Construction Corporation began to build a shortened version of the power tunnel before deciding on a method of power distribution. A special "Extra" edition of the *Niagara Falls Gazette* announced that Niagara Falls was to be "the Great Manufacturing and Electricity Center in America." At the very least, power could be brought locally to a large new mill region in Niagara Falls, and to that end the corporation acquired 1,580 acres over a two-mile stretch of land above the state reservation. Almost immediately, the Pittsburgh Reduction Company became the first tenant on this land when it transferred its aluminum manufacturing operations from Pittsburgh to take advantage of the inexpensive, year-round power the Niagara Falls Power Company offered.[20]

Despite the facilities to increase Niagara's local industries, the primary goal of the Niagara Falls Power Company (and the only chance, according to advisers, to make the venture pay) was to find a way to send the power to the burgeoning manufacturing city of Buffalo. If this pioneering venture in bulk electrical power transmission were to become economically viable, abundant electricity might ultimately be sent to cities within a 300- to 400-mile radius of Niagara Falls.

Although no efficient technology for power transmission existed in 1890, expectations were heightened. Europeans had successfully transmitted limited amounts of power by means of compressed air and direct and alternating current electricity since the 1870s. When queried by the Cataract Construction Corporation about the feasibility of this long-distance transmission, Thomas Edison cabled a positive reply to the firm. Having succeeded in his other technologies, Edison anticipated a quick solution grounded in electrical science.[21]

Edison's optimism notwithstanding, electricity remained a questionable source of industrial power. Most electric use was in lighting, and the electricity used for power was the Edison-backed direct current, which proved inefficient over even short transmission distances. At best, widespread adoption of the Edison system required several power stations in the different parts of a city, which made the direct-current system an extremely expensive and cumbersome option.[22]

Alternatives to the Edison system were even more problematical in 1890. One highly regarded possibility, the Faure battery, leaked too much energy and proved to be too impermanent. Alternating current, which could be stepped up to high voltages for speedy transmission, seemed the most likely option. Since the mid-1880s, however, alternating current engaged direct current in what the press referred to as the "battle of the currents." Staunch defenders of direct current, led by Edison, exaggerated the dangers and uncertainties of alternating current. Edward Dean Adams, the first president of the Cataract Construction Company and historian of the Niagara Falls Power Company, claimed that in 1889 the foremost textbook on electrical transmission contained only a brief mention of alternating current in the preface; alternating current seemed to be a promising option for the distant future only. Finally, while the flamboyant Tesla was at work on an alternating current motor by 1890, his invention was "still a prophecy rather than a completely demonstrated reality."[23]

Because of the technological uncertainties, the engineering community continued to debate the most viable method of distributing Niagara's power. As Francis L. Stetson, a director of the Niagara Falls Power Company and its most outspoken advocate, admitted, "In 1890, I was advised that power could be transmitted from Niagara to Buffalo, not by electricity, but only by compressed air, and . . . my adviser was Mr.

George Westinghouse." Even when the Cataract Construction Corporation commissioned the construction of two powerhouses, electricity had not been settled on. The initial plan called for the second plant to be designed for transmission of compressed air.[24]

Despite technical problems and uncertainties, the fame of Niagara Falls continued to attract attention to the project. The Cataract Construction Corporation advertised Niagara Falls whenever it recruited personnel, initiated new research projects or engineering systems, or sought greater capitalization. Adams reported that the corporation considered it good business policy to slip in references to the Niagara cataract. After all, "the falls still remained as a delight and wonder, while its observers pondered its problems of nature and entertained dreams of science applied."[25]

The most comprehensive strategy for culling up-to-the-moment technology on how to best utilize Niagara's immense power was the creation of the International Niagara Commission of 1890–91. This agency, which sat in London and was presided over by Sir William Thomson (later, Lord Kelvin), focused the eyes of the world's engineers on Niagara. The blue-ribbon commission solicited plans from top engineers and engineering houses and intended to award monetary prizes to the best scheme for developing Niagara's power, for distributing that power, and for combined development and distribution of the power. In the view of Niagara Power Company chief engineer Coleman Sellers, the commission gave the Niagara Falls project instant legitimacy and credibility:

> It has brought the scheme before the world with a prestige that cannot be measured by dollars; it has enlisted the interest of the whole scientific world; it has made the company command the confidence of the world and won for it the respect, as wise, far-seeing cautious business men and not followers of any one or more visionary schemer or inventor.[26]

Despite receiving fifteen European and five American entries, the International Niagara Commission decided not to award a prize in the category of combined power production and distribution. For the next two years, work on the hydraulic system continued as the Cataract Construction Corporation groped for an efficient and profitable technological solution to the transmission problem. In fact, the corporation delayed completion of the power plant in order to find the most efficient power type and method of distribution. By avoiding making a commitment to a plan until the last possible moment, the corporation hoped to avoid adopting a system that might be obsolete before it was operational.[27]

Tourist exhibitions of alternating current set crucial precedents for the implementation of Niagara's electrical system. At the Frankfurt Exhibition of 1891, engineers harnessed hydropower from a waterfall 100 miles away at Lauffen, converted it into alternating current, and sent it to the exhibition. The Lauffen waterfall powered a symbolic artificial waterfall as well as the manufacturing center of the fair. Only after the successful installation of alternating current at the World's Columbian Exposition did the Cataract Construction Corporation commit itself to the use of this form of power distribution. The Chicago fair foreshadowed what Niagara would do on a massive scale. When on May 6, 1893, the Cataract Construction Company made its decision to adopt alternating current, the inextricable link between alternating current and Niagara Falls was struck. Thereafter, the Niagara power development ushered the nation and the world into a new technological era.[28]

Although Niagara's tourist appeal contributed to the creation of a new, electrical Niagara, technological advances fueled the debate over the site's natural splendor. The most volatile issue of the harnessing of Niagara was not its engineering merit, which was indisputable, but environmental and sentimental concerns. Public outcry over the desecration of Niagara, accompanied by dire predictions that its future as a resort was doomed, persisted even after the state reservation was created in 1885.

These fears were well founded, because such experts as Lord Kelvin believed technology would inevitably supersede nature; he anticipated a day when no water would flow over the precipice. In his opinion, the utilitarian Niagara offered greater interest to tourists than nature. An article in the *Literary Digest*, "Is Niagara Doomed," announced that the day would come in the industrial age when Niagara would be turned on and off. Not only would industrial development prove more "beautiful" than nature, but the Falls in total harness "would furnish a spectacle of even more impressive grandeur than that now displayed by the uncontrolled cataract." As power development gave Niagara over to engineers and industrialists, nature lovers and preservationists saw the power interests as the bane of nature at Niagara.[29]

Nonetheless, despite warnings from the Commissioners of the State Reservation at Niagara, both electrical power interests and tourist promoters had cause for optimism for electric Niagara. Electricity was already associated with America's beloved icon figures Benjamin Franklin and Thomas Edison, and no one on the American cultural scene in the late 1800s inspired a greater sense of possibility and expectation than Edison. What Edison did to augment interest and faith in electricity, Niagara Falls would do on a grander scale. Intricate details of the harnessing of Niagara flooded scientific and engineering journals, such as *Scientific American, Cassier's Magazine,* and *Engineering Magazine.* The entire July 1895 issue of *Cassier's Magazine* explained the major components of the Niagara Falls Power Company project. Replete with an article on "Niagara in History" and numerous photos and illustrations, the issue conveyed the message that the Niagara electrical works had to be seen to be fully appreciated.[30]

In addition to this coverage in professional journals, newspapers and general-interst magazines also published thorough descriptions of the electrical accomplishment at Niagara. Niagara Falls did much to give electricity an appealing popular image. The dynamic Nicola Tesla made headlines by announcing that his invention of a multiple-phase electrical motor would make it possible to power the world with electricity from Niagara Falls. *Cosmopolitan, Munsey's, McClure's, Harper's Weekly,* and other popular magazines ran articles that followed the "harnessing," "chaining," "diversion," "capture," or "end" of Niagara. These articles, in addition to updated editions of tourist guidebooks, treated powerhouses and tunnels as additional sublime attractions at Niagara and glorified the engineering takeover of the landscape. Readers learned that the most expensive, extensive, and important engineering undertakings occurred at the site of the world's greatest natural landmark. Photographic images and illustrations paid tribute to this "progress." Niagara was undisputedly the "electrical Mecca of the world."[31]

Tourist literature helped convince the public that the power company's project belonged at Niagara. Guidebooks called on the tradition of progress by pointing out the centuries-old quest to utilize Niagara.

The first Niagara sawmill dated back to 1725, and since that time "doubtless hundreds of men with a mechanical turn of mind laid awake o'nights, thinking of the fortunes that could be made by turning well-wheels with this mighty stream." Indeed, if the uniquely American role was to transform energy, Niagara offered American engineers their greatest glory and challenge. As long as Niagara's waters tumbled over the cataract without serving humankind, the Niagara landscape would be incomplete and Americans were dissipating their birthright.[32]

Perhaps the most insistent and prolific advocate for this position was Peter A. Porter. Porter, the grandson of Peter B. Porter, was a visionary local power developer, politician, and guidebook writer. His essay "The Niagara Region in History," the only nontechnical article in *Cassier's* "Niagara Power Number" of July 1895, waxes most admiringly on Niagara's inspiration to human endeavor. Since the days of Hennepin, there had been no place where "the attention of mankind has been more, and in more ways, attracted than to this Niagara region." In a later history, *Niagara, an Aboriginal Center of Trade* (1906), Porter noted that Niagara Falls served as a portage and meeting place for Native American trade. Although, over the intervening centuries, attention shifted to scenery, the hydraulic developments of the 1890s allowed the area to "again become a really great center of trade" and productivity. In Porter's view, Niagara Falls had at last returned to its rightful roots and could begin to fulfill its commercial potential.[33]

New Niagara advocates also lauded the artistic merits of the inspiring waterpower development. Whereas poets and artists had failed to capture the true essence of Niagara, perhaps engineers could succeed. The most devoted proponents of vast power utilization at Niagara Falls saw a poetry in the cataract in harness. The Niagara section of *The Romance of Modern Engineering* offered a rhapsodic vision of a Niagara not going to waste but ceaselessly working for the betterment of humankind. An article by Curtis Brown in the September 1894 issue of *Cosmopolitan*, "The Diversion of Niagara," found inspiration in the utter ease with which Niagara would be able to turn a thousand mills. "Poetry certainly lurks in the idea of an energy that can toss off lightly, without missing it, a far greater power than ever was before obtained from any one source."[34]

While hinting that poetic paeans to Niagara's natural scenic charms had grown stale, "The Diversion of Niagara" suggests that the engineer

NATURE GIANTS THAT MAN HAS CONQUERED
BY RAYMOND PERRY
GIANT NO. 2—WATER-POWER

LAST month we told of the first nature giant man had tamed —the Wind. The second nature giant that man learned to control was the power of flowing water. We all know that water rises from the ocean as vapor and, dropping as rain on the mountains, makes its way in rivers to the ocean again. The explanation is simple enough, but when we see a mighty waterfall like Niagara, we realize at once that we are in the presence of a powerful giant who can do the work of armies for us, if properly harnessed. But it was long before man learned how to do this.

Up to that time each one had to grind his own grain, a little at a time, by rolling it between two flat stones; but when he learned the use of the water-wheel, he was able to grind with larger stones, such as he himself could not even move, and produce enough meal for his own use and a whole village besides. And now, to crown all, we have the turbine, which takes vastly greater power from the passing water.

The manufacturing industries have made our country famous the world over, and the giant water-force is doing its full share in turning the wheels. We can also see the power of water in use in a canal-lock by means of which a boat may be taken uphill; and in hydraulic mining where it digs the dirt and washes out the gold at the same time. The modern systems of sanitary plumbing, safeguarding the health, and of irrigation, by means of which vast tracts of desert lands are made to bloom, both depend upon the power of falling water.

Enthusiasts for a New Niagara promoted their vision widely. Here is an illustrated page from a children's magazine (1911), showing a conquered Niagara.

had given Niagara a new and more palpable meaning:

> Perhaps the new dignity conferred upon Niagara by the engineer
> will give future poets inspiration for better verse, and will help
> to dispel the feeling of disappointment that comes to almost every
> imaginative person at first view of the Falls.[35]

The photos accompanying the text give evidence of this new meaning.
A scene of the Niagara rapids uses the caption "Wasted Energy"; the
spectacular view of Niagara's water falling over the precipice represented
"the transformation of energy"; other new attractions include "a twelve
hundred Horsepower Turbine" and "the discharge of the hydraulic Canal." Contemplation of the perfect efficiency of a harnessed Niagara
would provide a more inspiring, more ennobling, and more thrilling
experience than the contemplation of untrammeled nature.[36]

Despite Niagara's utilitarian "destiny," enthusiastic commentators reassured skeptics that a harnessed Niagara would not lose its distinc-
tiveness as a natural spectacle. "The Diversion of Niagara" proclaims
that the harnessing of Niagara is no indignity, that instead the cataract
"might be said to be amusing itself by lending a small part of its strength
to these labors—a diversion in a double sense." With its torrential waters
undiminished, Niagara Falls would freely serve humankind while retaining its beauty and grandeur.[37]

According to New Niagara enthusiasts, Niagara Falls power development was just another part of the natural landscape at Niagara. Visitors
marveled at the new power plants along the riverbanks, at the edge of the
cataract, and on the side of the gorge. The technological order integrated
massive powerhouses, tunnels, and penstocks with the trees, vegetation,
and gorge-side rock formations. Despite preconceptions that any endeavor of such magnitude would have diminished the cataract, power
advocates stressed that one of the most reassuring aspects of the Niagara
venture was in fact its limited impact on the landscape.[38]

It is not surprising that the Niagara Falls Power Company emphasized
its support for the state reservation. Company pamphlets hailed the
need for the reservation and endorsed its inviolability while also reaf-
firming the principle that Niagara was a resource that invited utilization.
Edward Dean Adams proclaimed that, in addition to enhancing appre-

ciation for nature, the reservation inspired visions of Niagara's utility. While visiting the reservation, he said,

> the engineer inquires as to the source, the quantity and regularity of flow and proposes means for controlling the water and developing and distributing its power for myriad uses. . . . The far-seeing citizen and the statesman, concerned with the conservation of our natural resources, deplore the waste of energy and wonder why so little is being used.

New Niagara advocates noted that Thomas Evershed developed his blueprint for the vast harnessing of Niagara while he was an engineer for the Niagara state reservation. A deep desire to preserve Niagara's scenery intact motivated his plan.[39]

Confident that the New Niagara did not usurp nature, tourist promoters and power developers alike championed the engineer's additions to the Niagara landscape. Spokesmen for the New Niagara proudly publicized each new step in harnessing Niagara as positive events worthy of study and as offering delights for tourists. Eminent electrical engineer Coleman Sellers saw the import of the power development for tourism even if his interpretation of previous tourism at Niagara Falls was naive. "For the first time in the history of Niagara Falls," he said, "attractions other than those furnished by nature are offered." In *The Niagara Book: A Complete Souvenir of Niagara Falls,* issued for the world's fairs of 1893 and 1901, Sellers's chapter "The Utilization of Niagara's Power" addressed the public's curiosity about the projects of the Niagara Falls Power Company. And *Paul's Dictionary of Buffalo, Niagara Falls, Tonawanda & Vicinity* of 1896 explained that as waterpower actually was utilized, power facilities were of "interest to the world of mechanics and to every visitor to Niagara Falls."

Indeed, it is now assured that whereas in the past, Niagara Falls has won its distinction mainly as affording the greatest natural scenery of its kind in the world, the time is at hand when the place will, because of cheap electric energy, possess the distinction of being the greatest manufacturing center in the world.[40]

The romance of the Niagara Power Company's utilization of Niagara Falls power first focused on the great power tunnel. This 6,700-foot-long, 21-foot-high, and 18-foot-wide horseshoe-shaped tunnel immediately became a tourist attraction in its own right. As a commentator noted: "When the passenger alights at the railway station here, he stands directly over it." Tours aboard the *Maid of the Mist* steamboat, which passed by the tunnel outlet, as well as booklets such as *The Great Tunnel at Niagara Falls: A Story of a Bore That Is Not a Bore,* addressed the public's curiosity. The 1892 version of the New York Central Railroad's "Four Track Series" booklet, *Two Days at Niagara Falls,* devoted three pages to the construction of the great Niagara tunnel. Even the map room of the Cataract House hotel displayed a large model of the tunnel.[41]

Not only did the tunnel represent a tremendous capital investment, but the three-year project through solid rock became a structural landmark to rival Niagara's natural sublimity. Bored through solid rock and reinforced over its entire length with multiple layers of brick, the tunnel project was, according to critics, "probably the most perfect piece of continuous rock boring to be found anywhere in the world." A Michigan Central Railroad gift book told readers that more than a thousand workers labored around the clock on this, the greatest hydraulic tunnel in the world. The twenty-eight lives lost during construction further ennobled the tunnel as one of humankind's great, though costly, engineering feats and a source of pride for Americans. The lowliest Niagara Falls tunnel worker, though working in cramped and dangerous conditions, could claim a dignity in the triumph of nation-building. In return for the few years of arduous tunnel-blasting, the nation would be rewarded with an energy supply for centuries.[42]

The great Niagara tunnel extended from the focal point of the new electric Niagara—the Niagara Falls Power Company powerhouse. Edward Dean Adams noted that "the visitors at Niagara Falls increased at the first evidence of active construction of the power-plant."[43] All Niagara Falls power plants, whether they were built on the American or Canadian side of the cataract, immediately faced the scrutiny of tourists. These large structures intruded on the riverbanks and cliffsides within the view from the state reservation; on the Canadian side, they stood within the reserved confines of Queen Victoria Park itself. The power

The first great project of the Cataract Construction Company was a 6,700-foot-long power tunnel that took three years to complete. This photograph shows the tunnel during construction in 1892.

companies, tourist guidebooks, and visitors hailed the electric power plants as the central feature of the New Niagara.

Edward Dean Adams outlined the requisite features of the first power plant of the Niagara Falls Power Company. It had to provide suitable housing for "the torrents of Niagara." The powerhouse, "designed to be the largest in the world," was to be a symbol of the power and beauty of the great cataract. "It should be *attractive,* artistic in grandeur, dignified, impressive, enduring and monumental"—and, he added, *protective* and *instructive.* According to Adams, visitors should leave with as clear an impression of the heroic power plants as they had of the cataract. "The souvenir pictures carried away by the visitors should include one or all three of the powerhouses."[44]

Before the Niagara Falls Power Company Powerhouse Number One was constructed, powerhouses suffered from architectural neglect. Few were built by architects, let alone by one of America's most renowned architectural firms. Historian John R. Stilgoe located only a few articles on powerhouse design in architectural journals between 1880 and 1930. Engineering journals, which discussed the features of powerhouses in detail, equated merit and beauty not with aesthetics but with efficiency. Plants serving a factory works might even be makeshift structures grafted onto the landscape at the site they served. Built for machines rather than people, most were enormous but poorly designed structures whose utilitarian function obliterated any artistic pretense.[45]

In 1892, before it had even decided on the mode of power production and distribution, the Cataract Construction Corporation contracted the architectural firm of McKim, Mead & White to design and build two powerhouses on the inlet canal near Port Day. McKim, Mead & White was perhaps best known as the designer of the Boston Public Library. It had also already done private commissions for some of the directors of the Cataract Construction Corporation, including Edward Dean Adams, who lived in one of the Villard houses in New York City. Although Charles McKim, William Mead, and Stanford White had no prior experience designing powerhouses, hiring their firm was a master stroke for the Cataract Construction Corporation. McKim, Mead & White's abiding commitment to public architecture (utilizing local themes and historical associations) dovetailed neatly with the power company's interpretation of the meaning of Niagara Falls. The very fact that the power developers hired such a renowned firm demonstrated their concern not only for aesthetics but also for the symbolic significance of the power plant.[46]

Powerhouse Number One was built in bayed sections set off by "circular topped windows that are 14 feet wide and 15 feet two inches high." Originally 140 feet long, the powerhouse reached a length of 450 feet when all its eleven turbo-generators were installed. The arching of each section successively added a vertical element to the building's horizontal extension. This "unique and impressive" architectural effect kept the design "so well proportioned that a stranger does not estimate the parts nearly so large as they are." Because the power plant did not burn coal, no coal towers, coal bins, or ash heaps were necessary, and the building could remain a harmonious entity. The harmony was further ensured by the smooth capping effect of the roof. Later, the design of the Trans-

The Niagara Falls Power Company plant, showing Powerhouse Number One (right) and the Transformer House (left) at the turn of the century. (Courtesy, Buffalo and Erie County Historical Society)

former House (1893) and Powerhouse Number Two (1901–3) completed the complementary effect.[47]

Disdaining ordinary brick, McKim, Mead & White used native stone excavated from the tunnel and the wheel pit as a shell around the steel framing of the powerhouses.[48] Because similar stone lined the inlet canal, the canal and powerhouses were extensions of each other. Most important, this stone-brick masonry allowed the powerhouse to claim symbolic affinity with the natural landscape at Niagara. The masonry was rough-trimmed to avoid any sense of artificiality. Its solidity connoted permanence and stability and also protection, which was a crucial foil for the highly speculative venture contained within.

The Niagara Falls Power Company powerhouse marked the first design in five years by McKim, Mead & White to return to a heavy, naturalistic idiom reminiscent of the work of Henry Richardson. A triumphal arch connoted the sublimity of the structure and lent majesty to the powerhouse entry. By subsuming the mundane within the noble, the firm created a monument to modern American industrial and technological civilization. A new, representative American building—the electrical powerhouse—united science and art, order and progress. Regular geometric forms, solidity and massiveness, suggestions of Renaissance palazzos, and the great arch heralded a new American civilization to rival the great accomplishments of classical and European civilizations.[49]

Like other McKim, Mead & White commissions, the Niagara powerhouse hailed the union of the arts. Beyond the alliance of architect and engineer, it also welcomed the landscape architect's art and the sculptor's art. Neat, parklike grounds surrounded the structure. In 1895, Stanford White and Frederick MacMonnies, one of America's foremost sculptors and a favorite contributor to the work of McKim, Mead & White, collaborated on a flagstaff in front of the powerhouse. This ceremonial space further monumentalized the powerhouse and affirmed the structure's worthiness for its site.

Another affirmation of the high art and organicism of the Niagara Falls Power Company powerhouse was evident in the entrance archway. The huge triumphal arch bore a sculpted company seal, also designed by MacMonnies. Because "a seal in a powerhouse is an innovation," Edward Dean Adams insisted that

> the seal was the crowning touch to the architectural setting of the Niagara power-houses which distinguished it from former power-houses and gave a new significance to Niagara power. The part of the ordinary mill which housed its water-wheels, or the typical city electric plant of the early nineties alongside of railroad tracks and amid piles of coal and ashes gave no suggestion of architecture or seals.[50]

The seal's circular design featured a paddling Native American chief, Niagara, standing in a canoe but trying to slow the vessel against the strong currents of the rapids. The outer rim of the seal was emblazoned with a border of local fish and fossils, metaphorical images that en-

Entrance to Powerhouse Number One in 1924. McKim, Mead & White designed
the building as a symbolic monument to America's modern technological
civilization.

sconced the power plant in the Niagara landscape and at the same time
offered a paean to progress. "The Niagara seal represents in a high
degree the wonder of nature and the art of man; the romance of a dying
race and a science of a new century." As the visitor entered the Niagara
Falls powerhouse, the Indian chief, fish, and fossils forged the link
between one world and another and signified the transformation of the
age of nature to the age of technology.[51]

As a great work of public architecture, the Niagara Falls Power Company powerhouse of McKim, Mead & White set the aesthetic standard

for future powerhouse construction at Niagara Falls and elsewhere. Later Niagara powerhouses, on both the American and Canadian sides of the cataract, also attempted to monumentalize the power venture and yet subsume it within the natural landscape. In Canada, electrical works entered the reserved landscape of Queen Victoria Park beginning in 1900. The Canadian government and the power companies justified such incursions on reserved territory as beautifying measures; in exchange for the right to erect facilities within the park, the power companies paid rent and promised to beautify the landscape. Because two of the three companies that built powerhouses in Queen Victoria Park were controlled by American capital, these power ventures were already keenly sensitive to environmental and aesthetic concerns.[52] Guidebooks and power company pamphlets highlighted the Ontario Power Company's expenditure of $1 million on handsome Italianate-Renaissance palazzo designs for its powerworks. The company's screen-house featured a broad promenade that offered a spectacular view of the rapids. Similarly, the Distributing Station, situated on a bluff in Victoria Park, became "by far the most pronounced landmark on the Canadian side."[53]

Even as the power companies likened their works to palazzos and monumental landmarks, they continued to stress the restrained, unassuming qualities of the new structures. "In building the powerhouse, the instructions to the architect were to design a structure with dignified lines, but as inconspicuous as possible," according to one contemporary. Niagara powerhouses in the Canadian park or along the riverbanks were designed to blend into the landscape and to suggest harmony with the natural topography and vegetation. In response to charges that the powerhouse construction had scarred the landscape, tourist literature noted that the new islands and channels formed during the construction had added picturesque nature spots and viewing stations to the landscape. Far from supplanting the natural world, the powerworks had augmented it.[54]

In an address before the American Civic Association in 1907, Francis V. Greene, president of the Ontario Power Company, noted that from a strictly engineering standpoint a blocklike, factory-style powerhouse would have met the company's needs. The power venture's commitment to Niagara's scenery, however, was that nothing short of the world's most tastefully designed powerhouse would satisfy the company. The company asked the public to tolerate a temporary, unattractive construction while it guaranteed a permanent, aesthetic, natural-looking site. Greene realized that the powerhouse visitor was also a nature watcher. The only difference in the New Niagara from the old, Greene maintained, was that now the parks and electrical companies gave hundreds of thousands of visitors easy, convenient access to and enjoyment of the natural landscape, while technology served humankind limitlessly.[55]

As important as the outside appearance of these electrical structures was, the key to the new, electric Niagara lay within the powerhouses. The interior of the power plant housed the world's most advanced machinery and complex technology, and in an age of technological enthusiasm, many of Niagara's visitors—from the world's leading scientists to H. G. Wells to the readers of *Ladies' Home Journal*—found the powerhouses to be the region's most significant attraction.[56]

The chance to see the world's most modern and powerful machine, the dynamo, was a highlight of a visit to Niagara Falls. What the steam locomotive was to the steam era, the dynamo was to the electricity age: it inspired obsessive attention from turn-of-the-century thinkers. Henry Adams, who traveled to world's fairs seeking an understanding of the modern world, equated the dynamo to a miracle. This mystical energy-transforming machine symbolized infinite force and heralded a new world spiraling exponentially into the future. H. G. Wells saw Niagara Falls dynamos as "human will made visible, thought translated into easy and commanding things." For Wells these dynamos were "clean, noiseless, and starkly powerful . . . noble masses of machinery, huge black slumbering monsters, great sleeping tops that engender irresistible forces in their sleep." Silently, human accomplishment had triumphed above Niagara's roaring elemental waters.[57]

Unlike the great steam-powered boilers and machines (such as the Corliss engine), which were a clanging maze of moving belts and shafts, Niagara dynamos were remarkable for the simplicity of their streamlined forms of cold, black steel. According to Wells, the 5,000 and 10,000 horsepower Niagara dynamos would fit comfortably into the living room of a cottage. Coleman Sellers noted that these machines would attract interest precisely because they were so uninteresting.

> The electrical generators in the Power House will of themselves show perhaps little that is especially attractive, either as to mas-

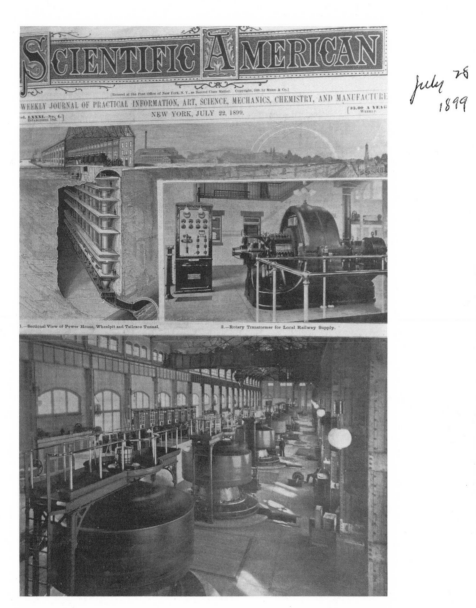

SCIENTIFIC AMERICAN

[Entered at the Post Office of New York, N. Y., as Second Class Matter. Copyright, 1899, by Munn & Co.]

WEEKLY JOURNAL OF PRACTICAL INFORMATION, ART, SCIENCE, MECHANICS, CHEMISTRY, AND MANUFACTURE

Vol. LXXXI.—No. 4.]
[Established 1845.]

NEW YORK, JULY 22, 1899.

[$3.00 A YEAR.
WEEKLY.

July 7th 1899

1.—Sectional View of Power House, Wheelpit and Tailrace Tunnel.

2.—Rotary Transformer for Local Railway Supply.

Popular magazines and scientific journals rushed to publish images of the Niagara Falls power plant. The rainbow in the upper right suggests that the plant was a suitable addition to the Niagara landscape.

sive proportions or intricate and curious machinery, but they will be wonderful for their subtlety.[58]

How thoroughly this modern technology contrasted with steam-driven powerhouses and the first electric powerhouses. Powerhouses of the steam era required human work to keep them going and suggested images of worn-out, grimy toilers actively stoking machines or attending to breakdowns in the intricate system of belting and shafting. As Stilgoe has shown, Americans were familiar with the interior of powerhouses as mazes of "pistons flying, balance wheels spinning, and drive shafts revolving." One contemporary tribute to the Niagara Falls Power Company powerhouse stressed that even "the typical power station of a decade ago was a chaos of electric wires which were festooned from the ceiling and crossed and recrossed each other in every direction." It was not only difficult but also dangerous to enter a powerhouse.[59]

The Niagara Falls Power Company power plant balanced technological requirements with aesthetic taste and tourist convenience. The interior design of the powerhouse ushered visitors to convenient viewing platforms.[60] Natural light filtered in the immense open space of the plant. A neat, orderly appearance prevailed, because conduits and casings kept the wiring carefully hidden, "it being impossible to find a trace of this most important part of the installation." Photographic images of control boxes and switchboards showed a clean, functional arena in which toil, dust, and clutter had no place. H. G. Wells reported that "the dazzling clean switchboard, with its little handles and levers, is the seat of empire over more power than the strength of a million disciplined, unquestioning men." Controlroom switchboards suggested calculation and precision—the perfect realization of technical efficiency. Francis V. Greene boasted, "To those who comprehend what tremendous forces are here controlled, this silent room is a most impressive spectacle."[61]

Only a few attendants oversaw the entire operation of each Niagara Falls powerhouse, and the neat, easy manner of these workers conveyed the clean, effortless, and leisurely aura of the electricity age. In the controlroom engineers directed the flow and distribution of the com-

Controlroom of a Niagara Falls power plant in 1907. Observers were struck by the clean, sleek interior with its state-of-the-art machines, dials, and switches. (Courtesy, Buffalo and Erie County Historical Society)

pany's electricity output. These heroes of the electricity age were extensions of the controlroom machines, dials, and switches. "The well being of so many thousands depends on the small band in the powerhouse, that it becomes an absolute necessity for each man to be specially trained, alert, resourceful to meet any emergency that may arise," wrote a contemporary. By the flick of a switch, these experts activated machines that altered the course of business and life effortlessly over great distances.[62]

Power transmission was the most ethereal and magical aspect of the Niagara electrical system. Harnessing power was one wonder, but "the transmission of Niagara—the play of Niagara power on a wire and delivery of it to every conceivable market within a two hundred mile radius is the second wonder; one greater than the first, for Niagara has entered the transmission era." The general public stood little chance of understanding the conversion of power from the plunge of Niagara's waters into transmittable energy. Electrical current originally at 2,200 volts was "stepped up" to 60,000 volts for high-speed long-distance transmission. Arching power lines draped on tall poles stood as the only tangible evidence of the enormous power potential on its way, moving invisibly at a lightning-fast pace.[63]

The culminating step in the utilization of Niagara Falls was the productive use of electricity. The enormous quantity of energy available over the electrical lines added to the wonderment of the system. One pamphlet said:

> The mystery of it all seems rather to increase than to be dissipated when one calls to mind the hundreds of cars miles away, speeding in every direction, the hundreds of thousands of electric lights turning night into day and the countless mills and machines performing the hard tasks, all driven by the forces developed before one's eyes and sent out over mere copper cables from the group of silent, turret-like pieces of mechanism without cog or belt, pulley or cam.[64]

Although guided power-company tours traced the course of Niagara power from the genesis of an idea to its use in industry and the home, real examples abounded outside the immediate confines of the generating station. Visitors at the Niagara Falls Power Company could also look toward the horizon to see a great industrial zone built on the power company's enormous land holdings. The tenants included metallurgical, chemical, and paper companies. As the industrial zone grew, it merged into the model workers' town of Echota, which provided family housing with up-to-date sanitation facilities and lighting courtesy of Niagara electricity and the Niagara Falls Power Company. Even more impressive was that power company visitors could follow the Niagara River more than twenty miles to Buffalo, where the company first transmitted 1,000 horsepower in November 1895. Long-distance electrical transmission provided light, propelled trains, and powered machinery of all kinds.

The most vivid example of electrical transmission for tourists in the late 1890s and early 1900s was Niagara's gorge-side electric railroads, a new form of transportation that familiarized masses of riders with Electric Niagara. The electrified tracks of the Niagara Falls Park & River Railway on the Canadian side and the Niagara Falls & Lewiston Railroad, or the "Great Gorge Route," on the American side sped thousands of pleasure riders on a spectacular trip through Niagara's natural and artificial attractions.

Speed and thrill, the illusion of danger, views of the unexpected, and the magical effects of nighttime searchlights drew the public to the electric gorge-side excursions. As John Kasson has shown in his book on Coney Island, *Amusing the Million,* mass participation in the wonders of modern technology and machinery promised a giddy escape from mundane reality. Much like the new roller-coasters at Coney Island–type amusement parks, these popular joyrides diverted fear of the technological sublime at Niagara into an enjoyable sensation that reaffirmed the pleasure-giving benevolence of electric technology.[65]

Whether they merely passed by on the electric railroads or actually entered the powerhouses, visitors to Niagara Falls found the area's electric landscape to be an instant tourist attraction. As Edward Dean Adams had hoped, the dawn of the electricity age inaugurated yet another tourist boom at the Falls. The possibilities of new technology and industry quickly captured the imagination of visitors.

A Niagara Falls Power Company powerhouse registry log reads like a who's who of turn-of-the-century dignitaries, capitalists, and engineers. Many visitors came with letters of introduction. Engineering societies and engineering students looked to Niagara Falls to keep up-to-date with the most progressive electrical developments. Foreign engineers toured the facilities in hopes of taking knowledge back home. Others who were dubious about alternating current and the Niagara methods found that the trip to the Niagara facilities erased their skepticism. Investors and engineers looked at the Niagara power works as a potential pattern for power systems in New York City and other locales.[66]

The more tourism the Niagara Falls power plants generated, the more company officials basked in the glory and legitimacy that such visits conferred. Edward Dean Adams's company history of the Niagara Falls

Power Company chronicled the praise of American and foreign engineers and such notables as Theodore Roosevelt. Francis Stetson, chief advocate for the Niagara Falls Power Company, stressed that although more people went to Niagara to see nature the most significant attraction of the region was not necessarily its scenery:

> If hundreds of thousands of people come here to see the scenic glory of the Niagara, I will ask you to see the character of the names that are written in that book [power company registry]— men who have come there to study and admire, from Lord Kelvin and from the great Chinese Viceroy; and the last inscription of William McKinley is written in that book before he went back to meet his death an hour afterwards. If the Falls attracts 800,000 people a year, those power houses have attracted the choicest and most intelligent people of the world.

According to Stetson, Niagara's most knowledgeable and powerful visitors went to see its powerhouses.[67]

Stetson's elitism notwithstanding, visits to the power plants became an increasingly democratized experience. Beginning in 1900, the Niagara Falls Power Company organized twenty-five-cent guided public tours from 9:00 A.M. to 5:30 P.M. Monday through Saturday, and from 10:00 A.M. to 4:00 P.M. on Sundays. Adams stressed the educative role of the powerhouse:

> Visitors wished to understand the process, know what became of the water diverted, and how it would be possible to translate the water-power into an electric power that would escape to Buffalo unseen, over simple wires, and these move the pumps of that city's water-works, the trolley cars in its streets, and take the place of steam engines in its factories.[68]

Among the tour attractions was a scale model of the entire Niagara Falls Power Company operations. Visitors could also read the important statistics of the development. Pamphlets described the water diversion and hydroelectric energy conversion processes. Through careful management of the tour, the power company ensured that visitors received a

Aerial view (1905) of Niagara Falls showing the three power plants in Queen Victoria Park then under construction and the industrial development immediately beyond the New York State Reservation. This drawing appeared on the cover of *Scientific American*, 1905.

positive image concerning the technological harnessing of Niagara Falls.

By the time of the Pan-American Exposition of 1901, the side trip to Niagara Falls often presented visitors more with a chance "to put the visitor in touch with the most marvelous electrical power development of the present time" than a chance to commune with nature. A balance between the attractions of nature and the attractions of technology kept the sight-seeing interesting and enlightening. The *Ladies' Home Journal* urged tourists to tour the powerhouse when "seeing Niagara for the first time." The *Index Guide to Buffalo and Niagara Falls* noted that "after visiting the wonders of nature, it is instructional to pass to a wonder of modern engineering" at the Niagara Falls Power Company.[69]

Tourist travel accounts at the turn of the century increasingly gave detailed descriptions of Niagara's technological, rather than natural, sublimity. For many Niagara tourists the novelty of experimental power development superseded interest in the cataract. While love of nature remained a far-from-universal passion, the gripping electrical works on display at Niagara Falls held implications for all Americans. By examining human constructions at Niagara, visitors gained a peek into the future of Niagara and of the nation. As Coleman Sellers insisted, Niagara remained the ultimate American tourist attraction not only for the engineer but also for the general public, "who cannot but be impressed with the magnitude of the undertaking and the thought of this great power being turned to the uses of man."[70]

Though opposition from preservationists mounted as an increasing number of power companies secured charters to divert Niagara's waters, tourist statistics indicated that the power advocates and promoters of the New Niagara had won their struggle for legitimacy. During the first fourteen years that the Niagara Falls Power Company charged for tours, the company collected $46,441. Beginning in 1918 the tour was free and the number of visitors soared. Edward Dean Adams reported that on a single day in 1926, exactly 3,264 visitors entered the Niagara Falls powerhouse.[71]

Tourist literature, accounts in the popular press, and growing familiarity with electricity all helped lure visitors to the power plant, and great power plants, rather than nature, came to symbolize America. As Thomas Parke Hughes explains in *American Genesis,* by the late nineteenth century foreign visitors marked the United States as a complex technological society rather than nature's nation. Since the late 1800s the American version of the Grand Tour featured requisite visits to the Brooklyn Bridge, massive factories, subways, and great industrial cities. When he visited the United States in 1911, British writer Arnold Bennett stated that he had no interest in seeing the great Falls of Niagara, but instead wanted to see electrical powerhouses in America, "where they are more wondrous." To him, power projects were America's "great material and poetical achievements."[72] Nowhere was this powerhouse America better represented than at Niagara Falls.

5

Electricity's Throne

Niagara Falls and the Utopian Impulse

When scientists and financiers first agreed on a working blueprint to harness enormous power from "Electricity's throne"—Niagara Falls—the *Niagara Falls Gazette* urged its readers to extend the bounds of their imaginations.[1] "The millennium has not come exactly, but the most gigantic engineering, mechanical, and financial enterprise of the nineteenth century is about to be developed." While remaining popular as a summer resort, Niagara seemed destined to grow both up and down the river until it incorporated Buffalo in its magical development:

> Aye, imagine thousands of great manufactories lining the river front, mammoth docks, and wharves and warehouses hitherto unthought of; innumerable workingmen's homes bordering on a series of broad boulevards leading up from Niagara Falls to Buffalo.[2]

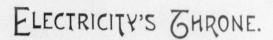

ELECTRICITY'S THRONE.

NIAGARA FALLS THE
ETERNAL HOME OF THE
KING OF THE NINE-
TEENTH CENTURY. . .

The Greatest, Cheapest Power.

WHAT THE HARNESSING
OF NIAGARA MEANS TO
THE WHOLE OF THIS
GREAT COUNTRY . . .

America's Smokeless Manchester.

THE CITY OF RAREST
BEAUTY AND GRANDEUR
CANNOT ESCAPE ITS
MANIFEST DESTINY OF
GREATNESS. . . . . .

BUFFALO:
NIAGARA PRINTING COMPANY.
1895.

Front cover (above) and back cover (right) of *Electricity's Throne* (1895), one of several promotional booklets for utopian real-estate schemes envisioned for Niagara Falls and vicinity. (Courtesy, Buffalo and Erie County Historical Society)

GRANDEUR

POWER

GREATNESS

The harnessing and transmission of Niagara Falls power was one of the most dramatic technological breakthroughs of the late nineteenth century. The new electric Niagara Falls not only raised issues of technology but also tapped a flood of cultural and imaginative possibilities, inspiring hyperbolic predictions for the future. From scientists to engineers, financiers, tourist promoters, and tourists, everyone anticipated ever-bolder power projects and manufacturing and development plans.

Such elaborate oracles for power use spawned a half-real, half-imaginary image of Niagara that coincided with prevailing American ideals and values. All these schemes shared a belief that technology would solve the pressing problems of modern society. Niagara boosters and industrialists typically spoke in the same voice as utopian developers. Thus, each additional electrical powerhouse and industrial enterprise "verified" the coming great manufacturing center. The massive use of the cataract's hydroelectric power would ultimately bring planning, organization, efficiency, and harmony to all spheres of life. Its clean, non-resource-draining energy would allow nature to continue to flourish while creating a truly aesthetic metropolis.

Precisely because technology promised so much at Niagara Falls, however, the euphoria over an anticipated limitless utopian future was matched by outrage over the desecration of the cataract and its surroundings. Heirs to the tradition of Frederick Law Olmsted wondered whether the New Niagara Falls was a dystopia—a horrid place of desecration, pollution, and blight. The diligence of the naysayers kept the public aware of the stakes of technological development at Niagara Falls and sounded the underlying ambivalence over technology's role in American culture.

The outcry of preservationists forced developers and utopians alike to justify their futuristic schemes. Developers could not get away with merely considering the bottom line. Instead, they, like the utopians, framed their comprehensive urban plans with fidelity to nature. Nothing short of a clean, aesthetic, majestic, trouble-free, and prosperous course for the future at Niagara Falls would be acceptable. Nonetheless, as the bold forecasts reassured an anxious public that Niagara's natural scenery would be preserved if not improved, their insistent message hailed the imminent creation of a new Niagara—a metropolis. Thanks to the persistence of the technological oracles and the debates they inspired, the eyes of the culture remained focused on Niagara Falls. As the metropolis took shape, both in new schemes and in reality, Niagara Falls promised to be a model for the rest of the nation.

The signing of the Niagara Falls power contract in 1890 marked another epic advance in the "era of technological enthusiasm." By the late nineteenth century the United States was truly "technology's nation." Foreign visitors regarded the country as a great building site. The last years of the 1800s and first years of the 1900s witnessed the construction of the Brooklyn Bridge and skyscrapers; the birth of automobiles, airplanes, and subways; the invention of the phonograph, the wireless, the telephone, and the motion picture; and the development and perfection of the incandescent light bulb and a rudimentary electrical system. Americans welcomed each technological wonder as another momentous sign of progress.[3]

This string of achievements lent itself to fertile imaginations as distinctions between the fact and the fiction of technological possibility blurred. When a spate of utopian novels appeared between 1883 and 1910 (the most influential of which was Edward Bellamy's 1888 *Looking Backward*), the brand of utopianism was technological utopianism. Although technological utopianism never became a coherent movement, its advocates shared several assumptions about technology and progress. Above all, in their novels, tracts, addresses, and development schemes, technological utopians believed in the inevitability of progress and possessed an abiding faith that progress and reform could be brought on by technology alone. They dismissed the negative consequences of growth as temporary, correctable aberrations; they optimistically worked for solutions to ensure a better, if not perfect, America in the immediate future.[4]

Utopian writers outpaced only by degree the reformers, city and national planners, professional organizations, centralized corporations, and even conservationists, who also shared a belief that technology properly used would be the most likely solution to the woes of American society. As it anticipated real settlements and changes in the landscape, this utopian conjecture became emblematic of the cultural meaning of Niagara Falls at the turn of the century.[5]

In addressing these ideals and values, let us not forget that while utopian works offered alternatives to the disorder of modern American life, their very appearance suggested cultural malaise. Utopian writings become more frequent during periods of upheaval and dislocation. In the exciting, hopeful, but tumultuous milieu of the late 1800s, the traditional authority of cultural custodians such as ministers, parents, politicians, editors, and teachers seemed outdated. Profound change lay behind the collapse of America's secure Victorian world-view: this was an era when rural residents left the countryside for the city, when farmers became wage-earners, and when millions of foreigners arrived in America.

Technological utopians offered attractive messages to a culture searching for order in an increasingly urban, impersonal, interdependent, and machine-driven society. Their visions for the future reflected poignantly the concerns of the age and served as pointed critiques of contemporary society. Thus, the accumulation of *technological* utopianism in the late nineteenth and early twentieth century revealed and expressed the prevailing cultural anxieties over the paths that progress and technology were taking.[6]

In real engineering, mechanical, and financial enterprises at Niagara Falls, equating development with utopia was a stretch. By 1880, industrial development had already produced the tawdry mills and disfiguring conditions that led to calls for a Niagara Falls state reservation. This early, small-scale development paled next to the awesome grandeur of the Falls and the Niagara gorge. After 1890, however, utopianism at Niagara Falls assumed a new urgency. The signing of the power contract in 1890 marked a true watershed in Niagara's history. Now equipped with huge investments and the world's foremost engineering talent, the Niagara Falls region prepared to develop on an order of magnitude heretofore undreamed of.

So great an aura of anticipation prevailed in the late nineteenth century that size alone connoted the magnificent future. One formula for predicting Niagara's future involved computing anticipated population from total horsepower used. The Niagara Falls Chamber of Commerce gushed over statistics that revealed that by 1890 in other waterpower centers, such as Lowell, Holyoke, Manchester, Lawrence, and Lewiston in New England, and Minneapolis, Minnesota, there were 4.98 persons per unit horsepower. After estimating the harnessable Niagara Falls power capacity conservatively at 550,000 horsepower, the Chamber of Commerce projected a population of 2,739,000. No wonder tourist tracts predicted that the city of Buffalo would become a suburb of Niagara Falls![7]

Nor were these figures predicted only by the Chamber of Commerce. The scientific and engineering community continued their toasts to Niagara's future after the Niagara Falls Power Company began producing power. The world's leading authority on alternating current systems, Nicola Tesla, remained inspired by Niagara's awesome potential.

> Tesla, looking for the first time upon the great whirling dynamo in the power-house of the Niagara Falls Power Company, saw pictured in his mind's eye a vast city stretching from one end of the Niagara Frontier to the other; a great industrial community the like of which the world has never yet known; a splendid city of great factories, whose wheels should be driven by the silent, wonderful electrical force generated from the mighty rush of waters past the city's doors; a city of millions of people of untold wealth, the manufacturing and industrial center of the whole civilized world.

Edward Dean Adams, New York financier and president of the Niagara Falls Power Company, noted that expectations for Niagara's electricity age ran so high that "to have predicted the future would have been more difficult than it is today to foretell the conditions a generation hence if a hundred times our present output is brought into service."[8]

New technological prospects extended beyond population statistics and industrial output, and instead addressed crucial contemporary issues and anxieties and pointed toward revolutionary improvements in the quality of life. Engineer Clemons Herschel insisted: "The future development of the Buffalo–Niagara Falls district, as a manufacturing centre, no less than as a place of residence, cannot fail to be one of the marvels of the fast approaching twentieth century."[9]

America's most spectacular natural landmark would not only be transformed into a city but also be a model city for the rest of the United States and the world. The massive use of hydroelectric power would bring a revolutionary efficiency to all spheres of life. Environments would be clean and smoke-free. The burdens of life would be eased for laborers and for women, and all citizens would have increased opportunities for prosperity and pleasure. And because the Falls would remain a protected wonder of nature, "the greatest national park in the world would be accessible to every inhabitant."[10]

This insistence that Niagara Falls would become a great metropolis was typical of progressive reform and utopian thinking. But the romance of progress did not entirely mask a lingering ambivalence over the role of technology and of the city in American culture. Late-nineteenth-century Americans faced the paradox that technological progress, which was equated with cultural and social progress, traveled in tandem with an increase in social and environmental ills. The last decades in the century saw cataclysmic economic slumps, unprecedented labor strife and worker misery, rampant disease and rising infant mortality rates, grotesque pollution and desecration of the urban landscape, and, with the arrival of hordes of new immigrants, an increasingly foreign cast to life in America.[11]

Cities may have been focal points for these problems, but they were also the site of the culture's most noteworthy progress and cultural accomplishments. Dreams of the ideal city in America predated the Puritans. Forecasts for the New Niagara followed in a long line of utopian correctives offered to the distasteful characteristics of life in America's cities. In the New Niagara version of utopia, Niagara would achieve an ideal "middle landscape." Niagara Falls and the sylvan verdure of the reservation would inspire an industrial city that remained smokeless, green, and tree-filled. Factories, homes, and gardens would share the landscape in harmony, and perhaps even more important, the utopian Niagara Falls promised to uphold national pride, morality, harmony, and prosperity through the healthful, clean, fantastically productive, and toil-less characteristics of electricity. Benevolent technology guaranteed the future of this ideal city.[12]

To gain insight into the idealized expectations of the New Niagara, it is useful to look at three of Niagara's more elaborate schemes from the 1890s and early 1900s. Leonard Henkle, King Camp Gillette, and William T. Love each postulated a utopia located at Niagara Falls, and each offered a cure for the most urgent problems facing the United States. Their cures confronted Niagara's older image as a supreme spot of sacred nature. In their respective utopian visions, however, nature is no longer supreme at the Falls, but is both subservient to and preserved by technology. Not coincidentally, each of these three New Niagara utopians presented his vision as a legitimate business proposition, and each wedded beauty to utility. Ultimately, the Niagara utopias sought subscribers and promised to reward enlightened investors with civic virtue and enormous profits.[13]

In the early 1890s one of the more provocative utopian blueprints for Niagara Falls attempted to combine Niagara's natural wonderment and popularity as a tourist destination with its new technological capabilities. The utopian plan of the Reverend Leonard Henkle of Rochester, a radical Greenbacker and sometime inventor, affirmed the continuing spiritual significance of Niagara Falls in American culture. For a civilization adrift in excessive competition and misery, Henkle recognized the continuing spiritual hold that Niagara Falls had on the American consciousness. Reminiscent of Olmsted and Charles Eliot Norton, who spoke for nature and envisioned the Niagara Falls state reservation as an antidote to modern industrial society, Henkle believed that Niagara still offered the best hope for the moral regeneration of a world in turmoil. Henkle's vision of the New Niagara, however, postulated moral regeneration centered around electrical technology, not around a religion of nature.

Henkle attracted the attention of *The World* with his scheme to construct a giant dual Dynamic Palace and International Hotel across the Niagara River. Designed to be built right at the crest of the cataract, this immense, half-mile-long and quarter-mile-wide monumental edifice was to be a $40 million Congress of Nations. Forty-one nations of the world would each send delegations and be represented symbolically by a giant column at the palace. The Dynamic Palace promised to be

> the grandest work of architecture on earth: the most immense in proportions, original in design, comprehensive in purpose and beautiful in appearance that has ever been conceived by the ingenuity of man: combining the most surpassing artistic beauty with the grandeur of the Falls. Solomon's Temple, St. Peter's at Rome,

St. Paul's at London, combined with all the architectural achievements of modern times, would not equal this stupendous structure. Built of granite, marble, steel, copper, glass, onyx, and aluminum, it must stand a thousand years.[14]

The entire structure would welcome up to 70,000 tourists and pilgrims for prayer and spiritual negotiation of the world's problems.

While he alluded to venerable pilgrimage destinations, Henkle acknowledged this new mecca's thorough debt to the electricity age at Niagara. Although Henkle pledged to contribute $50,000 annually to maintain Niagara's parks as "companion attractions of this great palace," higher beauty and grandeur derived from the monumentality, structural originality, and modern materials of the great Dynamic Palace. Plans for the palace envisioned it as a city unto itself. The near limitless industrial and energy potential of the Falls would serve the various levels of the palace and the hotel, and one level would be a great power plant, another a gigantic railroad terminus, another the world's largest hotel.

Thanks to the great Dynamic Palace and humanitarian stewardship, Niagara would remain the greatest attraction of the modern age. Each week 40,000 to 60,000 visitors would take advantage of cheap railroad fares to travel not to the Falls but to the great Dynamic Palace. Much like Olmsted's Niagara reservation, the technological palace pointed to spiritual uplift, education, and social harmony. Typical of the New Niagara, however, was that the palace presented, according to one broadside, "an [investment] opportunity never before offered to this or any generation, whereby each may so well promote his own welfare while he helps to mould the moral destiny of nations."[15]

At the same time that Henkle sought subscriptions for his Dynamic Palace, an enigmatic American inventor and entrepreneur devised a more elaborate utopian scheme for Niagara. King Camp Gillette embodied the American fascination with technology, and his boyhood penchant for tinkering culminated in his invention of the disposable razor. Although Gillette assumed the role of a conservative entrepreneur, he never let his razor empire squelch his romantic sense of the possibilities of technology to transform the world. Indeed, he envisioned Niagara as the guarantor of a technological utopia to supersede capitalism itself.[16]

By the 1890s, Gillette had joined other technological utopians in the belief that the world was at a crossroads. He believed that America (and global society) was sick, plagued everywhere by dishonesty, vice, greed, and crime. Chaotic capitalist competition, according to Gillette, produced all of society's woes. As an example, he noted that the temptation to acquire wealth at all costs had led food producers to disdain high standards of purity, and that harmful, even poisonous, adulterated foods resulted.[17]

A more dire consequence of this competition, however, was the exponential increase in the permanent and underprivileged wage-earning class. Laborers became the dupes of the few who successfully concentrated capital and controlled the economic system. Living in toil and drudgery, the lowly wage-earner was the great victim of the struggle for existence. Turn-of-the-century labor strife manifested the rage born of the worker's plight.[18]

In *The Human Drift* (1894) and *The World Corporation* (1910), King Gillette propounded solutions to these problems. Inspired by the displays of progress at the 1893 Chicago World's Fair, Gillette formulated a technological utopian vision to free the world from misery, poverty, and crime. Electricity would be the key. As the cleanest and most efficient source of energy in the world, it promised happiness because it placed the least burden on manual labor. Electricity's mastery over nature would allow modernity to advance "immeasurably beyond any civilization" the world had yet seen.[19]

To realize his electric utopia, Gillette envisioned a day in his own lifetime when an all-encompassing, supercorporation would transform the world through efficiency. Taking America's great vertically and horizontally integrated corporations as a paradigm, the popularly subscribed "United Company" would undercut capitalist production and distribution, thereby effectively crushing all competition. Managed by 125 "directors," the "United Company" itself would assume the role of organizing the government and conducting the business and services first of the nation and then of the world.[20]

Such efficiency would be possible if Niagara Falls were the center of the United Company. Gillette publicized his views at a time when the American public had learned of the wondrous harnessing of Niagara. In fact, Niagara gave immediate recognition and credibility to Gillette's plan. Photographs of the untrammeled Niagara rapids and cataract in *The Human Drift* attested to the potential of the New Niagara. A technological utopia could be located around Niagara Falls because the "demonstrated fact" of Niagara power allowed nature to "assume new meanings and ends." Niagara's inexhaustible energy represented "a natural power far beyond our needs." Moreover, once a pipeline was built to utilize the entire drop of water between Lakes Erie and Ontario, the horsepower output of the Falls would be doubled to 12 million. Gillette continued:

> Here is a power, which, if brought under control, is capable of keeping in continuous operation every manufacturing industry for centuries to come, and, in addition, supply all the lighting facilities, run all the elevators, and furnish the power necessary for the transportation system of the great central city.[21]

Gillette's "Metropolis"—the name he gave his model city—extended throughout the territory within a forty-mile rectangle issuing from Niagara Falls. Five million men and women would gain employment building Metropolis. Funding for the project would be no object, because everyone would want to invest in the great company and because Niagara power guaranteed the swift, economical, and aesthetic transformation of the landscape. The various bureaus of the United Company—manufacturing, food-processing, education, and architecture—would be seated at Niagara; only the agricultural and mining fields and overflow-product warehouses, as well as, ironically, vacation retreats, would be located outside Metropolis.

As the United Company serviced the top one hundred cities in the land, the processing of goods, services, and ideas through the company offices promised to create even greater centralization at Niagara. Gillette believed the superior efficiency and standard of living at Niagara Falls would entice the entire population to settle there. In an ironic switch from the older image of Niagara as the symbol of untrammeled nature and the garden, now Niagara Falls, or Metropolis, "would be our home, and North America our farm."[22]

As he envisioned Niagara's rise to the world's great metropolis, Gillette recalled the idealistic aesthetics of Chicago's White City. Metropolis promised to be a "perpetual world's fair." The electrical technology first foreshadowed on a small scale at the Columbian Exposition would take permanent form in a comprehensive, beautiful, and modern landscape. The New Niagara would overcome all engineering problems. "Converted into the electric current, it would drive all the machinery of production, and in the form of light convert 'Metropolis' into a fairy land." Great, immaculate manufacturing plants would stand in stark contrast to the cramped, poorly ventilated structures that typically harbored the forlorn laboring classes. Because "thousands of [Niagara] turbines" would do the work formerly consigned to laborers, Gillette's technological utopia promised to be a new landscape of vitality and excitement: "Like the heart of a sentient being the city would pulsate with life through its millions of arteries of copper and steel, and stand a living, breathing monument of man's combined and highest intelligence."[23]

In Gillette's vision, the technological beauty of this model city gave constant joy to its inhabitants. Mammoth, brightly colored apartment houses or hotels would house as many as 60 million residents. Plans called for the symmetrical arrangement of these "conservatories" to extend from Niagara to Rochester. Air-conditioned, glass-enclosed walkways substituted a managed atmosphere for the uncertainties and inconveniences of normal weather. Carefully manicured and planted walkways gave inhabitants the feeling of a vacation resort in their permanent residence. Parklike grounds and gardens filled in the landscape between the residence complexes.

> Can you imagine the endless beauty of a conception like this—
> a city with its thirty-six thousand buildings each a perfectly distinct and complete design, . . . each building and avenue surrounded and bordered by an everchanging beauty in flowers and foliage?[24]

Every scene of human, architectural, intellectual, and recreational interest would flourish at the metropolis centered at Niagara Falls. Technology conserved and idealized nature. No wonder Gillette anticipated that "Metropolis" would suggest the beauty of the Arabian Nights.[25]

In our late-twentieth-century consciousness, Love Canal near Niagara Falls has come to symbolize the horrible consequences of technology run amuck: the toxic waste on which a Niagara neighborhood was built condemned a landscape as it condemned its inhabitants. Yet the plans for the original Love Canal in the 1890s and early 1900s bespoke only the wide-eyed technological possibilities of the New Niagara. Local real-estate developer William T. Love devised a plan to channel water from the upper to the lower Niagara River via a canal to a tract of land northeast of the cataract. Love billed this 15,000-acre plat as "the most appealing and beautiful town site in existence." Clearly the 140,000 horsepower secured in the 290-foot drop of the canal guaranteed the "beauty" of the town. Here Love and his Niagara Falls Manufacturing Company hoped to create one of the greatest manufacturing cities in America.[26]

Calculating a ratio of five persons per unit horsepower, Love anticipated that his town, aptly called "Model City," would be a suburb of Niagara Falls with a population of 700,000. It is not surprising that he looked to the factories he would sell cheap power to as essential building blocks of his scheme. In Model City:

> When the factories are there, the people will be there—the people are the City. There is ample time after that for building operations—great factories, stores, office buildings, schools and churches—all new, modern lighted, and HEATED by electricity—Street Railways, Sewers, Water-Supply—everything requisite for an ambitious modern city—the BEST of everything is good enough for us.[27]

Love acted as the ultimate authority in all early Model City matters. He was confident he could "locate factories by the score" in Model City, largely because power would be so inexpensive. Love promised to award power free for forty years to any factory that would employ one person per horsepower used. Claiming to have already signed up a client to 35,000 horsepower, he insisted that "one institution will get [free] power that, elsewhere produced by steam, would cost $500,000 a year." Other "factories handicapped by high rents, high-priced power, poor railroad facilities, crowded quarters, etc.," were sure to follow this example. Factoring-in Model City's other advantages of productive country, benevolent climate, attractive scenery, and abundant railroad service, the company prospectus called the site "par excellence, the location of the world for such an enterprise as ours."[28]

Like Niagara's other utopian developers, Love believed the New Niagara offered an escape from the historical problems of urban and industrial life. Seven years of planning and technological improvement promised to eliminate the waste that was "always incident to the tearing-down-and-building-up process of growth of all cities." At Model City, the by-products of technology—sewers, water pipes, electrical lines and wires—were to be put out of sight and out of harm's way in alleys; streets would not have to be torn up for repair. From the start, the Model City Company boasted of hiring landscape engineer and town planner Nathan P. Barrett, whose extensive portfolio included planning the company town of Pullman, Illinois. With ample resources to secure aesthetic planning and nearby entertainments and amusements, Model City promised to fulfill the ambition of its founder.[29]

The inevitable prosperity generated from Niagara power foretold an uncity-like city. The allocation of 1,000 to 2,000 acres, and $500,000, for parks and permanent exhibition grounds, and an additional $12 million for building purposes (including homes for 150,000 factory workers) ensured that Model City would be "a city of homes." It is significant, that "no down payment, for lot or building, will be required of steady, worthy men"; Love wanted workers to have easy access to ideal housing in nice neighborhoods. Company planning and high standards also banned such evil influences as saloons. Thus, "starting right, our citizenship will be right."[30]

Love also hoped to create a truly ideal community by starting new cooperative industrial plants in Model City each year, which would give workers governance in their own affairs and preclude strikes and labor unrest. An "Industrial University" would offer practical training in technical studies for everyone, thereby adding to the quality of production and increasing the life opportunities of all citizens. The university would become "one of the greatest schools on the American continent" and add to the reputation of Model City "as a monument to the progressive spirit of the age—to the genius, goodness and greatness of the American people."[31]

Love's vision wound up as a failed real-estate proposition. Beyond acquiring the state charter for the Model City plat, building a factory, and commencing early work on the canal, he never secured the investment necessary to convert the landscape into a "model city." Yet, in a day far removed from the tragic fate of the Hooker Chemical Company's toxic Love Canal, William T. Love's plan bespoke the unbridled enthusiasm for the New Niagara. To the end, he insisted that "Model City promised the greatest likelihood of investment success in the world":

> The utilization of this power will create the next great municipal development on this continent and will place new cities on the map. Thousands will secure homes and employment here, hundreds will make fortunes on the rapid rise in real estate, that must follow this great development, and hundreds of millions of dollars of taxable property will be added to the wealth of the Empire State.[32]

Niagara Falls never matched the visions of its boldest utopian romancers. In the eyes of Niagara boosters, however, the cataract did achieve a certain technological splendor. New Niagara enthusiasts tried to convince businessmen, tourists, and the general public just how beneficial electricity had been to the Niagara region.

Although initial hopes for Niagara power focused on long-distance power transmission, an efficient, inexpensive long-distance transmission would have obviated the need for industrial development in the immediate vicinity of the cataract. Instead, lingering transmission inefficiencies led to a more encouraging and lucrative ramification of the electricity age for Niagara Falls: development at Niagara itself. Abundant, unending, and cheap power was a great incentive for industries to locate at Niagara Falls. The Pittsburgh Reduction Company began making aluminum in Pittsburgh in 1889, but when the Niagara Falls Power Company offered its power at $20 per horsepower in 1892, the firm relocated its entire aluminum operations at Niagara.[33]

Headlines in the *Niagara Falls Gazette* regularly announced the arrival and expansion of new manufactories, including the Pittsburgh Reduction Company, Carborundum, Union Carbide, Norton Abrasives, and the Natural Food (Shredded Wheat) Company. Business bred more business, especially in the electrochemical and electrometallurgical fields, where by-products from high-heat processes formed new chemicals and abrasives. Most of these industries and processes did not even exist before the late 1890s. Indeed, by 1901 Niagara Falls emerged as one of the great production centers of the United States.[34]

Almost overnight the electricity age converted Niagara into a vital boom town. Less than two years following the announcement of the power contract in 1890, the villages of Niagara Falls and Suspension Bridge united to form the new City of Niagara Falls. From a region with less than 9,000 inhabitants in 1890, Niagara Falls became a dynamic city of nearly 20,000 by 1900 and 30,000 by 1910. By 1905, Niagara Falls was the fastest growing city in New York State, and in 1914 some 11,000 Niagara Falls workers held jobs spawned by the advent of hydroelectric power.[35]

Real development approximated fantastic expectations for the New Niagara just enough to perpetuate them. The former sleepy tourist hamlet stood poised for the future with an attractive blend of the natural order (embodied in the parks on each side of the cataract) and the new technological order (embodied in the adjacent manufacturing zone).

Despite this purported balance of the natural and the technological at Niagara Falls, the conversion of Niagara into a sublime technological complex elicited dismay and outrage because the cataract still symbolized America's original, untrammeled nature. The Niagara Preservation Movement of the 1870s and 1880s had, in fact, revivified Niagara's associations as a place of nature. Not unlike other American urban growth in the late nineteenth and early twentieth centuries, however, development at Niagara Falls revealed some of the darker, unnatural aspects of modernity and deeply offended Victorian sensibilities. Niagara's industrial zone, which spread two miles above the cataract and one mile below it, was remarkable for its filth and foul air. Smoke-spewing factories and mills along the cliffbanks and riverbanks gave Niagara the same hideous fascination as Pittsburgh. Above the upper rapids on the American side, "tall red chimneys rise over a flourishing colony of low red factories, and trailing clouds of soot stain the sky and the smooth reflecting surface of the river." The mills, chemical companies, advertisements, waste piles, and sheds "under the very shadow of the reservation, not two thousand feet from the plunge of the American Fall, huddles as foul and unsightly a milling village as ever dishonored a river's brink."[36]

Because advances in productivity exceeded corresponding advances in the living and working environment, Niagara became a dubious place to live. The Tunnel District, created during construction of the power tunnel, proved a particularly loathsome zone of slime and degradation. This workers' ghetto of shanties and tenements bred pestilence and crime. Violence, promiscuity, corruption, social unrest—indeed, all social ills—prevailed in the Tunnel District and threatened the entire social fabric of the City of Niagara Falls. No wonder Niagara seemed to fulfill the most dire predictions of moral and physical decay arising from urban development.[37]

These deleterious consequences of large-scale development in no way dimmed the enthusiasm of Niagara's boosters. Repudiating mounting evidence that power plants, chemical companies, and other manufacturers befouled the environment and diminished the natural sublimity of the cataract, New Niagara advocates lauded the area surrounding the cataract as a place to live. By 1897 the Niagara Falls Chamber of Commerce proudly announced that the two miles between Niagara Falls and Suspension Bridge had filled in "with business houses, the handsome dwellings of the well-to-do citizens, and the cozy cottages of the middle class." And most important, they claimed, electricity catalyzed growth that was clean, quiet, healthful, and beautiful.[38]

Advocates of technology focused on the Niagara Falls Power Company's model village of Echota (rather than on the dismal Tunnel District) as the contribution of the electricity age to living standards in the New Niagara. From its initial plans in 1893, the Niagara Falls Power Company hoped that Echota (an Indian word for "shelter" or "place of refuge") would counteract the notion of the deleterious impact of large-scale manufacturing on domestic life. Company towns were not uncommon in the late nineteenth century, but the power company's decision to hire the renowned architectural firm of McKim, Mead & White to design a workers' neighborhood according to a middle-class ideal was unprecedented. The first forty-two houses, many of which were attributed to Stanford White, featured varied floor plans in single-family, duplex, and four-unit structures. These spacious designs contrasted with

Street in Echota, the company town for workers of the Niagara Falls Power Company. The architectural firm of McKim, Mead & White was hired to design the neighborhood according to a middle-class ideal.

the typically monotonous, cramped, and shoddy quarters of the industrial labor force. Because each house was wired for electricity, power-company workers had electric light and heat before many of the well-to-do at Niagara Falls. Moreover, each house had its own lawn with sidewalks and faced toward a wide, tree-lined, macadamized, electrically lit street.[39]

By erecting Echota on swampland, the Niagara Falls Power Company had reclaimed "a district not fit for comfortable residence" and turned it into "an ideal healthful village." Echota was a complete village, with a hotel, a store for general provisions, a fire department, and a railroad station. Built on 84 acres, the village was served by "an ample supply of water for domestic purposes and a sewerage and drainage system by which all sewerage is conveyed to a disposal house, where it is chemically treated and rendered innocuous."[40]

According to *The Romance of Modern Engineering*, Echota gave immediate evidence of the technological promise of the future under the supervision of America's best civil engineers. Niagara Falls guidebooks and railroad tourist brochures immediately hailed Echota as a model town. Indeed, Budgett Meakin included Echota in *Model Factories and Model Villages*, his 1905 report on visionary industrial ventures. The Niagara Falls Power Company's workers' town proved worthy of emulation by other progressive-minded companies.[41]

Echota foretold an organic future for the New Niagara where industry, nature, and community would be harmoniously integrated. A chapter on Niagara in *The Romance of Modern Engineering* announced: "A great city is springing up with mushroom speed—a city free from smoke, gas, ashes—an ideally clean city." Magazine articles in 1901 with such titles as "The Future in America" and "The New Niagara: A City of the Future" set the tone for cultural focus on Niagara and announced that the magic electricity age metropolis was at hand. In its 1903 series "Progressive American Cities," the *National Magazine* selected Niagara as "one of the marvels of the industrial age." "That which impresses forcibly the visitor to Niagara Falls now is not only the falls, but the city and the wonderful industrial center that is being established there."[42]

One Niagara-boosting account described the experience of a world traveler who returned to Niagara Falls after a forty-year absence. The New Niagara was as wondrous as any place he had ever visited. The monumental buildings on the horizons were factories; majestic structures he thought were art galleries were in fact powerhouses. Incredulously aware that he was in a great industrial center, the returning traveler marveled at the clean air and wondered whether all the manufacturing operations were closed. On the contrary, the demand for Niagara's products meant that Niagara's factories never stopped production. The narrator informed his guest that the cleanness of electricity accounted for Niagara's healthful environment. At great expense, Niagara Falls was now without pollution; it had eliminated the smoke nuisance and had erected a clean, silent, and aesthetically triumphant industrial order. The visitor emerged a total convert to this new Niagara.

> I have seen nearly all the noted places in the world and since my first visit here have always maintained that my feeling of enchantment was more largely aroused over the sights at Niagara Falls than elsewhere, and now I am as greatly surprised over the view of this immense industrial growth as I was at my first view of the Falls, because I can safely see that, in all my travels, I have never seen such a group of large manufacturing plants as can be seen here from this one point of view.[43]

Niagara's tourist appeal guaranteed that the New Niagara would be exposed to a steady stream of visitors, who generally embraced the New Niagara with enthusiasm. So while Niagara Falls was neither a closed nor a planned utopian community, it was a great dramatic stage. Technological development at Niagara turned it into the "mecca of electricity." In the infancy of electrical science, experts expected the technological advances to continue and the ramifications of Niagara Falls power to be limitless. Tourists and the magazine-reading public, in addition to men of science, anticipated new engineering wonders and further power-harnessing at Niagara. The abundance of futuristic schemes and the repeated association of Niagara Falls with technological utopia testified to the cultural prominence of the New Niagara and the faith in technology and progress to remake the world.

Yet, because neither Leonard Henkle's nor King Gillette's nor William Love's utopian vision for a Niagara utopia was realized, Niagara wanted a tangible project to display its fantastic potential to a truly mass audience. By the turn of the century, great expositions and world's fairs most closely embodied technological utopian views. In addition, these fairs were huge tourist attractions. The New Niagara Falls seemed to realize its promise as it dominated a world's fair in 1901. At the Buffalo Pan-American Exposition, a temporary city—inspired by the New Niagara—thrust Niagara Falls to the forefront of the national consciousness.

6

The Spirit of Niagara

Niagara Falls and the Pan-American Exposition of 1901

Throughout the summer of 1901, hundreds of thousands of tourists witnessed the operations of a unique powerhouse of the Niagara Falls Power Company. The powerhouse—a working scale-model of the company's Niagara Falls plant—was located in the Electricity Building of the Pan-American Exposition in Buffalo. By removing a small section from the wall of the powerhouse, the power company enabled visitors to look down into the deep cut of the wheel pit and view the turbines in the waters below. Thanks to this astonishing utilitarian exhibit, many more tourists gained an appreciation for the inner workings of Niagara's powerhouses in Buffalo than in Niagara Falls during the run of the exposition.[1]

The display of power in the Electricity Building represented only a

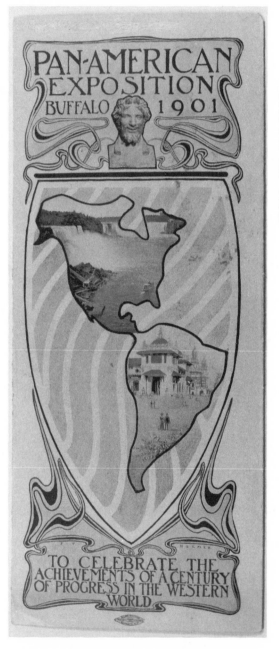

PAN-AMERICAN
EXPOSITION
BUFFALO 1901

TO CELEBRATE THE
ACHIEVEMENTS OF A CENTURY
OF PROGRESS IN THE WESTERN
WORLD

Brochure from 1901 Pan-American Exposition in Buffalo. Exposition organizers exploited the tourist lure of Niagara Falls in official promotional literature. Here Niagara symbolizes America and American progress. (Courtesy, Buffalo and Erie County Historical Society) tiny fraction of Niagara's influence on the Pan-American Exposition and on Buffalo itself. During the six-month run of the exposition, more than 6 million Americans entered the Buffalo fairgrounds. This great exposition to celebrate a century of progress was organized around the idea of drawing the western hemisphere into closer cultural and commercial connection. Yet, the exposition and the cataract were so closely allied that Niagara Falls became a symbol for the aesthetic, commercial, and ideological goals of the fair. From exposition advertising to the general scheme of the exposition grounds, from the exposition's sculpture and color scheme to its machinery and manufacturing, Niagara imbued all aspects of the fair.

Although the Pan-American Exposition is remembered as the site of the assassination of President William McKinley, the plans for the fair revealed the pervasive cultural impact Niagara Falls had at the beginning of the twentieth century. Niagara's civic leaders, tourist promoters, and power advocates shared the belief that the utopian promise of Niagara Falls and its electric energy would become evident during a world's fair. Even after it lost its chance to host the Pan-American show, the New Niagara gained the world's attention during the Pan-American Exposition.

The world's fair provided a stage for Niagara's long-distance electrical transmission precisely because the Pan-American Exposition was sited at Buffalo. Most important, the New Niagara of the world's fair offered the nation aesthetic improvement and brought harmony to the city. Its synthesis of nature and technology foretold a highly complex, technological, and productive—yet joyous and beautiful—landscape. Unlike the fantastic dreams of Niagara's utopian future, however, the Pan-American Exposition embodied the palpable marvels of the City Beautiful Movement. Never were the visions of the New Niagara so real as in the six months of the Buffalo Pan-American Exposition.

Given the expectations for the new electricity age, it is not surprising that Niagara Falls became the focal point for a world's fair. Beginning in the second half of the nineteenth century, such expositions put American culture on parade. No other institution celebrated American accomplishments in the arts and sciences like America's world's fairs. The fairs presented rare opportunities to elevate the nation's taste. They showed millions of Americans what American artists were painting and sculpting and what Americans were inventing and manufacturing. Because the sheer scope of this accumulation of cultural artifacts created temporary exposition villages or cities, fair locales demanded planning, coordination, and services beyond the usual ordering of the landscape. By the time of the 1893 World's Columbian Exposition in Chicago, America's world's fairs had become models for city planning and ideal city life.[2]

The functions of the fairs were educational, aesthetic, and commercial. Above all else, however, their function was progressive, for if world expositions lured travelers to see representative cultural accomplishments and historical development, they also let them peek into the future. Beginning with the Centennial Exposition in Philadelphia in 1876, America's expositions introduced the public to the nation's and the world's latest technology. As the fairs idealized technology and progress, they presented the latest advances and experiments in all facets of life. At a time when Americans were prone to flights of futuristic fancy, these expositions expressed and vivified American utopianism.[3]

After the Columbian Exposition of 1893, the next great American world's fair was to be the Pan-American Exposition. First scheduled for 1899, it was to crown a century of progress that had witnessed the emergence of the western hemisphere as a leading and independent force in the world. Niagara's boosters, who were never keen on Pan-Americanism, nonetheless insisted that Electric Niagara in the 1890s best encapsulated American progress. As soon as Niagara Falls became a great center for power development, then, it emerged as a likely host for an international exposition. Niagara's massive electrical works, the wonders of electrical power transmission, and the utopian possibilities of a nearly limitless use of power all conjoined in the prospect of a world's fair at Niagara Falls.

By 1897 the site choice for the Pan-American Exposition boiled down to a contest between Niagara Falls and Buffalo. The Niagara site actually was to have been Cayuga Island, which was located five miles from the cataract. The distance between the island and the power plants would display the safe and efficient transmission of electricity. Taking the Chicago world's fair as their model, Niagara boosters envisioned the largely unsettled and overgrown island being converted into an extensive and even permanent wonderland lit and powered by Niagara power. What better way to pay tribute to a century of progress than to feature the most revolutionary advance of the era—Niagara electricity.[4]

When Congress selected Cayuga Island to host the exposition (originally scheduled for 1899) the *Niagara Falls Gazette* claimed that the fair promised to be a huge success. Millions of tourists, many of them potential investors in Niagara's burgeoning future, would see Niagara at its best. Niagara's newly formed Chamber of Commerce immediately published a booklet entitled *Niagara Falls: The Greatest Electric and Power City of the World*. The booklet highlighted not only the unmatched diversity of attractions at Niagara, but also the boundless industrial potential of the Niagara region. When President McKinley came to Niagara for a groundbreaking ceremony on Cayuga Island in 1897, Niagara's utopian promise seemed about to be realized.[5]

The Spanish-American War, however, spoiled these early plans for the Pan-American Exposition. Although the war forced postponement of the exposition until 1901, when the fair site shifted to Buffalo, Niagara's boosters remained undaunted. Some questioned why a great fair to celebrate Niagara electricity would take place along the slimy banks of an unknown creek (the Scajaqueda). But Buffalo won out over new competition from Detroit, which sought to host the fair for its centennial celebration, because "those interested were emphatically of accord in the opinion that the site should be as near the Falls as possible because of the world-wide fame and universality of the attractiveness of this great cataract."[6]

The Pan-American Exposition, whether at Cayuga Island or Buffalo, was a promotional windfall for Niagara Falls. Just as the occasion of the exposition in the Niagara region would lure millions to the fair in 1901, Niagara's proximity to Buffalo guaranteed that travelers would frequent the more famous tourist site. Enticed by a world's fair, tourists who had not considered Niagara as a resort might once again look to it as the primary destination for their summer jaunt. In turn, Niagara Falls once again captured the imagination of the nation and the world.

Buffalo's Pan-American Exposition opened on May 1, 1901, and lasted until November 1. For the nation's eighth largest city, holding such an exposition offered both the immediate benefits of a season of extraordinary tourism and the chance to promote its outstanding commercial and cultural advantages. Nonetheless, while fair organizers "ever kept in view of doing for Buffalo and the Pan-American Exposition the very best thing that could be done,"[7] locating the great exposition at Buffalo proved to be an ambivalent enterprise. The idea of holding an exposition at Buffalo, according to cultural commentator Herbert Croly, was "not in itself a happy idea." He viewed Buffalo as a "minor American city."[8]

Indeed, Buffalo's prominence "derived partly from internal commerce and partly from its proximity to Niagara Falls." Where once the Erie Canal had ensured Buffalo's prosperity, now Niagara Falls and the transmission of Niagara's electrical power were directly responsible for ushering in a new and more prosperous era in Buffalo's history. Croly said, "The strength in the Buffalo Exposition consisted not in the least in its being Pan-American, but in its being genuinely and typically American." This unique "Americanness" derived from Niagara Falls. "An exposition, on the other hand, is as contemporary almost as a daily paper, and as American as electricity and Niagara Falls can make it."[9]

Thanks to Buffalo's proximity to the Falls, the Pan-American Exposition was momentous in the history of American advertising. *Profitable Advertising* reported: "It is universally admitted that no similar enterprise has ever been so well advertised, and the methods used have met with the public's unqualified approval." Rather than flooding the public with picturesque images of Buffalo, the promotional department exploited Buffalo's connections to Niagara Falls. Officials realized that the proximity of Niagara Falls might induce distant travelers to attend the Buffalo exposition.[10]

Pan-American fair pamphlets prove the point. *The Pan-American: Its Purpose and Its Plan* made little mention of Buffalo and presented not one picture of the Buffalo cityscape. Illustrations of the exposition buildings are interspersed between photos of Niagara, and the effect was to suggest that the fair was actually located at Niagara. Early leaflets such as *The Pan-American, Thirty Minutes from Niagara Falls* discussed the plans for the exposition around a series of photos of the cataract and the Niagara gorge, and souvenir photograph collections almost always included views of Niagara Falls. Likewise, for their Pan-American promotion, railroad companies issued special booklets with views of the cataract—any special identification with Niagara Falls made the railroads' routes to the exposition more desirable. Even postal stamps commemorating the exposition at Buffalo featured scenes of Niagara Falls.[11]

Although early advertising showcased picturesque Niagara scenery to induce travelers to journey to Buffalo, the predominant image of Niagara Falls at the Pan-American Exposition proved to be strikingly manmade. Advertising strategies increasingly glorified the New Niagara of sublime technology. According to *Profitable Advertising,*

> At its inception the management wisely decided to give its [Niagara's] principal features the widest publicity possible, and as a result of this policy, which has been consistently and persistently followed throughout, there is not a civilized country on the globe that is ignorant of the wonderful enterprise now progressing to the thunderous music of Niagara.[12]

This conscious identification of the Pan-American Exposition with the New Niagara is best seen in the exposition's quasi-official emblem. Evelyn Rumsey Cary's nine-color "The Spirit of Niagara" was the most successful poster of its era. In 1901, *Profitable Advertising* called it the most effective advertising poster of all time. In addition to the 1.5 million color copies of "The Spirit of Niagara" (ranging from 3 by 5 inches to 2 by 3 feet), a black-and-white version appeared in the nation's daily newspapers and boosted the number distributed to nearly 10 million.[13]

What is most striking about this emblem of the Pan-American Exposition is the substitution of Niagara Falls for Buffalo. Beneath the nude goddess in front of the cataract are the bold letters "NIAGARA." Niagara Falls, crowned by a rainbow, stands as the fertile inspiration and engenderer of the exposition. The disproportionately tall cataract, which dominates the pictorial space, joins with the hazily outlined lighted exposition buildings in the background, conveying the idea that the power of the Falls illuminates the exposition and drives its exhibits. Long-distance power transmission is as efficient as if the buildings were right above the cataract. The exhibition buildings become the symbolic replacement for factories, which of course occupied the real landscape above the Falls. In eliminating the natural, verdant surroundings of Niagara and substituting a wondrous, built landscape, "The Spirit of Niagara" gave the American public a bold and brilliant image of the New Niagara.[14]

Evelyn Rumsey Cary's "Spirit of Niagara" became the
unofficial emblem of the 1901 Pan-American Exposition,
appearing on posters and in newspapers all over the nation.
Here it adorns a souvenir guide for the exposition.
(Courtesy, Buffalo and Erie County Historical Society)

The Pan-American Exposition crystallized tourist awareness of Niagara's electrical and industrial developmental possibilities. During the summer of 1901, it was virtually impossible to think of either Buffalo or Niagara Falls without also thinking about electricity. Even those who journeyed to Buffalo with no intention of going to Niagara Falls would be forced into contemplating the wonders of Niagara electricity and its service to humankind. "The mighty power which thunders at Niagara, transformed to magic currents of supreme intensity, will here illuminate the grandest works of man."[15] Powered by Niagara Falls electricity, the Pan-American Exposition recapitulated the accomplishments and progress of the nineteenth century as it tendered a glimpse into the future.

The chief feature of the fair was electricity. Even before the exposition began, organizers specified that only electricity could be used to power and illuminate the fair.[16] Calls to run the Chicago exposition by Niagara power were mere pipe dreams in 1893,[17] but eight years later at Buffalo long-distance transmission was the great technological triumph of the world's fair. Popular magazines reported that Niagara Falls supplied a "practically unlimited supply of electricity" to the Pan-American Exposition. In fact, the Niagara Falls Power Company transmitted 5,000 horsepower. First stepped up to 22,000 volts at the power company's distribution house in Niagara Falls, this high-voltage current traveled by insulated lines to Buffalo, where it was reduced to 11,000 volts. In the Electricity Building, eighteen step-down converters further reduced the current to 1,800 volts, at which point it was sent out to the transformers near the exhibits and stepped down to a usable voltage. The ease of this power transmission and its remarkable results pointed fair visitors to the Niagara Falls Power Company. Numerous commentators joined exposition organizers in concluding that visitors to the Pan-American fair would want to visit the source of Niagara electricity: the Niagara Falls Power Company powerhouse in Niagara Falls.[18]

The Pan-American Exposition was the first time that electricity formed the chief organizing theme of a fair. An area encompassing 1,390,000 square feet was illuminated, requiring (not including the electrical materials of the midway) more than 900 arc lights, 200,000 incandescent lamps, 400 miles of electrical wires, and 94 large-size underwater searchlights in the fountains.[19]

Such statistics could only suggest the mind-boggling magnitude of the electrical works and functions at the Pan-American Exposition. Visitors to world's fairs expected to encounter technology's proliferating advances, and in the interval since the Chicago world's fair, engineers had perfected bigger and more powerful motors and electric machines. The Buffalo fair featured exhibits that served as "a grand advertising scheme for the display of the inventions, manufactures and industrial enterprises of the Republic."[20]

These displays frequently revealed an explicit link to Niagara Falls. The Niagara Falls Power Company's working miniature power station in the Electricity Building provided one such link. The Natural Food Company, maker of the Shredded Whole Wheat Biscuit, opened its new factory at Niagara to coincide with the opening of the Pan-American Exposition. Chemical company exhibits featured the new chemical processes that utilized the continuous power of Niagara and the high heat of Niagara furnaces. Electrochemical and electrometallurgical exhibits were a unique addition to the fair.

While technical complexity precluded the general public from comprehending many exhibits, the Pan-American Exposition also offered electricity for the masses. In one exhibit, a new storage battery by Edison pointed to the day when Americans would be able to pick up electricity in a bottle. Visitors marveled at x-rays, phonographs, a model telephone station, and akouphones, which allowed the deaf to hear. Another exhibit promoted cooking with electricity. New household appliances gave Niagara electricity immediate relevance for the everyday lives of women visitors.[21]

Perhaps the most dramatic convergence of nature and Niagara Falls electricity occurred in the electric incubator machines on the midway. The juxtapositioning of incubator babies and Niagara Falls presented "the weakest and the most powerful manifestation of nature's power." Just as Niagara Falls promised limitless energy for human use, the tiny babies symbolized the nation's limitless future. The babies were ultimately "the power sent here in fragile human forms to rule the falls, and other manifestations of crude power, regulate nature and do the work of embellishing and cultivating the globe." Thanks to the tender application of Niagara in nursing the incubator babies, these "little human dynamos" would one day rule Niagara.[22]

The New Niagara's care for the tiny incubator babies demystified natural processes and took the terror out of Niagara Falls and electricity. The mixed metaphor of babies and dynamos revealed the union between the technological and the natural world. Babies nurtured by life-giving Niagara electricity rendered the lingering notion of opposition between humans and nature anachronistic. Thanks to technology, Niagara, man's once-terrifying "seeming antagonist is in the deeper sense his most tender and inspiring friend, . . . whose very opposition but strung the other's sinews and hardened his muscles for the victory."[23]

During the Pan-American summer, Niagara electricity also spawned new forms of popular entertainment. An experiment with high voltage by the Niagara Falls Power Company produced artificial thunder and lightning, and the lightning bolts spelled "NIAGARA." For a small fee, visitors could listen to the roar of the Niagara cataract over a telephone line. And on the midway, technical effect combined with a phantasmagoria of sensation to create the hilarious and exuberant spirit of amusement parks. Some 2,000 incandescent lamps illuminated F. W. Thompson's "Aerocycle." According to Mary Bronson Hartt, the "Darkness and Dawn" concession had been so improved by new technical effects since the Omaha fair that the entire original "theatre" was now a waiting room for the current expanded show.[24]

The great sensation of the midway was Thompson's fantastic voyage in "A Trip to the Moon," an electrical ride that eventually became a permanent fixture at Coney Island. Thompson earned fame as America's first great ride-maker and professional midway-show promoter. Although he studied classical painting under muralist Kenyon Cox, Thompson suppressed his more subtle artistic instincts to give the public a raucus, wonderful technological flight of fancy. Electricity powered his mooncraft's wings and gave riders the sensation of rising above the clouds. The two distinguishable landmarks as viewed from "space" were Niagara Falls and the Pan-American Exposition's great illuminated grounds and Electric Tower.[25]

Neither individual exhibitors, incubator babies, the midway, nor the triumph of long-distance transmission could tell the true story of Niag-

A TRIP TO THE MOON.

The great air ship is here shown poised above Niagara Falls, while the ray from its powerful search-light illumines the Pan-American Exposition, and the true sweep of the Niagara River is shown between; and beyond the lights of Buffalo. This is easily the first of the Midway attractions for novelty and audacity of conception. The traveler enters a great landing-dock, from whence, in company with two hundred and fifty others, he steps on board the air-ship Luna. The fastenings are cast off, the great wings beat, the ship begins to rise, or seems to, the earth drops rapidly away until it becomes a mere receding ball, other planets appear, increase in size and brilliancy and are left behind, and finally the moon draws nearer and nearer, and the air-ship settles down upon its surface. Then follows disembarkation into the streets of the moon-city, with visits to the people and the shops and bazars of Luna. After one of the most thoroughly enjoyable trips possible of conception the air-ship returns to earth once more.

The most popular attraction of the Pan-American midway was F. W. Thompson's electrical ride known as "A Trip to the Moon," which created the sensation of rising above the clouds. Shown here is a fanciful re-creation of the ride that appeared in *With Pen and Camera at the Pan-American Exposition*. Niagara is at bottom right. (Courtesy, Buffalo and Erie County Historical Society)

ara's dazzling impact on the exposition, however. Commentators were quick to note that Niagara's influence defied limitation.

> The electrical exhibits cannot be contained in a single building; they are everywhere. Niagara power drives the trolley which carries you to the grounds, turns the wheel of countless machines

in Machinery Hall; whirls the electric fans which cool the theatres in the midway; illuminates the cycloramas and other electrical effects and illusions; makes possible the powerful searchlight on the Electric Tower which sends signals to Toronto; glows in the blended colors of the Electric Fountain, and blossoms in a whole firmament of electric stairs which make up the glory of the Pan-American illumination.[26]

Such an entertaining array of electrical innovations made the exposition into "a new edition of a world encyclopedia." Even the ignorant visitor left a "genuine worshipper of the genius that can generate the marvelous mechanical devices."[27]

Organizers of the Pan-American Exposition feared that in the years following 1893 public enthusiasm for world's fairs had waned. No longer could the simple hosting of a world's fair or a re-creation of the White City be counted on to lure tourists and investors into the host city. Consequently, Pan-American planners sought new ways to capture public attention and patronage. The exposition's chief architect, John M. Carrère, of the New York architectural firm of Carrère & Hastings, stressed the importance of the visitor's "first impression" of the fair. Because the visual impact of the landscape might well determine the success or failure of the privately funded Buffalo venture, organizers wanted to create a stunning environment of beauty, joyous entertainment, and education.[28]

The Buffalo exposition realized this goal by using playful colors and fanciful ornamental details in the style of the Spanish Renaissance. The exuberant Spanish motifs gave the fair a look that contrasted sharply with the stern Beaux-Arts classicism of the Chicago fair. But Niagara's influence was also crucial in creating a visually stunning impression. The artistic aim of the exhibition was to use color and electricity to amuse, awe, and educate the public. Through a combination of readily abundant electricity, the commitment of Superintendent of Electrical Exhibits G. F. Sever to exploit the nighttime wonders of electricity, and the well-known electrical-display skills of Luther Sterringer, the fair offered "a greater opportunity for esthetic experiments than have ever before been possible anywhere."[29] Edward Hale Brush wrote:

> It is intended to have the exposition so attractive both by day and by night that the visitor will scarcely know when it is the most pleasing and beautiful. The electric illumination will be on an unprecedented scale, marvelous in beauty as well as absolutely unique.[30]

By fully exploiting the visual impact of electrical illumination, the Pan-American Exposition became the first world's fair to be primarily both an outdoor and an evening spectacle. The fair implemented an architectural scheme whose full effect was evident in its nighttime design. Artificial light was everywhere. Fair organizers set building specifications for individual buildings and for the Court of Fountains based on the fair's electrical displays. Hundreds of thousands of incandescent lights outlined the perimeter of the halls as well as much of the sculpture. The electrical engineers decided to use 8-candlepower lamps in place of the standard, harsher 16-candlepower lamps or older arc lamps in order to bathe the grounds in a soft, warm glow. Moreover, whereas standard electricity is instantly turned all on and all off, Luther Sterringer created a great dimming switch to gradually bring on and intensify the light. The entire process took about a minute, and no previous electrical display had ever so magically accentuated the transition between day and night.[31]

Electrical illumination proved so popular that tourists left the midway to revel in the nighttime transformation of the Court of Fountains. Even visitors who argued that the Pan-American Exposition paled in comparison with Chicago's fair still were awed by the electrical wizardry of the Buffalo fair at sunset. *Cosmopolitan* magazine's editor, Robert Grant, told the story of two friends whose initial disappointment in the Pan-American Exposition led them to retreat to the solace of nature at Niagara Falls. But Grant called them back to Buffalo:

> I took upon myself to assure them that if they departed without seeing it [night-time illumination] they would be guilty of a cruel wrong to themselves, and that the spectacle was worth a voyage across the Atlantic. They regarded me skeptically, but they con-

sented to go with me on the following evening.[32]

Upon viewing the nighttime display, Grant's friends reacted by echoing age-old tourist conventions for describing Niagara's sublimity. Now, however, Niagara's sublimity comprised the engineering triumph of illumination from long-distance power transmission, not just pristine nature. Feeling incapable of doing justice to the spectacle, the onlookers warned: "The description of what follows will be trite enough to those who have seen it for themselves." Because the exposition at night was, like the cataract, a one-of-a-kind wonder, awestruck tourists exalted the sensations they felt in its presence. Anyone who saw it, said *World's Work* editor Walter Hines Page, experienced a "new kind of brilliancy." He continued: "You are face to face with the most magnificent and artistic nocturnal scene that man has ever made." Such a visual wonder was worth a transatlantic journey.[33]

The New Niagara shaped the Pan-American Exposition in ways that were not limited to electrical effects or exhibits. The entire architectural design, as well as the decoration, sculpture, and color scheme, embodied a progressive vision of human history. Starting at the esplanade, buildings and sculpture in tandem portrayed humankind's evolving triumph over nature. Heavier architectural design denoted the naturalistic qualities of the Forestry, Mines, Horticulture, and Graphic Arts Buildings. The Machinery, Electricity, Manufacturing, and Liberal Arts Buildings that lined the Court of Fountains represented more-advanced human genius and were treated with more-delicate architectural features.

All over the fairgrounds, allegorical statuary figures told the story of American accomplishment from the days of the Native Americans to the harnessing of Niagara Falls. Along the Court of Fountains, bolder or heavier sculptural detail gave way to lighter and more delicate detail. This progression reached a culmination at the head of the court, where Paul W. Bartlett's "Genius of Man" symbolized all other work and pointed to the Electric Tower.[34]

The allegorical history told in architecture and sculpture culminated in Niagara Falls. At the end of the Court of Fountains, "the Electric Tower, representing the crowning achievement of man, is dedicated to the great waterways and the power of Niagara that is utilized to generate the current which runs the Exposition." The sculpture on the tower and in the cupolas of the tower's pavilion base dramatized the harnessing of Niagara. Sculpture renditions of the Great Lakes in the pavilions suggested the immediacy of Niagara Falls. The center shaft of the Electric Tower embodied Niagara Falls in the 74-foot artificial waterfall that released 35,000 cubic feet of water per minute. Twin opposing statues by George Grey Barnhard flanked the artificial cataract. On the right stood "the Great Waters in the Days of the Indian"; to the left stood "the Great Waters in the Days of the White Man."[35]

Like the sculptural works, artistic coordinator C. Y. Turner's decorative color scheme harmonized with the didactic architecture of the exposition buildings. Upon entering the grounds at the Esplanade, visitors distinguished deep colors. Where architectural and sculptural detail were heavier, a cruder color scheme of primarily oranges and greens conformed to the emphasis on nature's resources and on more primitive human life. Closing in on the Electric Tower, ruddy colors gave way to more subtle ones. In Turner's scheme, ivory, gray, and greens stood for refinement.[36]

Although the color scheme of the Pan-American Exposition owed allegiance to the exuberant hues of a Spanish village, Turner's choice of a Niagara shade of green for his focal color verified Niagara's organizing role at the fair. As used by Turner, green represented power. Turner explicitly acknowledged the significance of the New Niagara in the color scheme:

> Since I wished in some way to emphasize the great power which was being used to run the Exposition, the beautiful emerald-green hue of the water as it curls over the crest of Niagara Falls seemed to me a most fitting note to carry through the exposition, and I therefore adopted it and this color is found on some portion of every building.[37]

Because the green of Niagara "comes out everywhere," as Walter Hines Page noted,[38] Niagara continued to serve as an inspirational and uniquely American icon. Indeed, artists, engineers, and architects all used Niagara Falls in a complementary manner. For Turner, Niagara's color stood for progress and refinement. Similarly, because no original sculptural work stood beyond the Electric Tower, Niagara received the last word in the exposition's record of American history. Although Niagara Falls might have appeared to be a symbol of primeval American nature or an obstacle in humankind's early battles with nature, it instead represented American civilization's highest accomplishment. Barnhard's "Great Waters" chronicled an abridged history of development at Niagara Falls. After "the Great Waters in the Days of the White Man," viewers looked to the rising Electric Tower, and to the future.

The Court of Fountains at the Buffalo fair proclaimed a grand city-center landscape of civic pride, dignity, and sociability for an urban, democratic society. As impressive as this arrangement of buildings was, the most riveting structure on the Pan-American Exposition grounds was the Electric Tower. This tower gave the Buffalo fair an up-to-date architectural modernity that was quite distinct from Chicago's Court of Honor of 1893. Architect and critic Claude Bragdon called the Electric Tower "the high C of the entire architectural symphony, being artfully led up to by the converging perspective lines of the adjacent buildings, the planting and terracing, and by the arrangement of basins, cascades and fountains."[39]

Designed by John Galen Howard of New York, the Electric Tower was "the one purely monumental building in the grounds." Whereas all other pavilions on the grounds seemed festive and exuberant, the Electric Tower most closely resembled a tall office building. In the late nineteenth century, skyscrapers represented another uniquely American contribution to the technological sublime. These elegant structures were instant attention-getting landmarks and symbols of progress.[40]

Reaching a height of 400 feet, the Pan-American Electric Tower stood three times taller than all the other exposition buildings. Ninety-four searchlights shone on the artificial waterfall. The tower's vertical steel shaft and staff facade suggested modern design and modern materials. At the top, Herbert Adams's crowning brass statue, "Goddess of Light," symbolized electricity. The centerpiece for all exposition searchlights, outlined with innumerable incandescent lamps, and employing electric elevators that gave visitors access to new heights, the Electric Tower was the exposition's great monument to the role of electricity and technology in modern life.[41]

SEARCHLIGHT ON ELECTRIC TOWER

The Electric Tower was the architectural highlight of the exposition and a powerful symbol of the electricity age inspired by Niagara Falls. (Courtesy, Buffalo and Erie County Historical Society)

To convey the Electric Tower's direct connection to Niagara, a giant searchlight in the tower beamed toward the Falls. The tower also featured the blue-green coloring that suggested "the water as it curls over the crest of Niagara Falls"—the precise moment when its power potential was greatest. Likewise, the artificial falls sculpted into the tower evoked "the propinquity of Niagara itself, and . . . [made] the stable architecture of its environment vibrate with living energy. Often and often do we return to it, and always with a new perception of its felicity and power." In size, color, beauty, sublimity, and organizing impact on the landscape, the Electric Tower was the structural and metaphorical equivalent of the New Niagara at the Pan-American Exposition.[42]

As it soared above the Spanish architecture of the exposition, the Electric Tower sparked associations not only of business energy but also of the supremacy of the United States. In his study of America's world fairs between 1876 and 1916, Robert Rydell shows that, in all the fairs of this period, organizing ideas about race, nationality, and progress confirmed the economic and political hegemony of the United States over the other nations in the hemisphere.[43] As the focal piece of the Buffalo exposition, the Electric Tower, with less of the Spanish Renaissance color and ornamentation, impressed visitors with its aura of strength, majesty, boldness, and prosperity. Looming high above everything else at the fair, the tower proclaimed a world made in the image of the United States. It also emphasized that America had what the Latin American countries did not—electricity.

Although it was a symbol of power and of American superiority in a jingoistic era, the Electric Tower also represented the altruistic and humanitarian role of both Niagara Falls and the United States. The delicate "Goddess of Light" statue beckoned electricity, under American stewardship, toward a new golden age of peace, warmth, and mutual trust: electricity and scientific genius—great agents of democracy—would improve the universal condition of humankind. Ultimately, the Electric Tower offered the philanthropic promise to lessen life's burdens and improve the standard of living for all.[44]

Tourist accounts of the Pan-American Exposition acknowledged that the Buffalo fair had created a realm of magical enchantment on its grounds. Visitors "were suddenly transported into surroundings, as different as possible to those by which they were ordinarily accustomed, and every aspect and suggestion of which were festive and entertaining."[45] Unlike previous electrical illumination at world expositions, the lighting at the Buffalo fair bathed visitors in a soothing, welcoming glow that had "a warmth, a strangely human element, that is not usual with electric lamps." In this "City of Living Light," ordinary visitors could forget the workshop and the monotony of everyday life. Somehow the temporary nature of the exposition added to the impact of the colorful Spanish architecture. The "architecture has made a flourish to thrill the heart for a summer." Mary Bronson Hartt, Walter Hines Page, and Julian Hawthorne were among the many commentators who concluded that the Buffalo exposition was more compelling than the strenuous Chicago and Paris world's fairs. Said one critic: "Certainly the Pan-American is well worth visiting, if only for this sensation" of being in a completely new environment.[46]

Mass cultural institutions, such as world's fairs, offered unique opportunities to influence popular taste and educate the populace. One principal justification for a great exposition was the elitist hope that a fair's visual impact might elevate what was believed to be the crude aesthetic sense of the ordinary American. By introducing a "holiday mood" into the fairgrounds and officially embracing the midway as part of the fair proper through easy connection to the Court of Fountains, the organizers appealed to all segments of society. According to Walter Hines Page, families of all types frequented the fair. Fair organizers, however, managed the exuberance of the Pan-American Exposition through careful orchestration of the fair's symbolism. The lavish ornament of the exposition was subsumed in a grand concept that marked the harmonious integration of nature and technology and provided clear didactic lessons.[47]

According to Columbia University President Nicholas Murray Butler, the Buffalo exposition was the first American exposition to be ideally suited to the improvement of popular taste. In "The Educational Influence of the Exposition," Butler noted that, unlike the huge Chicago fair, the Pan-American Exposition was compact and comprehensible. Instead of dulling the senses with riotous variety and wearying scope, the Pan-American offered visitors sensations that could actually be comprehended; the Buffalo fair compelled thought. From the exposition buildings to the waterways, the lighting, the landscape gardening, the sculpture, and the color scheme, the exposition presented a unified image. Consequently, visitors might learn the lessons of good taste more easily. "Even a layman in the arts cannot fail to notice the deep esthetic impression that the Exposition makes upon himself and those about him."[48]

Because the Pan-American Exposition was so new and festive, however, some critics urged caution. Its color scheme and overall vivid aesthetic impression shocked the conservative taste of some commentators. Herbert Croly questioned the efforts of fair organizers to surpass all previous expositions. In his view, the "Rainbow City" took gaiety and picturesqueness to garish excess. Tawdry coloring and decorations, especially away from the Court of Fountains, ran wild. "It is intentionally novel and gay," said Croly. "The desire for advertisement, the necessity of creating a sensation may well drive subsequent expositions still further in the same direction."[49]

Croly reminded his readers that the Pan-American Exposition was temporary, that because its architects and engineers had no need to concern themselves with the everyday imperatives of structure and permanency, they designed for effect only. Had not the unlimited use of Niagara's electric power produced a riot of sensations, rather than a truly functional use of a benevolent power? Croly's biggest fear was that this experimental novelty might become so popular that it would dominate everyday construction. Frivolity would then supersede reason, and a visually stunning urban landscape might ultimately prove illusory, useless, and dangerous, he said.[50]

Yet, those who doubted that the Pan-American Exposition foretold a golden future were in the minority. Although the exposition may have been a great illusory construction, and thus similar to Chicago's "White City,"[51] many contemporary critics noted that Buffalo's "Rainbow City" constituted a genuine functional, if temporary, city. The exposition city was clean, sanitary, and provided up-to-date services. Niagara Falls power supplied the Pan-American fair with all the essentials of the modern city—driving the motors of its transportation system and lighting its streets and buildings. Behind the dazzling display lay "the triumph not of Aladdin's lamp, but of the masters of modern science over the nature-god, Electricity."[52]

The working splendor and beauty of the Pan-American Exposition represented an ideal that contrasted with the more characteristic, turn-of-the-century American cityscape. Urban reformers bemoaned the disorder and discord of American urban space. A typical American city massed an "inharmonious jumble" of tawdry architecture, and even where good buildings existed, local quirks in the landscape and lack of harmony muted their aesthetic impact. Indeed, the contrast between the exposition's Niagara-inspired "Rainbow City" and Buffalo's permanent cityscape provided a crude reminder of America's urban ugliness: "three miles away are a thousand ungraceful shapes piled garishly together, and here this dream of perfection." Echoing Thomas Cole's laments of seventy years earlier, the Pan-American showed that ugliness and squalor were the products of carelessness and lack of attention to things beautiful.[53]

Thus, the Pan-American Exposition infused new life into the City Beautiful Movement, which was an attempt to ameliorate the ugliness of America's urban landscapes. Its leadership comprised Beaux-Arts architects, artists, enlightened businessmen, editors, and activist citizens. The movement harkened back to the village improvement societies of New England in the 1850s, which were motivated by citizen action and civic pride and in which any aesthetic or practical improvement redounded to the benefit of the community. In its updated form at the dawn of the twentieth century, the City Beautiful Movement embraced the variety of modern urban life. The appearance of a factory was as important as the condition of a park. Indeed, the movement welcomed the aesthetic challenge of improving all realms of the city.[54]

City Beautiful activists, such as architect Claude Bragdon and writer, reformer, and city-planner Charles Mulford Robinson, believed that the Pan-American Exposition's aesthetic triumph would stir up popular discontent over everyday mundane conditions. The common man, once exposed to this fair, could not help feeling the "vague discontent with the environment of hideousness in which he, for the most part, dwells." More important, after seeing the possibilities of electricity and the logical organization of the electric city, Americans would work for a better environment. A renewed civic pride in public architecture and in how the landscape looked would bring much-needed changes to the city.[55]

This missionary impulse to realize a higher aesthetic was especially evident in the color scheme of the Pan-American Exposition. Commentators noted that the Buffalo exposition rejected modern architecture's avoidance of bright color. Indeed, following the adulation for the White City, white had become the favorite color in the United States. By 1901, many architectural critics hoped that "if the Buffalo Exposition can stimulate American architects to pay more attention to color values in their designs, it will have made at least one valuable contribution to American architectural progress."[56]

In fact, the exposition's color scheme stimulated precisely this attention at Echota, the model workers' town built in Niagara Falls by the Niagara Falls Power Company. When the town needed repainting in 1901, the Niagara Falls Power Company acted on the inspiration of the color scheme of the Pan-American Exposition. The company chose Reginald C. Coxe, president of the Buffalo Society of Artists, to give Echota a similar color scheme.[57]

Soon the entire community of Echota came under the artist's aegis. Coxe chose restful and complementary colors. Grays, greens, and warm reds predominated, and blended in with the local vegetation. "Echota will offer none of the harsh contrasts so familiar in village landscapes; but with its cool grey-greens will become a part almost of nature's picture." The International Traction Company joined in by painting its station and waiting room, and the Bell Telephone Company allowed Coxe to choose the color for the telephone poles. Down to each clothesline, everything in the town received the artist's attention. The result was a "color symphonic town, in the heart of a manufacturing district, [that] now stands for all the world to see—a new sight for Niagara!"[58]

From stylistic coherence to technological splendor, the Pan-American Exposition suggested the importance of experts. As John Brisbane Walker said, the heroes of the Pan-American were its engineers, architects, and sanitation experts. The magnitude of staging a world's fair, and the extensive use of electricity at the Pan-American fair, required a thoroughly planned city. Never before had engineers and architects, landscape-gardeners and artists, businessmen and artists, experts and politicians worked together with such cooperation. The Pan-American Exposition was an object lesson in "what men working in harmonious effort may accomplish for the delight of all."[59]

In setting up the "Rainbow City," the artists and technicians not only utilized the highest scientific and aesthetic knowledge but also insisted that they could reproduce these effects after the exposition. The Court of Fountains suggested a vibrant city center; fountains and grand buildings could bring people into community, foster civic pride, create favorable first impressions of a city, and soften industrial skylines. If the lessons of the exposition were applied properly, "sanitary advantage will be considered in a scientific way, and homes and factories will be outlined with reference to the highest advantage of the entire community."[60] Indeed, once the American voter and the politicians realized "that there are men competent and ready to make that environment beautiful as soon as he and his fellow choose to demand their aid,"[61] the Pan-

American example would become a great antidote to the unattractive everyday environment.

Although historians commonly credit Chicago's White City with launching the City Beautiful Movement, the term "City Beautiful" became current only after the Pan-American Exposition. The Niagara-inspired fair fostered hope for future aesthetic urban environments—the very fact that the exposition took on its magnificent aspect so suddenly (thanks to technology and expert planning) suggested that other cities too might be able to beautify quickly. Critics hailed the temporary city erected on the Buffalo fairgrounds as a prophecy of "The City of the Future." Likewise, Albert Shaw, in his "Real Value of the Exposition," speculated that the fair offered a model for new possibilities for cities. Herbert Croly anticipated that no other institution would be able to match the influence that world's fairs had on art and architecture. The Buffalo exposition's new ideal promised to spur experts on to great achievements and to give them the determining role in America's aesthetic growth. According to Julian Hawthorne, the exposition city "glows with the promise of things to be."[62]

Indeed, as "The New Niagara: 'Exhibit A' of the Pan-American Exposition" pointed out, the Pan-American Exposition manifested the utopian promise of Niagara. Thanks to Niagara's example, the nation promised to "Niagarize" and utilize other waterfalls to harness power and transform the environment into one of supernal beauty. Julian Hawthorne hoped that the exposition at least demonstrated on a small scale what Niagara and America might accomplish on a large scale. Sounding the profound American faith in the future, ordinary travelers speculated that, in twenty-five years, "you will see something like this—the golden city!" As Hawthorne said, "All the world will then be an Exposition."[63]

Ultimately, the Pan-American Exposition suggested a new world, and no more comprehensive example of the potential of the new, electrical Niagara Falls could be found than at the Pan-American Exposition of 1901, which displayed the entrance of the New Niagara into all facets of modern life. Thanks to Niagara's magical influence, a contemporary writer wrote,

> never before was Ariel so enthroned. The Exposition is his, the crowning features of its architecture are in his honor, and he will

shed his light and play his pranks in every corner. Why should he not? He is leagued with Niagara's cataract, and his power is commensurate with that mighty flood. It will be an impassive and unimpressionable spectator indeed, who can regard the moving machinery, the glowing lights or the play of colored fountains, knowing that the life of all is that the world's shrine of beauty, the Niagara cataract, without feeling a new thrill for the glory of human achievement, a new aspiration for international amity and the progress of the race.[64]

The Pan-American Exposition showed how Niagara's nature and technology could be utilized in dramatic ways to refocus the nation's aesthetic consciousness. So pervasive was this influence that, as I show in the next chapter, Niagara's transformative power promised redemption for even the more mundane aspects of everyday life.

7

"The Wonder of the Age"

Shredded Wheat and the Natural Food Company's Model Factory

In 1914 the Shredded Wheat Company's advertising director Truman De Weese explained that the company, known as the Natural Food Company until the previous year, took every opportunity to familiarize the public with "The Home of Shredded Wheat," because not all Americans could visit the company's factory in person. Since 1901, the year the Natural Food Company moved to Niagara Falls, Shredded Wheat advertising images had done much to ingrain the massive, architecturally resplendent model factory "Home of Shredded Wheat" in the national consciousness. The company's task was easier because the food factory was located at Niagara Falls.

Although Niagara Falls remained America's most popular natural landmark, by the late 1800s the public had also embraced a wondrous

"The Home of Shredded Wheat." The Natural Food Company built this model factory in 1901. Also known as the Natural Food Conservatory, it attracted 100,000 visitors a year. (Courtesy, Buffalo and Erie County Historical Society)

artificial landscape at Niagara Falls. Amid utopian projections that touted this New Niagara as the next great manufacturing center in America, Shredded Wheat and Niagara Falls remade the image of the most mundane, neglected, and scorned of all building types—the factory. Immediately upon opening in 1901, the works of the Natural Food Company, which produced the Shredded Wheat Biscuit, attracted tens of thousands of visitors. The *Niagara Falls Gazette* even reported that the one million people expected to visit Niagara in 1901 would mean "one million converts to Shredded Wheat."[1]

The Natural Food Company's model factory at Niagara Falls was the embodiment of America's romance between nature and technology. Designed to be a tourist attraction to rival the Falls, the "Natural Food Conservatory," or Shredded Wheat Factory (the company was renamed the Shredded Wheat Company in 1913), fulfilled the vision of its founder, Henry Perky, while it offered a corrective to the chaos and destruction of industrial capitalism in modern America. In this way, the plant closely resembled other model factories at the turn of the century that sought to win public approval and a greater market share by inviting scrutiny of plant operations and by practicing and promoting enlightened labor relations.

Unique among progressive manufacturers, however, was the plant's location at Niagara Falls, which guaranteed unprecedented free publicity and attention for the Natural Food Company. The company's progressive goal was to synthesize nature and technology for the benefit of humankind and the environment, and tourism played an integral role in realizing that goal. The famed tour of the Shredded Wheat Factory demonstrated both the wonders of technology and the benefits of enlightened management. Visitors toured an immaculate, hygienic workplace and afterward were served the "perfect" meal and heard lectures by custodians of culture who decried everything tawdry in the Niagara landscape. From its mass-produced natural shredded-wheat biscuits to its intricately planned building and grounds, from its worker-welfare programs to enlightened management, the Shredded Wheat Factory was presented as an ideal industrial venture that heralded hope for an era of industrial splendor.

The Natural Food Company was the creation of Henry D. Perky. Born in Ohio in 1843, Perky studied law and served briefly in the Colorado state legislature before he entered industry. An entrepreneur with a spiritual bent, he plotted a new direction in his career after he attributed his recovery from a long illness to a dietary regimen of pure whole wheat. Almost immediately after recovering, Perky became not only a cereal manufacturer but also a food expert, a reformer, and an educator. Upon moving to Worcester, Massachusetts, he founded the Natural Food Company, the New Era Cooking School, and *The Oread*, a journal of domestic science. By the late 1890s the cornerstone of Perky's benevolent and democratic program for social betterment, pedagogy, and prosperity was his natural whole-wheat biscuit.[2]

The simple 3-by-4-inch biscuit produced in Perky's Worcester factory made an immediate impact in a volatile cereal revolution that swept over America's breakfast tables in the 1890s and early 1900s. The cereal industry grew so rapidly that by 1904 Battle Creek, Michigan, the home to Post and Kellogg's, also served forty-two other cereal-makers. Machine-processed ready-to-eat grain cereals offered alternatives to home-cooked meat, eggs, and bread breakfasts and were ideally suited to the flux and fast-paced lifestyle of the nation. Relentless marketing schemes both embraced that lifestyle and acknowledged its physical and psychological toll. The claims that Perky and other cereal-producers made for their foods addressed the public's anxieties about the nation's health and morality, as well as concerns about the purity and nutritional value of manufactured foods in the era before government regulation of foods. The highly publicized personal histories of Perky, Post, and Kellogg bolstered their cereals' claims as effective and efficient health foods.[3]

According to its inventor, Henry Perky, the Shredded Wheat Biscuit—"the Wonder of the Age"—was a great panacea for all personal and societal woes. Natural Food Company booklets such as *The Vital Question* and *The Happy Way to Health* attributed all kinds of problems—from indigestion and constipation to crippling diseases, infant mortality, promiscuity, crime, lack of productivity, and business failure—to nutrient-depleted processed foods and a disorganized diet. The life-giving qualities of the Shredded Wheat Biscuit, however, were said to overcome the problems of an artificial diet. The biscuit allowed the body to "live in harmony with Natural Law," advertisements asserted, stating that this "Wonder of the Age" produced sound teeth, bones, flesh, and muscles, good nerves, and—most important—healthy, productive, successful people. The unique qualities of the Shredded Wheat Biscuit provided specific benefits to all types of people in the incredibly diverse cultural milieu of turn-of-the-century America. Laborers, businessmen, women, children, athletes, invalids, the elderly—and everyone who ate Shredded Wheat—could count on getting the proper nourishment for their daily tasks.[4]

By the time Perky had left Worcester for Niagara Falls in order to expand company operations, the precooked, ready-to-eat Shredded Wheat Biscuit had entered the nation's households and general stores. Echoing other charismatic cereal manufacturers, such as Charles W. Post and John Harvey Kellogg, Perky emphasized the crucial link between his natural, health-building food and industrial peace and efficiency. His enlightened management at the Worcester works, coupled with strict hygienic standards and a happy workforce of healthy girls who were well schooled in domestic science, helped publicize his business as an ideal progressive enterprise. Thanks to a popular product and keen advertising, the Shredded Wheat Biscuit became a profit-making food.[5]

Despite Perky's claims for this natural food, it was only after the Natural Food Company relocated to Niagara Falls in 1901 that the Shredded Wheat Biscuit truly entered the nation's consciousness. Perky leaped at the chance to bring his operations to Niagara Falls, where he could take advantage of cheap electric power and an ideal factory location bordering the New York state reservation. He secured investments from William B. Rankine, Darius O. Mills, and several other New York financiers, all of whom had bankrolled Niagara's electrical development. Fresh from the triumphant electrification of Niagara, they were ready to exploit Niagara's potential for a new industrial order. One booklet of the day stated glowingly:

> It is a source of encouragement and gratification to those who are striving to attain certain attractive ideals in their relations between employees and employers that the harnessing of Niagara shall have made possible this place of light and beauty where cleanliness goes hand in hand with human kindness.[6]

The enormous showplace Niagara factory that Perky planned and based on the highest principles of architecture, technology, and management promised to attract the attention of Niagara tourists who were already captivated and amused by artificial additions to the landscape.

The free advertising from this high-profile enterprise was an incalculable marketing coup for the Natural Food Company. Long after Perky sold out his interest in Shredded Wheat, Niagara Falls remained the company's chief asset. Anyone who visited the Niagara plant, browsed through Shredded Wheat promotional literature, or noticed a Shredded Wheat advertisement saw the link between the biscuit and Niagara Falls. It is difficult to imagine a more inviting opportunity to exploit associations of nature and natural processes. The Natural Food Company, which used natural whole wheat, produced its biscuits at a site where nature was supremely beautiful and powerful. Because Niagara power harnessed nature's energy, nature itself was said to govern the production process. One company pamphlet suggested that baking Shredded Wheat with Niagara electricity was the modern-day equivalent to Native Americans crushing wheat grains and then baking them between heated stones. Thanks to the pure production process made possible by the New Niagara, nothing was added to or taken away from the natural whole wheat. In an era of adulterated foods, Niagara Falls nature and technology allowed the Natural Food Company to manufacture the "Wonder of the Age."[7]

The Natural Food Company promoted the Shredded Wheat Biscuit and its sibling, the Triscuit (a baked shredded wheat wafer) as Niagara Falls foods. The seal of the Natural Food Company depicted an Indian grinding-pestle with Niagara Falls in the background (until 1993 all boxes of "the original Niagara Falls cereal" featured an idealized image of Niagara Falls). Trade cards boasted that the company owned more than 900 feet of frontage on the Niagara River and that the factory's rooftop observatory overlooked the upper rapids. Images of the cataract and the rapids appeared next to pictures of the biscuit. Advertising cards exaggerated the union between Niagara Falls and Shredded Wheat by depicting the factory nearly immersed in the cataract. Other views juxtaposed photographs of the factory's immaculate interior with the cataract. Elaborate store display boxes designed in the shape of "The Home of Shredded Wheat" featured Niagara Falls and a wheatfield in the background. The high visibility of these images helped further link the Shredded Wheat Biscuit to the technological and natural symbolism of Niagara Falls and established an indelible popular identity for the product.[8]

Niagara Falls and Henry Perky were a perfect complement to each other. Niagara Falls offered Perky unique possibilities for the production and marketing of Shredded Wheat. His enterprise was precisely the type of factory that the Niagara Falls Power Company and Niagara-boosters had hoped would locate at Niagara. When it announced plans to begin operations at Niagara Falls in 1901, the Natural Food Company played a key role in shaping Niagara's development. With its capital of $10 million, the company inaugurated an investment boom in Niagara Falls. Moreover, although Niagara Falls entered the twentieth century with more than 265 manufacturing plants, the factory, also known as the "Natural Food Conservatory," was a catalyst in the emergence of the city "as one of the marvels of the industrial age."[9]

To adequately appreciate the euphoria over the arrival of the Natural Food Company at Niagara Falls, we should recall the anticipation that attended the large-scale harnessing of Niagara's power. Many leading scientists, engineers, and developers, as well as Niagara-boosters, forecast the rapid conversion of Niagara Falls into a manufacturing mecca and population center. If Niagara Falls only approximated the per-person horsepower totals of New England mill towns, its projected population would exceed 2 million.[10]

Such hyperbolic predictions, however, brought home the demographic realities of the "new" Niagara. Despite a healthy growth rate, in 1900 the city of Niagara Falls had a population of barely 20,000. Newly arriving chemical and metal enterprises consumed tremendous amounts of power but employed few workers. By contrast, Perky announced that more than a thousand men and women would work in his company's great factory. Although that proved to be an exaggeration, the company workforce of five hundred was the largest contingent of workers at any Niagara Falls plant. The Natural Food Company rekindled visions of a populous industrial metropolis and catalyzed expectations for similar ventures.[11]

Perky's enterprise also promised to help the New Niagara regenerate the industrial landscape of twentieth-century America. His charismatic leadership of the company was typical of City Beautiful enthusiasts, who wanted to improve America's urban centers and industrial zones by appealing to community pride. The City Beautiful Movement was not a radical movement. The social and economic makeup of its advocates differed little from that of their opponents, who saw the city in purely utilitarian terms; City Beautiful members participated fully in commercial-industrial society and valued private property. But City Beautiful advocates such as Perky did share a belief in an organic city and in the malleability of citizens. By making their surroundings beautiful and healthful, they expected to achieve a more profitable, productive, stable, and happy urban order. Thus, Perky's public lectures and the well-publicized beautification projects of the Natural Food Company helped motivate interest among the other owners and managers of businesses and manufactories, newspaper editors, real-estate specialists, and investors, as well as the Niagara Falls Chamber of Commerce and the Businessman's Association, that had a stake in improving on Niagara's industrial image.[12]

By 1900 that image was partially in need of repair. Niagara itself resembled less and less the promised clean and magical utopia of the electricity age. Following the harnessing of electrical power, water diversion charters gave power developers the right to, potentially, dry up Niagara's great natural spectacle. The newly relocated, unaesthetic factories that lined the Niagara's riverbanks and the power companies' lands further spoiled Niagara's sylvan splendor. Niagara's industrial landscape stretched for acres and acres devoid of trees or greenery. Among the greatest offenders were the massive Carborundum and Pittsburgh Reduction Company plants. Huge smokestacks atop windowless, barnlike structures belched forth a blinding layer of vile smoke. The *Niagara Falls Gazette* regularly noted the putrid stench in the air from chemical and electrometallurgical plants. Contamination in the water supply threatened to bring on a cholera epidemic. Despite the supposedly clean Niagara electricity, Niagara Falls had become one of the least healthy areas in New York State.[13]

Niagara's myriad industrial establishments introduced the problems of factories everywhere in America in the late nineteenth century. Factories had come to symbolize the discord and disease that permeated the modern city. Fuming smokestacks, formerly a signal of productivity, now betokened inefficiency, waste, and pollution. Factory-building commissions typically were assigned to hack architects or mere builders, and while the three-to-five-story factory building emerged as a type in the nineteenth century, in most cases these structures were remarkable for their lack of harmony and poorly conceived for the production processes that took place inside. Unappealing, combustible, and often shoddy structures exacerbated the growing hostility between owners and laborers in the era of the "robber barons."[14]

In the Gilded Age, ugly factory buildings symbolized the condition of the nation's industrial workforce. The plight of workers became increasingly degraded and tenuous by the late 1800s. Workers logged long days in unsanitary and unsafe working conditions, only to return home to squalid and congested living accommodations. Company towns of worker housing were often the worst offenders, as companies gouged employees for rent and provided only minimal facilities. No wonder tensions between management and labor erupted into open conflict in such events as the Haymarket Riot, the Pullman Strike, and the Homestead Riot.

Most industrial operations retreated from direct public scrutiny. Only employees ventured into industrial zones and industrial buildings; huge walls and fences and windowless facades marked factory complexes off from their surroundings. One contemporary wrote:

> [Though] there is nothing more fascinating than to see how things are made, . . . very few manufacturers admit visitors to their plants, either from the real or fancied danger that the visitor will be injured by machinery, will learn trade secrets, or distract the attention or get in the way of employees.[15]

Even the rare well-built factories were situated in degraded industrial zones, such as Niagara's mill and manufacturing district, but reformers directed their social ire at factories and the factory management that built them.[16]

By the turn of the century, concern for public image, technological efficiency, and industrial peace, as well as the lure of greater profits, led a small number of model progressive companies in England and the United States to make reform a principal goal in the industrial endeavor. These establishments, including the Natural Food Company, took the lead in using both modern technology and good taste to establish an enhanced working environment. They tended to be large and powered by electricity, and because many of them invited public inspection, they emphasized beauty, efficiency, cleanliness, and labor peace.

Proponents of reform manufacturing believed that healthy conditions, together with character-building programs in the workplace, would ultimately defuse labor resentment and mold workers to middle-class standards of order and efficiency. The welfare or social-betterment agenda of these model factories promised to enrich the lives of plant operatives and to reestablish common interests between management and labor.[17]

At the pioneering National Cash Register Company (NCR) of Dayton, Ohio, management deemed that an attractive factory setting, scrupulous hygiene, and a system of organization that provided for worker representation and input led to a more efficient operation. At no other factory in the world had "capital . . . professed to study the higher interests of labor" so thoroughly. NCR strove to win the loyalty of its workforce by establishing programs that attended to worker health, education, and morale both in and out of the workplace. As *The Nation* said about the foremost American model factory, the affairs of NCR took on national significance because of the company's devotion to the welfare of its workers, "not only in the hygenic and esthetic conditions in the factory but in the houses, [and] grounds of its employees."[18]

One of the industrial enterprises that modeled itself after the National Cash Register Company was the Natural Food Company. The *Niagara Falls Gazette* greeted the announcement of the groundbreaking in December 1900 for the Natural Food Company factory with the revelation that "the famous features of the NCR plant at Dayton will be reproduced." Arnold Shanklin, an NCR manager, explained his company's system in a lecture series at the Natural Food Company plant. Henry Perky even lured Edward A. Deeds, one of the managing engineers of the Dayton plant, to his operations at Niagara Falls. The successful duplication of the NCR system at Niagara Falls led Robert Patterson Jr., general manager of the NCR works, to vow to send "all the foremen of his works to Niagara Falls to look over the grand plant of the Natural Food Company."[19]

Much like other image-conscious Gilded Age titans, such as NCR's Patterson and the cereal magnate C. W. Post, Henry Perky brought an insistent vision to the operations of the Natural Food Company. Although the whole-wheat biscuit suggested the Natural Food Company's respect for an older, purer, and more natural era, Perky's forward-looking message left no doubt about his commitment to progress and to enlightened management practice. An article in *World's Work* magazine hailed the factory as "the kind that wise manufacturers are coming to believe in . . . for their employees." No technological convenience, no safety concern, no sanitary facility, no relief from drudgery, no beautification project was too costly or insignificant for his company. When workers went on strike for higher wages during construction of the plant, Perky intervened to grant the workers what they demanded and they returned to work the very next day. The *Niagara Falls Gazette* exclaimed: "Certainly there can be found no one more interested in the welfare of mankind than Henry D. Perky." His goals included harmony and prosperity throughout his business empire.[20]

Perky's civic-minded generosity redounded to the good of Niagara Falls and ultimately the nation. Henry Perky and the Natural Food Company continually professed outrage over the noise, smoke, and pollution of Niagara's manufacturing zone. Contamination of the environment proved especially problematic for a food maker that wanted to claim the absolute purity of its natural food product. The *Niagara Falls Gazette* reported that Perky went to the International Paper Company and told its president to "stop that malignant smoke in your plant or else I won't come to Niagara." Unwilling to share a neighborhood with chemical companies, and aware that the industrial zone would inevitably spread farther up the river from the Falls, Perky ultimately rejected an offer to relocate his company on the grounds of the Niagara Falls Power Company.

Instead, Perky set his sights on the choice property that bordered the Niagara state reservation, "far away from the smoke of factory or railroad."[21] Updating Olmsted's views on nature, Perky stressed that nature's redeeming influence made the Natural Food Company a better industrial enterprise. He located his factory on the border of Niagara's preserved lands not because he wanted to displace scenery with utilitarianism but because he recognized that there was an affinity between nature and an ideal production environment. In turn, the businesses and residences bordering the "home" of Shredded Wheat would benefit from the company's naturalistic construction and fidelity to nature. Easing fears that his Natural Food Company would further usurp the picturesque beauty of the state reservation at Niagara, Perky claimed he had situated his operation in front of the rapids above the Falls to safeguard the rapids from other manufacturers. Now "nobody but God Almighty can interfere with them." In the first decades of the new century, Niagara's best custodian seemed to be the Natural Food Company.[22]

At the edge of the state reservation and the Niagara River, majestic residences lined the lots on Buffalo Avenue. The list of Buffalo Avenue homeowners read like a roll call of the New Niagara's first families. Perky purchased 10 acres for his plant and hastily demolished several houses. Some lamented this encroachment on nature and neighborhoods. A letter in the *Buffalo Express* noted that the Perky plant would

> make work and help keep the region busy and prosperous. But
> it is with a keen regret that we read of the proposed destruction
> of several of the finest residences at Niagara Falls. That city can
> ill spare them. For a city of its size and ambition, Niagara Falls
> is singularly unattractive in its residence portion.

Even Shredded Wheat literature acknowledged initial community
outrage over Perky's brazen infringement on Niagara's choicest
neighborhood.[23]

To counter these charges, the *Niagara Falls Gazette* dismissed the
efforts to confine the Perky plant to a factory zone as anachronistic and
illogical. Because the plant was to be a monumental structure built of
glazed brick and glass, its beauty would surpass that of the displaced
residences. Now, with the New York State Reservation as its yard, the
Natural Food Company had the ideal site on which to build its home.[24]

Set on a slight promontory facing the upper Niagara rapids and bordering on the state reservation, the Natural Food Company insistently
distanced itself from Niagara's more sordid industrial surroundings.
Following the cue of other "Crusaders for Fitness," who founded sanitariums, health resorts, and educational institutions, Henry Perky envisioned his Niagara grounds as the site of a great educational complex
and tourist resort.[25] He had previously converted Alfred Thayer's
Oread Castle in Worcester into a cooking and domestic science institute,
and he looked to build a more spectacular "Oread" at Niagara Falls.
And in April 1901 the *Niagara Falls Gazette* reported that Perky had
put aside $1 million of his personal fortune to establish "The Perky
Million Dollar Club," an institute to educate "healthy men." Perky
intended to live on the site, and several of the prominent residences he
acquired with the grounds were to be left as housing facilities for the
school's students and faculty.[26]

Perky ultimately spent little time in Niagara Falls before selling out
his interest in the Natural Food Company and the two schools of domestic science were never built, but it is possible to speculate on what
they might have been like. Perky's Worcester Oread offered a year's
instruction to girls in various branches of domestic science—including

cooking, sewing, household economics, sanitation, food chemistry, and bacteriology—as well as to those taking courses in psychology and pedagogy. An additional planned course in public elocution at Niagara would ensure that his Oread students were adequately prepared to hold demonstration cooking schools on the varieties and benefits of Shredded Wheat. Such demonstrations were designed to ease the traditional resistance of American women to manufactured foods and to show the culinary versatility and nutritional value of the Shredded Wheat Biscuit.[27]

Beyond this pragmatic, business function of the proposed Natural Food Company educational complex, student testimony from an Oread Collegiate Institute reunion in 1904 reveals that Perky intended to have the institute fill what he saw as a desperate need for domestic science teachers. Typical of other members of the educated northern bourgeoisie between 1880 and 1920, Perky shared an antimodern concern for the breakdown of traditional family institutions. He lamented that women grew up poorly equipped to fulfill their roles in the twentieth century. According to Henry Perky and other domestic science reformers, American society suffered because women did not know how to apply sound scientific knowledge to domestic tasks. By completely reversing the original academic mission of the Oread, "Mr. Perky . . . strives to show the value of a domestic training in an age which puts a high estimate on a purely literary and scientific education."[28]

The organizing element of Perky's grand Niagara complex, and the only component that was actually built, was the Shredded Wheat Factory. Yet from the time the *Niagara Falls Gazette* revealed the details of the endeavor at Niagara Falls, the Natural Food Company disdained the common label of "factory" to describe its operations. Flattering postcards of the plant proclaimed: "The Natural Food Conservatory, the Home of Shredded Wheat." A company-produced tourist booklet entitled *The Wonders of Niagara, Scientific and Industrial* announced that the company "changed factory to conservatory, and won the admiration of residents" on Buffalo Avenue. A conservatory was "a place for preservation or safekeeping of things" and "a public place of instruction"; it conjured associations of music and the arts—cultural endeavors that diverged from the typical perception of the factory world. No wonder female guides conducted tours through the Conservatory in much the same way guides escorted tourists through historic houses.[29]

In its quest to transcend the ordinary, the Natural Food Conservatory piqued public curiosity with the immense scale of its operations. The *Niagara Falls Gazette* called Perky's vision "as big a venture as the continent can show." Size alone gave the Conservatory majesty and set it up as an analog to the Niagara cataract. Henry Perky erected an industrial building with a "magnitude to dwarf any industry already here." Tourist literature indulged the passion for the gigantic statistics: the Conservatory used 4 million bricks, 200 tons of marble, 30,000 panes of glass, and 35 tons of paint, at a cost of $2 million. The company's 153-foot chimney exceeded the height of the Falls and was the second tallest structure in the area. At the time of construction, the Natural Food Company claimed that its factory was the largest industrial building in the world. So large was this five-story "home" that the mammoth National Cash Register factory in Dayton would have fit inside the Natural Food Conservatory.[30]

Despite this accent on size, Perky's commitment to create a model industrial institution enabled the Natural Food Conservatory to achieve a certain architectural grace. After considering designs from such architects as Albert Esenwein and C. W. Fisher, Perky hired Norcross Brothers to construct the factory. Unlike common, boxlike factories, the building articulated an imposing combination of modernism and romanticism that was typical of the ornate architecture of the turn-of-the-century American Renaissance. The plant's five-story symmetrical design consisted of a main central box with two flanking wings that dropped down to three stories on the ends. Steel framing allowed banded windows to dominate the edifice; brick served only as an outer skin on the structure. The Conservatory presented a rambling panorama, thanks to the thrusting forward of the central block, recessed flanking wings, alternately flat and pitched roofing, and turrets and cupolas. In a 1905 study of model factories, Budgett Meakin acknowledged that the building resembled "more a palace than a factory." With its massive lightness, commitment to modern glass and steel materials, use of the most technologically advanced machines and appliances, and homage to Niagara's majestic nature, the Shredded Wheat Factory was an ideal electricity-age industrial building.[31]

The grounds of the Natural Food Company complemented both the architectural splendor of the Conservatory and the neighboring natural scenery of the state reservation. Ten parklike acres, which included a tree-lined drive, gardens, and a public playground, suggested the setting of a college campus or an estate. Verdant surroundings, the landscaped plaza in front of the plant, and the flying pennants and flags that seemed to move in unison with breaking waves of the rapids further accentuated the organic presentation of the Home of Shredded Wheat. Trees, creepers, shrubs, manicured lawns, and winding paths (all features of the landscape design by Olmsted Brothers of Massachusetts) softened the image of the factory. The entire Natural Food Company landscape foreshadowed the later twentieth-century use of the corporate landscape to symbolize the wealth, power, and magnanimity of a manufacturing operation.[32]

Like the New Niagara power plants, the true wonder of the Natural Food Company was the inside of the factory building. Arriving tourists and workers (company ads boasted that the latter were also treated as "guests") entered immediately into the Conservatory's enormous, opulent lobby featuring oak furniture, leather upholstery, and a glass chandelier. These accoutrements suggested a hotel parlor or an aristocratic home, not a factory. Because the Victorian parlor served as a reception room for guests, it displayed the character of the "household." Historian Katherine C. Grier has shown that public parlors were "associated with the progress of civilized living"; while suggesting cultivation and education, these parlors allowed each visitor to "imagine oneself owning and using such a room." Grand, genteel furnishings in the Conservatory lobby indicated that parlor sensibility permeated this industrial home.[33]

After leaving the lobby, visitors followed the production process of the Shredded Wheat Biscuit and the Triscuit. With each step tourists advanced farther into this "home" that was filled with technical wonders of electrical manufacturing. Huge machines manifested the sublime productive capabilities of the plant. The company boasted that the Conservatory produced biscuits representing 116,297 miles of wheat per day, "enough to go around the globe five times." According to the tourist literature, ovens, shredders, and packing machines "always excited the interest and astonishment of visitors." Yet, the machines remained reassuring. The company's sealing machines "impress the visitor as being 'almost human' in their operation as they automatically open the flaps

The foyer of the Natural Food Company factory was opulent while also suggesting the homelike atmosphere the company strove to promote. (Courtesy, Buffalo and Erie County Historical Society)

of the cartons, seal them with dexetrine, . . . fold them together again and then paste a strip of paper over each."[34]

The Conservatory strove to inspire benign and entertaining interaction with futuristic technology. As part of the company's unique free lunch service to visitors, each guest deposited his or her menu card on a flatbed car of a miniature electric railroad that extended to certain seats in the lunchroom. Once the visitor pressed the button, the car whisked off to the Conservatory kitchen, returning moments later with the order complete. This little demonstration suggested the utopian efficiency depicted in Bellamy's *Looking Backward* and the fascination of a railroad switchyard. The whole operation was, according to *World's Work* magazine, "a feat that was almost magical."[35]

Futuristic technology helped make the Natural Food Conservatory a magnet for tourists, although this technology would have contributed nothing especially new to the industrial process if it had not set new production standards. No better reason for building the plant at Niagara Falls existed than the opportunity to utilize a completely electrical manufacturing process. This process proved beneficial in two ways. During an era when the public read muckraking exposés like Upton Sinclair's *The Jungle* and learned about a direct link between disease and poor sanitation and hygiene in food preparation, the Natural Food Company boasted: "In this plant are realized the most advanced twentieth century ideals—cleanliness, purest food, and hygiene."[36] Perky addressed a public-relations problem by using electricity and by demonstrating that his factory could live up to his claims. An advertisement for General Electric in 1914 heralded the industrial cleanliness of cereal manufactories such as Shredded Wheat:

> Not only has electricity made it easy for cereal companies to improve their output by regularity in the speed of machines, but the cleanliness of electricity, eliminating unsightly belts and dripping oil cups, has made it possible to give plants a tidiness and attractiveness that naturally led to the show-place plant for daily visitors.[37]

Dirt-free technology and modern sanitary facilities became important attractions that linked the technological sublimity of the New Niagara to the domestic associations the company craved.

The Shredded Wheat Biscuit itself embodied purity, thanks to technological processes. First, the Natural Food Company claimed to use only a superior strain of wheat. The untouched wheat was "shot automatically from wagons" into enormous cleaning machines. Next the wheat was soaked in cold water before it was cooked in monster kettles. Agitated throughout the cooking process, "the grains rub each other, friction loosens the woody fibre on the surface, and removes the minute insect life and eggs of insects which adhere to wheat." Following this purification process, the company shredded the wheat with "machinery especially invented and built for this purpose." Sharp blades cut the wheat to four-inch threads, which would leave the biscuits three inches across and half an inch deep. When so shaped, the biscuits were cooked in steel cylinders at 560 degrees for thirty-five minutes before being transferred to a second oven at a lower temperature and baked for six hours. The lightly browned, natural-looking biscuit, which resembled a bale of hay, was in reality a thorough product of the factory.[38]

The other product of the Natural Food Company—the Triscuit—went the Shredded Wheat Biscuit one better. Because it was baked entirely by electricity, the technological purity of the Triscuit stood unsurpassed. It was "filamented, formed, and baked in the electric machines of the Natural Food Company." As was possible only with an "electric food," "during the process of manufacture [it] is not once touched by human hands." The Triscuit's mechanically sealed packing, like the packaging of the Shredded Wheat Biscuit, prevented the contamination common to bulk foods and to foods packaged under less-stringent hygienic standards.[39]

The pure hygienic standards of the Natural Food Company applied not only to the baking process but also to the factory and to the company workforce. When World's Work, National Magazine, and such progressive industrial advocates as Nels Bengston and Budgett Meakin highlighted the features of the Shredded Wheat Factory, they insisted that what the company had done should be emulated by other companies that sought to ease the burden on their workers and to promote industrial peace.[40]

In contrast to the typical dark and dreary factory, the Shredded Wheat plant was a "Palace of Light," thanks to 844 large windows that made the building almost transparent. The naturally bright interior precluded the glare and heat that plagued ordinary factories. Likewise, the Shredded Wheat Factory featured the most modern innovations in ventilation science. Double-sealed windows shut out the impurities of the New Niagara atmosphere while intake vents and fans brought in new air from the outside. This air was then cleansed by sprayed water, which knocked dirt particles down onto the floor. The clean air then was forced throughout the factory by a duct system. A complete cyclical replacement of the air inside the factory took just thirty minutes.[41]

Indicative of the Natural Food Company's obsessive concern for purity is that no feature of the Conservatory stirred company pride as much as the luxurious design of the factory bathing rooms. The Natural Food Company installed numerous marble bathroom fixtures, and the

Interior views of the Natural Food Company factory from a 1905 gift book. The tour of the Conservatory showcased the elegant and elaborate facilities of the company's model factory. (Courtesy, Buffalo and Erie County Historical Society)

$100,000 showplace washrooms included "shower, and needle and tub baths, individual lockers, and other facilities encouraging cleanliness and neatness on the part of employees." In an era when few bathed frequently and when working-class hygiene lagged even more, employees could take baths on company time in bathing areas of the "most expensive and modern pattern." Workers changed into and out of work uniforms in the adjoining locker rooms. By providing the elegant marble and mosaic lavatory and bathing facilities that were symbols of status in the best homes, the company boasted that it created a homelike work environment.[42]

The Natural Food Company also served employees a lunchtime meal, and high standards of purity prevailed here too: "The food that is purchased and served to the employees in the two dining rooms is carefully examined, the milk is tested daily, the dishes are all sterilized, and the use of cold storage foods is prohibited." Meakin reported that the company "first sterilizes, then filters, and finally re-sterilizes its drinking water." A la carte company lunches "embraced a selection of foods prepared with reference to the tastes and physical necessities of the employees," although each offering featured Shredded Wheat. By organizing the workers' lunch hour, the company hoped to reinforce the family feeling among its operatives. At the least, the company expected to gain a more healthy and sober workforce.[43]

Turn-of-the-century industrial reform did not stop with programs that brightened, rationalized, and sanitized the work environment. Natural Food Company pamphlets acknowledged that the company "looks to keeping the standard of its employees up to the same high grade that characterizes everything connected with it." By the late nineteenth century, farsighted factory managers recognized the recuperative benefits of recreation. Proponents of social betterment insisted that proper leisure and recreation were "second only to the importance of good food and air for building up the worker's system." The company prominently displayed its recreational, educational, and character-building programs to the public, with the firm belief that what was good for the worker was also a powerful advertisement for the company.[44]

Each workday, the Natural Food Company stressed the uplifting value of Niagara's scenic nature. Unlike the monotonous and sensually numbing surroundings of most factories, at the Shredded Wheat Factory workers could look through their shop windows at the Upper Niagara rapids. Even more spectacular was the view from the Conservatory roof garden observation deck, a panorama of the rapids above the falls that Meakin recommended as "one of the picture spots of Niagara." Finally, winding paths and metal benches along the landscaped Conservatory grounds provided the soothing, passive recreation reminiscent of an Olmsted park. This use of a building design and siting to provide views and access to nature was far in advance of corporate thinking of the time period.[45]

Hoping to reform and monitor worker leisure-time pursuits, the Natural Food Company organized athletic contests and held summer outings. Outdoor facilities on the company grounds included a ball diamond, a tennis court, and a playground. The company also used part of its grounds for a garden plot for workers, and distributed seeds and plants and offered horticultural instruction. In addition to enjoying the nutritious fruits and vegetables of the garden harvest, workers might apply these gardening lessons to their own homes. Love of scenery, respect for beauty, and the long-range planning of gardens inculcated a conservative ethos.[46]

Indoors, the Natural Food Company sponsored a circulating library, shorthand and typing classes, and mathematical instruction. Company literature pointed out that these classes provided practical benefits to workers because they "helped to decrease their cost of living, provide[d] additional income and better themselves in every way." Other organized activities, such as daytime dancing, choral singing, instruction in musical instruments, etiquette classes, and involvement in various clubs, reinforced teamwork and discipline even as they exalted civic and domestic virtues.[47]

The social programs instituted by the company showed special concern for women's welfare and for a more rational management of the household. A "factory mother" helped female workers "to meet the troubles and perplexities peculiar to the sex." Female workers had their own dining room and received the company lunch free. During lunch, "Oread" girls lectured female operatives on the healthful properties of Shredded Wheat and preached the principles of domestic science.[48]

Just how well the workers at the Shredded Wheat plant absorbed these principles of system, domestic science, and social betterment was crucial to the tourist image of the company. While Henry Perky headed the Natural Food Company, factory girls exemplified his philosophy of domestic science and social betterment. Referring to factory workers as students, the *Niagara Falls Gazette* reported: "Mr. Perky's students are truly examples of the healthfulness of shredded wheat. He takes anemic girls, feeds them on this natural food diet, and the results are apparent."[49]

Long after Perky retired, cultural commentators noted that the healthy, cheerful-looking workers were products of an ongoing successful managerial organization. Social betterment programs relieved the drudgery of work and produced loyal workers who identified their interests with those of the company. At the Shredded Wheat Factory, workers were living advertisements for the Shredded Wheat Biscuit and the health-promoting ideals of the Natural Food Company. One contemporary wrote:

> As purveyors of food-stuffs for which especially nourishing properties are claimed, they [company managers] doubtless see in their [workers'] plump faces and pleasant smiles which result a valuable recommendation of their products.[50]

In its concern for the welfare of its workers, the Natural Food Company carefully oversaw the activities and behavior of its workforce. Recognizing that the plant operatives could not afford to live in the suburbs or take restorative vacations, Henry Perky tried to provide an appealing environment with ample recreational opportunities. These activities, as well as the company's refined atmosphere, exerted a measure of social control, but they also embraced the modern city. Certainly the company used dancing lessons, sporting events, and socials to try to eliminate dancehalls and saloons from worker culture, but its educative, cultural, and recreational programs were also useful to workers beyond the workplace. Skills the workers learned at the Conservatory could help improve neighborhoods as well as individual households. In addition to establishing respectful relations with management and reinforcing teamwork, production values, and discipline on the job, social betterment programs dignified labor by instilling in workers a civic pride, an enthusiasm for private property, and an awakened sense of life's opportunities.

From the first announcement of Henry Perky's plan to build a mammoth plant at Niagara Falls, expectations for tourism ran high. The *Niagara Falls Gazette* immediately called the venture "the Crowning Glory of Niagara Falls" and predicted that "every visitor to Niagara will be a visitor to the Natural Food Conservatory." Because Perky timed its opening to coincide with the 1901 Pan-American Exposition in Buffalo, interest in the plant soared at the outset. Tourists at the fair could see the Shredded Wheat exhibit in Buffalo and then visit the Conservatory at Niagara Falls. By the end of August 1901, the *Gazette* reported that "the massive, handsome, and modern plant of the Natural Food Conservatory is becoming one of the principal points of interest at the Falls, judging from the number of strangers who visit the works daily."[51]

Owing in part to the Pan-American Exposition, the fame of the Shredded Wheat plant spread. By 1903 the Natural Food Company's City Beautiful commitment led the *National Magazine* to feature Niagara Falls as one of the nation's rising progressive cities. In addition to company advertising, magazine articles, tourist literature, and guidebooks further touted the virtues of a visit to the Natural Food Conservatory. A Niagara Falls Board of Trade publication, *Niagara Falls of Today,* asserted that this plant was "one of the great surprises of America and has been read about and talked about so much that to go into details regarding it would be a repetition of what nearly everybody knows." While the Board of Trade exaggerated when it claimed that "nearly every visitor to the city" visited the Natural Food Company, the visitor rolls of the Home of Shredded Wheat annually numbered between 50,000 and 100,000.[52]

The Natural Food Company became essentially a tourist bureau in its own right. Not only did the company's popular cereal give Niagara Falls instant publicity, but the Natural Food Conservatory, with its 1,000-seat auditorium, provided Niagara with one of the nation's foremost convention facilities. In 1903 the *National Magazine* rated Niagara Falls and St. Louis, which was preparing for its world's fair, the nation's two leading convention cities. Because the Natural Food Company made the auditorium readily available, many reform-minded associations took their conventions to Niagara, and convention-goers witnessed firsthand the company's progressive endeavors. In all cases, the Natural Food Company propagated images of the model factory's new spirit of character-building and harmony between nature, home, and city.[53]

Tourists lined up to tour the Natural Food Conservatory. Despite the chagrin of some visitors who questioned the aesthetic appeal of a cereal factory, most of those who took the tour accepted the company's claims. An artist from the *National Magazine* who stopped at the Perky plant during a trip to the Pan-American Exposition found the factory to be the cleanest he had ever been in. One visitor wrote on a postcard:

> I have just gone through this wonderful plant and have seen them make shredded wheat. It is said to be the cleanest food factory

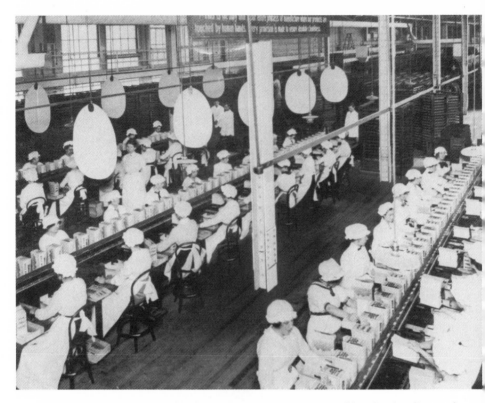

Workers packaging Shredded Wheat. Tourists were impressed by the cleanliness of the factory. A banner reads: "This is the only time in our entire process of manufacture where our products are touched by human hands. Every provision is made to insure absolute cleanliness." (Courtesy, Buffalo and Erie County Historical Society)

in the world. You certainly would like Shredded Wheat even better than you do if you could see it made.[54]

From free tour to free lunch, from the roof-garden view to the fascinating shredding and packing machines, the tour of the factory delivered wonder, education, and entertainment.

Visitors received a relentlessly didactic and moral lesson in dieting, cooking, and maintaining an efficient home. Everyone who stepped into the Natural Food Conservatory was a potential convert to Perky's philosophy of domestic science. The tour's emphasis on proper ventilation, worker comfort, efficiency, cleanliness, and hygiene gave visitors clear instruction in household management and the electric kitchen. The Natural Food Company promoted the Shredded Wheat Biscuit as a product capable of restoring individual health, remaking the American home, and righting the course of the nation, as well as reforming American dietary flaws.

At a time when management and labor stood in tension, when work became increasingly segregated from the home, and when image-conscious businesses separated their office headquarters from their production plants, the Natural Food Company preached that factory and home should be imbued with the same organization and values. Photographs of well-dressed workers leisurely eating lunch in the company dining room, playing the piano or gazing at pictures in the library, and attentively doing their jobs conveyed the joy of working at the Conservatory. All these activities constituted the factory experience. No wonder the Natural Food Company seemed to be the "happiest industrial organization" in the world.[55] The *National Magazine* concurred that the company had "brought to a happy consummation all of its plans and hopes for an ideal manufacturing institution."[56]

The company's "twentieth century" ideals proved to be an incalculable public relations windfall for the Natural Food Company and for Niagara Falls. The Shredded Wheat version of the new electrical future became the accepted doctrine of New Niagara boosters. Model industry and nature united to confirm Niagara as the nation's tourist mecca. Tourists moved effortlessly between equally sublime and instructive natural and artificial wonders; guidebooks even conflated the Shredded Wheat Biscuit with the great cataract. Although construction of the factory eliminated some of Niagara's finest residences, and although the plant abutted the state reservation, the immense structure staked a claim as a modern preserver of Niagara Falls. City Beautiful reformers applauded this futuristic hygienic, odorless factory. The Natural Food Company was the "crowning glory of Niagara," but even more, it served as a model for social reformers and industrialists as they attempted, in their own way, to shape America's future.

Epilogue

The New Niagara arguably reached its zenith in 1901. The opening of the Pan-American Exposition and the Natural Food Conservatory, the solution to the problem of long-distance power transmission, and the utopian promise of clean manufacturing near Niagara's monumental new power plants refocused the nation's attention on Niagara Falls. During the year of the Pan-American Exposition, nearly 3 million tourists visited Niagara Falls. For these visitors and others, the Niagara landscape symbolized the promise and progress of a new century. Nature and technology seemed to be in happy balance. Until World War I, the New Niagara strove to realize the glorious future foretold in 1901.

Impressive as the New Niagara was in the last decades of the nineteenth century and first years of the twentieth, however, the story soon became one of disappointment, even failure. Near the closing date of the Pan-American Exposition, Niagara Falls was humbled when Mrs. Anna Edson Taylor, a midwestern schoolteacher, successfully plunged over the Falls in a barrel. An article in the *Literary Digest* noted that, unlike other stunters who dueled with nature at Niagara, Mrs. Taylor was neither an athlete nor a professional daredevil. Thus Niagara, which a century earlier was too wild, too uncivilized, and too unassailable even for visits by female tourists, had been conquered by a frumpy, middle-aged schoolmarm. The general interest in this exploit—the culmination of a long sequence of stunts dating back to Sam Patch—further etched Niagara in the national consciousness as a site of catch-penny contests. When Mrs. Taylor followed in the footsteps of other Niagara daredevils by becoming a dime museum attraction, the vulgarization of Niagara seemed complete.[1]

To some observers, Anna Taylor's barrel trip symbolized the degradation of and limits on the raw power of the Falls. In the early 1900s, the myth of Niagara's infinite power was shattered. A "Decade of Stagnation"—as some New Niagara advocates characterized the interval from 1906 to 1916—saw Niagara Falls lose its leadership in American electrical power development. The area's original power facilities rapidly became obsolete, and government restrictions on water diversion from the waters above the Falls short-circuited the power companies' visions. America's educated middle class turned an increasingly wary eye toward the supposed marriage of nature and corporate technology. Newspapers, magazines, new preservation societies, even the national government, lamented the diminishment of nature at Niagara Falls. Far from realizing the utopian promise of 1901, the Niagara landscape reflected the harsh realities of the modern technological order. America's technological and developmental growth moved forward relentlessly, leaving the ideals of the New Niagara behind.[2]

Even among tourists, the special appeal of Niagara's improvements waned. Compared to the wonders leading up to 1901, new tourist attractions could not match the iconic purpose, education, and uplifting enjoyment of the bridges, parks, electric railroads, model factories, the first massive power plants, and the Niagara-inspired "City of Living Light" at the Pan-American Exposition. By the 1920s, Americans viewed Niagara Falls less as a place of special majesty and meaning than a divided landscape of industry and sentimental tourism.

The quick reduction of Niagara to a mere production center and commercial tourist attraction strained anew the long-simmering tension between tourism and industry, myth and reality, wilderness and development—in short, between nature and civilization. The glory days of the New Niagara pledged a harmony, or at least a balance, between these opposites. In the twentieth century, Niagara power plants ~~might~~ *were* have ~~been~~ built to harmonize with the Niagara environment, and developers might have professed their allegiance to Niagara's scenic wonders, but nature fought a losing battle in the Niagara landscape. Increasingly, over the objections of the New Niagara boosters, the underlying ambiguities of Niagara's continually revised synthesis between nature and progress were exposed.

Warning signs had emerged throughout the nineteenth century. Beginning in the 1830s, tourists' accounts lamented the tawdry aspect of Niagara; new additions to the landscape piqued ambivalence, even outrage, among visitors who came to revel in natural scenery. While the opening of the Niagara state reservation in 1885 fostered an illusion of nature protection, the results of Niagara's preservation showed that nature's victory was fragile at best and pyrrhic at worst. Almost immediately thereafter, Niagara's reserved nature faced assaults from all sides.

Tourist growth in the 1880s and 1890s and the need to accommodate thousands of daily visitors posed a major threat to nature. The new Niagara parks and expanding railroad and excursion schedules brought more and more visitors to Niagara. The superintendent of the Niagara reservation calculated that the Niagara region received 500,000 visitors in 1889. By 1905, some 800,000 people visited the waterfalls annually.[3] Despite pledging allegiance to Frederick Law Olmsted's ideal of natural treatment for the reservation, the reservation management could not resist a tendency to add more conveniences and improvements to accommodate these visitors. Although the reservation comprised Niagara's only enclave of nature on the American side, a street railway entered the mainland section beginning in 1901. The steam and electric railroads, especially the Great Gorge Route, displaced all nature in their paths, and the automobile as well added noise, smoke, and traffic to the landscape.[4]

Along with these intrusions of the city into the realm of nature, a lingering spirit of crass materialism plagued Niagara. Creative promoters eluded a ban on advertising on the reservation grounds by placing their immense signs in the river and on the gorge sides; bright and bold commercial images bombarded a captive audience. By the summer of 1901, Niagara's most insistent boosters decried the pestilential convergence of pickpockets, bunco men, gamblers, dope fiends, prostitutes, strippers, and ruffians on the Riverway just beyond the reservation. Thus, even after the creation of the Niagara reservation, Niagara still had its reputation as a disappointing and vulgar resort.[5]

On the Canadian side, the history of Queen Victoria Park bore out the accuracy of Olmsted's worst premonitions. Any plans the Canadian commissioners had of managing the park in harmony with the New York State Reservation went awry when they introduced nonindigenous plants and trees seemingly in order to "get as many varieties as possible" into the park. The Ontario Provincial School of Practical Foresty, Horticulture, Flora, and Botany operated within the park. Because Queen Victoria Park received no public monies for management and maintenance, the commissioners faced the problem of operating a self-supporting park that also was free to visitors. Ultimately, they settled on a strategy of renting concessions to private enterprise and corporations. The same civilizing impulse that turned the Canadian park over to the landscape gardener also sanctioned restaurants, hotels, trains and train stations, automobiles, and power company ventures within the park boundaries.[6]

With the approval of the Canadian government and the park commission, an electric railway and the power operations of three different power companies occupied some of the choicest land in Queen Victoria Park by the early 1900s. Dufferin and Cresland Islands fell victim to "an inextricable chaos of rock excavations." While new artificial attractions became a part of the landscape,

> utter devastation of the natural beauties of Queen Victoria Park, the demolition of islands and creeks, the excavation of the rock surface to the complete obliteration of well-known land marks, have been the accompaniments of the unparalleled endeavors and achievements here.[7]

The commissioners of the Canadian park admitted that technology had greatly displaced nature on the Canadian side of the waterfalls,

A "General View" of the Falls. This view of the Falls shows the extent to which modern civilization encroached on even the preserved landscapes at Niagara Falls. Queen Victoria Park especially embraced the latest technological advances. (Courtesy, Buffalo and Erie County Historical Society)

though they never embraced the Olmsted ideal that the park should be a pure pastoral oasis. They argued that because the Canadian park extended over a vast area and included land that otherwise would have been privately owned, they could at least preserve more of the beauty of that land by regulating the appearance of the landscape. According to the prevailing Canadian ethos, the scars on the landscape were warranted by such improvements as the trolley, which gave the working class cheap access to the park, and by the power plants, which promised to benefit all the people of Ontario. The Canadian park commissioners welcomed the park's ability to give uplifting lessons about nature and to demonstrate human control over nature. Charles Mason Dow conceded:

"The Park will abundantly sustain them in their contention that the park as a whole, with its wealth of electrical machinery, will then be of tenfold greater interest to the great majority visiting it."[8]

The creation of the New York State Reservation at Niagara Falls formally protected the scenery around the American side of Niagara Falls. Ominously, however, the establishment of the reservation opened the floodgates for power interests and manufacturers to exploit the areas outside the park. In 1885, New York State invoked its right of eminent domain to acquire the lands bordering the Falls for the Niagara reservation, only to return "control" of the waterfalls to private interests by granting liberal power-development charters to power companies between 1886 and 1896. As such nature defenders as Charles Mason Dow and Horace McFarland surmised, because Niagara Falls had for "so long been accepted as the synonym for limitless volume, measureless power, and endless flow," no one realized the limitations of Niagara's torrential flow. The state exacted no compensation in granting these rights and frequently placed no restrictions on the amount of water diverted. Thus, the great waterfalls at Niagara were still in need of protection.[9]

Although the reservation commissioners could not control the waters beyond reservation boundaries, they alerted the public to the dangers of water diversion above the falls. The reduction of water flowing over the cataract threatened to diminish and even dry up the great cataract. Andrew Haswell Green, commission president of the Niagara state reservation from 1888 until his death in 1903, doggedly sought protection for Niagara's scenic beauty from any agency that would listen. He used his annual reports to publicize the dangers of the power companies' privileges and to blast the state legislature for hypocritically committing itself to preserving Niagara's scenery but not preserving the be-all and end-all of that scenery, the Falls themselves. Spurned in his efforts to convince the state to guarantee the grandeur of the cataract, Green made formal appeals to the federal government. He called for international action to safeguard the waters of the Niagara River. The creation of an International Waterways Commission in 1902, which was charged with setting policy on navigation, development, and preservation of the inland waters of the Great Lakes, finally put Niagara under the aegis of an international body. Nonetheless, continued Canadian resistance to international action (the Canadians sought to protect their right to utilize Niagara power for their own economic expansion) frustrated the growing number of Americans interested in Niagara's scenic preservation.[10]

As private corporations gained legal control of the water flowing in the Niagara River, the tide of public opinion turned increasingly against the power-company interests. A mounting social-reform impulse, which encompassed the renewed efforts to save Niagara Falls during America's Progressive Era, signaled a response to the vast social and economic flux of the late nineteenth and early twentieth centuries. Educated middle-class Americans, who formerly might have channeled their energies into churches and missionary work, now created new social institutions and professions that wedded moral concern to expertise for the greater public good.[11]

New institutions came to Niagara's defense. City-dwellers who saw America's urban spaces as the crucible for the nation's most pressing problems initiated a back-to-nature movement that encompassed scenic and wilderness preservation. The nature-loving faction of the Progressive conservation movement espoused the sentimental value of preserving Niagara Falls. The American Scenic and Historic Preservation Society, an organization founded by Andrew Green in 1895 to safeguard the nation's cultural, historical, and environmental heritage, began an aggressive campaign of public education on the dangers of diverting Great Lakes water above Niagara Falls. Counting such social and business elites as power magnates Edward Dean Adams and J. P. Morgan as life members, the preservation society resembled the Niagara Falls Association in its prestigious membership and its mission to protect beautiful scenery.[12]

Much more influential than the American Scenic and Historic Preservation Society was the American Civic Association, a City Beautiful citizen lobby group under the leadership of printer J. Horace McFarland of Harrisburg, Pennsylvania. This group, which also devoted itself to such community issues as billboard regulation, the smoke nuisance, and home and garden beautification, led the fight for preservation of Niagara Falls. Its membership of more than 2,000 in 1905 comprised people with wide-ranging backgrounds in reform, scenic preservation, gardening, parks, and forestry. The American Civic Association could have had no better advocate than McFarland, who had a passionate love for nature and a relentless commitment to achieving an aesthetically appealing environment. His guidance of a comprehensive civic beautification project, as well as his prominence at the head of the civic association, made him the leading spokesperson of the City Beautiful movement in America.[13]

McFarland's strategy to save Niagara capitalized on one of the most influential forms of the Progressive reform spirit—the rise of modern journalism. At the turn of the century, newspapers and general-interest magazines boosted circulation by publishing investigative exposés of moral outrages, corporate abuses and greed, and political corruption. These often inflammatory, "muckraking" articles helped simplify some of the gray areas of modern life by creating stark heroes and villains for a society "searching for order."[14]

In the "muckraking" era, the press pinpointed the enemy threatening America's sacred birthright of Niagara Falls as the predatory, utilitarian-minded electrical power developers and the technological-industrial complex they constructed. Press coverage, which formerly lavished praise on the New Niagara and its wondrous technological possibility, now warned against the dire threats that technology posed. *Leslie's Weekly, The Independent, Everybody's, Ladies' Home Journal,* and *McClure's*—the very same magazines that had published paeans to the New Niagara a few years earlier—ran emotionally-charged pieces on the plight of the Falls. Articles with titles like "The Rape of Niagara," "Niagara Be Damned," "The Waste of Niagara," "The Desecration of Niagara," "The Crime Against Niagara," and "Niagara and the Plutocrats" roused public ire against the corporations and the monopolists that engineered power production at Niagara and planned even more devastation. As the *Review of Reviews* reported, "[corporate] men of colossal fortune who would ruthlessly destroy our greatest object of natural scenery" were to blame for conditions at the Falls.[15]

Even more telling were the technology-boosting journals *Cassier's Magazine, Popular Science Monthly,* and *Scientific American* that printed articles and editorials on "The Destruction of Niagara Falls," "The Menace to Niagara," and "Vandalism at Niagara Falls," respectively. Each magazine raised the issue of the moral implications of a desecrated Niagara Falls and disavowed the uncurbed rights of the power interests. *Cassier's,* which in 1895 had published its ode to the New Niagara in an entire "Niagara Power Number," lamented in 1905: "Niagara Falls are doomed." *Scientific American* acknowledged its role in promoting Niagara development but insisted that previous plans left the scenic beauties of the Falls intact. By 1905 the magazine deemed the "cold, hard, ugly utilitarianism" so pernicious a threat that it called for a halt to further power production plans.[16]

The years 1905 and 1906 represented a turning point in the public's perception of the new Niagara Falls. After a utopian "Decade of Progress," Niagara ceased to be an acceptable crucible for limitless technological improvements. The publication of McFarland's "Shall We Make a Coal Pile of Niagara Falls" in the *Ladies' Home Journal* proved to be the most influential attack on Niagara Falls development ever published. McFarland, calling Niagara Falls "the Monument of America's Shame and Greed," wanted to arouse a mass audience of outraged citizens. Both the Canadian park, which allowed power ventures on park lands, and the New York State Reservation seemed destined to be "merely the graveyards of a betrayed trust, from which we may see that which was once awe-inspiring canalled and turbined and wired into profit-producing work for a few of the betrayers."[17]

McFarland cast blame not only on greedy, self-serving power companies but also on politicians who gave Niagara's sacred waters away. The free invitation to take Niagara's waters smacked of graft to a public that was well aware of vote-buying for special privileges in the Gilded Age. How else could the state legislature's free gift of Niagara Falls to the power companies be explained when the state itself had to buy Niagara from private landholders to preserve the Falls?[18]

"Shall We Make a Coal Pile of Niagara Falls" outlined a strategy of citizen action to save Niagara through joint Canadian and American government control. McFarland urged each and every reader to write to President Theodore Roosevelt and Earl Grey, governor-general of Canada, and implored clubs, associations, and church groups to send petitions urging restrictions on water diversion. The stakes were eminently clear: "If the people act the Falls can be saved; if the people—you!—procrastinate the Falls are doomed."[19]

McFarland's article sparked a massive "Save Niagara" letter-writing campaign. No sooner had McFarland issued his public plea than a flood of letters reached President Roosevelt from concerned readers and from merchants associations, religious groups, and women's clubs. More than 100,000 women alone responded to McFarland's call to action. In a letter McFarland read at the hearings, Edward Bok, editor of the *Ladies' Home Journal,* stated that the support for McFarland's "Save Niagara" campaign was the most instantaneous and widespread he had ever encountered in all his years as an editor. Roosevelt, who met frequently with McFarland and the American Civic Association, became convinced of the public's fondness for Niagara Falls and stepped up federal efforts to pass national legislation limiting water diversion and to conclude a treaty with Canada to protect the waterfalls.[20]

In 1906 the American members of the International Waterways Commission acknowledged: "The glory of Niagara Falls lies in the volume of its water rather than in its height, or in the surrounding scenery." The commission warned that continued development of Niagara's waterpower would lead to the scenic destruction of the Falls. In the opinion of the American members, the economic benefits accruing from massive new power schemes paled before the "great loss to the world of the inspiration, aesthetic education, and opportunity for recreation and elevating pleasure which the mighty cataract affords." The enactment of the Burton Act of 1906 authorized the secretary of war to grant permits for water diversion and power transmission. The legislation imposed limits on the power companies' rights to divert water from the American side of the Falls and restricted the amount of electricity that could be transmitted from the Canadian side to the United States.[21]

As more and more Americans read about the evils of the New Niagara, power advocates rose zealously to defend their interests and investments. At and after the Niagara Falls hearings, a stream of experts— from engineers to Niagara's oldest inhabitant—testified that there had been no visible alteration in the Falls due to water diversion, although their evidence was often less than scientific. Clemons Herschel, a consulting engineer for the power companies, insisted that the river flow had varied by as much as 50 percent without any noticeable scenic harm. Ontario Power Company President Francis V. Greene compared the appearance of Niagara Falls in ten new photos with John Vanderlyn's Niagara paintings from the early 1800s, "so that you may see that even when 250,000 horse power is being taken out of the Falls there is no change in the appearance of the Falls."[22]

True to their faith in technology, developers claimed that they were actually preserving Niagara. Whenever nature took its natural course, they pointed out, the full force of the Niagara river current eroded the riverbed. Scientists had long ago forecast that one day the Falls would have eroded away to nothing. Already over thousands of years Niagara Falls had receded seven miles from Lewiston. Some experts estimated the yearly erosion of the apex of the Horseshoe Falls to be 6 to 8 feet a year, far more than the erosion at the sides. This meant that the bulk of water flowing over the Falls "was actually destroying the scene." If left unchecked, the developers argued, Niagara Falls would "commit suicide"; only a diminishment in the flow of water in the center of the river and a more even distribution of water over the entire Falls would preserve the characteristic horseshoe shape of Niagara Falls. Ironically, greater water diversion would guarantee Niagara's scenic majesty forever.[23]

Power advocates realized that if public pressure could prevail on government to limit water-diversion charters, the New Niagara might never fulfill its grand design for the electricity age. Not coincidentally, Peter A. Porter, whose grandfather, along with Benjamin Barton, purchased the lands bordering the cataract to found a manufacturing town, published his interpretative history *Niagara, an Aboriginal Center of Trade* in 1906, at the height of the controversy over the proper use of Niagara Falls. Porter believed the hydraulic developments of the 1890s allowed the area to return to its ancestral roots and "again become a really great center of trade." Power developers and aboriginal traders, however, made strange bedfellows—so strange that in the halcyon days of the power developers, as in 1895 when Porter wrote "The Niagara Region in History" for *Cassier's,* he made scant mention of this "aboriginal" foreshadowing of the great industrial Niagara. In the expectant days of the mid-1890s, Niagara's history signaled mind-boggling progress from the period when Native Americans ruled the unimproved landscape; in the contentious cultural climate of 1906, Porter used history to show the continuum of land use between the power developers and the Indians.[24]

Like Porter, Francis Stetson, chief counsel for the Niagara Falls Power Company, pondered the currents of change. "How many men at that time [of the granting of the company's charter] supposed that the riparian owner of 2 miles of water front, 7,000 feet above the falls and beyond the limitation of State ownership, was not entitled to take his own water out across his own land?" The power companies took enormous risks in investing in an uncertain plan to harness Niagara's waters and return them to the river without injuring the landscape. Because no one could prove any scenic diminishment of the Niagara torrent, and because the Niagara powerhouses had received architectural acclaim, Stetson believed the movement to deny power charters to the Niagara Falls Power Company and other power ventures at Niagara arose from an antimonopoly fervor in America.[25]

Beginning in the 1890s, this fervor encompassed antitrust legislation, calls for public regulation and even ownership of utilities, and social gospel reform. On the eve of the "Save Niagara" campaign, Ida Tarbell's muckraking exposé *The History of the Standard Oil Company,* which was serialized in *McClure's* and published in book form in 1904, raised the public's consciouness against trusts to a fevered pitch.[26]

During the hearings for applications for water-diversion permits, Stetson tried to overcome the image of the power concerns as ruthless, greedy monopolies by likening the Niagara Falls Power Company to the continent's initial pioneers. He pointed out that, in addition to being the first company to secure diversion rights from New York State, the Niagara Falls Power Company was the first to apply Niagara's great volume of water with turbines; it developed the world's largest dynamos and provided the first long-distance bulk transmission of electricity in the world. The $19 million in company investments exceeded all the other Niagara power ventures combined.[27]

Stetson further contended that when the state gave the Niagara Falls Power Company its initial monopolist powers, it attempted to serve the industrial development of the nation while conserving and beautifying the Falls. Having already spent more than $1 million on beautification, the power company challenged Secretary of War William Howard Taft to find an instance when it "failed to carry out the duty which we regarded as imposed upon us." Indeed, compared with the "irresponsible civic association" that unjustly abused it, the Niagara Falls Power Company was

> entitled, not to the carping and harsh criticism that has been
> exhibited and extended here, but to the thanks of mankind for
> what we have done in the extension of the useful arts and of
> the utilization of water courses, not only here, but throughout
> the world.[28]

Although Stetson pledged the Niagara Falls Power Company's fidelity to nature preservation at Niagara Falls, he and other advocates for the New Niagara echoed the "wise-use" viewpoint propounded by such conservationists as the Roosevelt administration's Gifford Pinchot. In the late 1890s, Pinchot had redefined conservationism (and had run afoul of preservationists) by advocating practical, scientific forestry in the nation's forest reserves. To accede to the preservationists' wishes, he contended, was to lock up an incalculable natural resource.[29]

Just as Pinchot in his capacity as the nation's chief forester sanctioned the controlled exploitation of the nation's forest reserves, New Niagara advocates believed the government should provide reasonable scenic preservation while it recognized the higher value of power production and transmission. Edward G. Acheson, the inventor of Carborundum, insisted that current power development had caused no diminution in the Falls and argued that the revolutionary implications of Niagara abrasives and graphite depended utterly on Niagara power and that any limitation of electrochemical production would be detrimental to the general public. An official of the Pittsburgh Reduction Company declared that the affordability of Niagara-produced aluminum led to the creation of more than fifty new companies that depended almost exclusively on aluminum; thousands more companies used aluminum or aluminum alloys to a lesser extent. Finally, the General Electric Company submitted a report on the industrial value of Niagara Falls that labeled the Falls the most valuable economic hub in the nation. By publishing statistics on the economic windfall that would accrue if power developers harnessed just 2 million of Niagara's 6.5 million available horsepower, General Electric hoped to convince the government commission and the public at large of the unreasonable cost of preserving Niagara's *entire* scenic majesty.[30]

Despite the pleas of Horace McFarland and the American Civic Association, and despite the federal government's conviction that the water diversion jeopardized the grandeur of Niagara Falls, the water-diversion hearings did not close the door on the New Niagara. No evidence showed conclusively that the power company projects had as yet diminished the Falls. The Burton Act, which was enacted "for the preservation of Niagara Falls," was a blow to power developers, but the provision in the law allowing for larger diversion and power transmission under revokable permits gave the power interests hope for the future. Even more so, the short duration of the legislation kept scenic preservationists on the defensive by requiring them to push for its renewal. By 1913, after only two renewals, the Burton Act lapsed completely. As the more liberal provisions of the International Treaty of 1909 went into effect, the "power companies immediately increased their capacity to the limit allowed by the treaty."[31]

Although joint international action to restrict the diversion of the waters above the Falls was aimed at guaranteeing the integrity of the Niagara landscape, the world crisis of the 1910s and the war preparedness campaign rekindled power developers' hopes of exploiting Niagara more fully. World War I created massive new demands for energy and industrial production. New Niagara boosters knew they would have to convince the public of the urgency of more comprehensive and efficient mass-energy production. Advocates for the New Niagara continued to look to technology for a solution that could calm the fears of the preservationists and preserve their own interests.

One radical technological solution—Kennard Thomson and Peter A. Porter's "Niagara Falls Junior" power project—proposed to harness an extra 2 million horsepower from the Niagara River without any additional diversion of the waters above the Falls. Instead, a second falls at Niagara, about 95 feet high, would result from construction of a dam across the lower rapids below the cataract. Thomson and Porter justified their plan with a characteristic American land-use maxim: "Niagara Power: What Nature Has Provided, Man Should Utilize." Calls to appropriate the enormous waterpower resource at the expense of the lower rapids echoed the rationalization of America's displacement of Native Americans from their land. The choice was between progress and the moribund way of the Indian. Just as the scenic preservationists had labeled the power company diversion plans a crime against God's birthright, Porter derided government limitations on Niagara power as a "sin." He insisted that the "State of New York ought [no] longer to allow such a source of benefit to its people, such a source of taxation and of revenue, to be disregarded."[32]

Responding to the imperatives of scenic preservation in the twentieth century, Thomson and Porter claimed that their development plans would both preserve Niagara Falls and improve on nature. A "Niagara Falls Junior" promotional pamphlet featured photos of the Niagara cataract with the caption "Our plan will save this from Destruction." The 2 million extra horsepower would not require any diminishment of the great waterfalls because water that had already passed over the Falls would be reused. Although their plan would have replaced the lower rapids with a lake, Thomson and Porter argued that because those rapids were not included in the Niagara Falls reservation, they were "not absolutely unique or an essentiality to Niagara's scenery." Instead, Porter insisted:

> As a compensation for the loss of these rapids there would be created a new falls—about 95 feet high; and new Rapids below the dam—and I firmly believe the new scenery of that lake and Falls would be quite as attractive as, more than full compensation for the loss of those rapids.[33]

An even more elaborate and widely discussed plan to alter Niagara's appearance captured headlines in 1915. The editor of *Popular Science Monthly* noted that as the bitterness between the nature lovers and commercial interests intensified, Dr. Thomas H. Norton, a visionary promoter of the chemical industry, had "outlined a scheme whereby it would be possible to satisfy those who only see the beauty of Niagara, and those who see only power going to waste." By constructing a mile-wide, 40-foot tall dam across the Niagara River at a point a half-mile up from the Falls, Norton sought to harness the entire 6 million horse-power of the waterfall. Such a plan would require that Niagara Falls be turned on and off daily. For fourteen hours each day, beginning at eight o'clock in the evening, the entire flow of the river would be diverted as the cataract served industry. Here the sylvan setting of Niagara's parks would be replaced by a mined and developed horizon. No other spot on earth could match the productivity of this "electropolis of the world."[34]

Norton contemplated not only the industrial splendor but also the touristic splendor of his scheme. He pledged that engineers would fasten a resistant steel shield to the crest of the falls to prevent recession of the falls and preserve Niagara's characteristic horseshoe shape. This enormous steel shield would have "the necessary architectural features to harmonize with the environment." Norton's plan offered tourists a new spectacle and new sensations. Visitors who gazed at the freely falling cataract between 10:00 A.M. and 8:00 P.M. could contemplate what the scene would be like when Niagara went dry: "Fancy the marvelously weird and fantastic sight of a moonlit winter's night as the cataract vanishes from sight and its roar ceases. Or fancy its sudden springing into joyful life and activity."[35]

Such a stunning scene of human control over nature, Norton believed, would captivate the imagination of tourists far beyond the unchanging, ceaseless flow of the undammed cataract. Combining "all the swift movement and stupendous grandeur offered by the sweep of the Johnstown flood, or the tidal wave of Galveston, free from the tragic terror and horrors of those cataclysms," the switching on and off of Niagara promised to be an unmatched spectacle. Norton asserted:

> Am I exaggerating when I state that 99 out of 100 of our fellow citizens would look forward more eagerly to the two swiftly enacted, spectacular grandiose events of the desired programme than to spending an entire day in contemplation of the falling water, clouds of spray, flitting rainbows and the varied panoramas of cliff and forest?[36]

The anticipated city and landscape attending Norton's project at Niagara offered an equally compelling vision of Niagara Falls. One colorful rendering shows "Niagara as it is not, but may be." Visitors enjoy

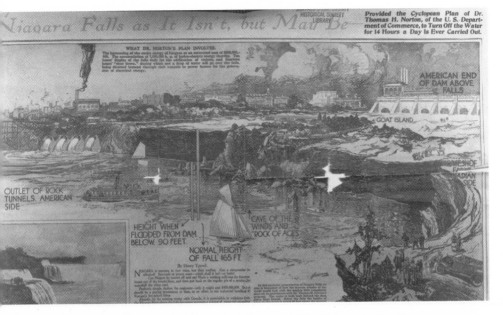

Dr. Thomas H. Norton's plan for a dry Niagara, 1915. Visionaries like Norton
sought a way to harness Niagara's full power without diminishing tourist interest.
(Courtesy, Buffalo and Erie County Historical Society)

exploring the dry cataract bed on donkeys, while others sail in the newly
formed lake basin between Niagara's bridges and the face of the Falls.
On the horizon, at the upper banks of the Niagara gorge near the Falls,
giant factories stand as public monuments. Depicted in grand classical
style, they connote not only the prosperity of this New Niagara, but
also the glorious harmony of the entire scene.[37]

In addition to the description of the Norton dam in the *Sun* and in
the special Sunday Supplement section of the *Herald American*, several
civil engineers attested to the feasibility of Norton's project. Compared
with the construction difficulties of the Panama Canal—another great
triumph of American culture—this scheme to utilize Niagara power to
the fullest was facile. Norton computed the cost of the initial phase of
the project at only $200 million, far less than the $500 million required
for the Assouan Dam. Even the outraged public denunciation of Norton's plan by Robert Underwood and the firm of McKim, Mead &

White seemed only to vivify the real possibility of a dry Niagara.[38]

If these fantastic and futuristic plans for the New Niagara were never realized and ultimately inspired only a ripple of interest, the New Niagara nonetheless rushed forward in the national consciousness. Once the nation moved inexorably into World War I, Niagara reassumed its role as a working symbol of the nation and of national progress. Technology boosters insisted that in the world's true time of need, the most valuable impact of Niagara Falls pointed to utilitarian service, not sentimental scenery. Before World War I, "the cheap power obtained made Niagara a laboratory where great ideas could be transformed into nation-benefiting enterprises."[39]

In a feature article entitled "Niagara at the Battle Front," *National Geographic* explained how during the war Niagara power and Niagara's technological industries multiplied the nation's production output, accelerated manufacturing speed, and heightened the durability of wartime weapons, vehicles, and supplies. The electrochemical and electrometallurgical industries that were so often reviled as the bane of the Niagara landscape by preservationists played a crucial role in breaking Germany's nearly monopolistic hold on the world's chemical production. Ultimately, Niagara Falls tipped the scales to victory to the Allied side, liberating humankind from despots. This supremely American achievement was fittingly commemorated with a two-page frontal-view photograph of the waterfalls captioned "Ceaseless flow symbolic of American purpose and resources."[40]

On the domestic front, the New Niagara continued to embody progress by revolutionizing life for women in a more peaceful manner. Niagara electricity sponsored a newfound joy in homemaking by keeping the houses of rich and poor alike warm, well lit, and fresh with circulating air. Electricity toilessly took over cooking, cleaning, laundering, and almost every common household task.[41] Niagara hastened new markets for the first electrical appliances. As early as 1901, exhibition halls in the Pan-American Exposition featured examples of edible goods baked in Niagara-inspired electric ovens.[42] An assessment of the pre–World War I era by officials at the Buffalo Electric Show of 1919 charted the forays that Niagara power made into domestic service:

> It was a busy era and the most majestic of all cataracts was giving of its power to the humblest of tasks, for in Buffalo each morning thousands sat down to Niagara boiled eggs, Niagara broiled bacon, Niagara toasted bread and Niagara percolated coffee. And when breakfast was completed many of the breakfast dishes were washed by Niagara energized dish washers. On Monday clothes were washed by Niagara; on Tuesday they were ironed by Niagara. . . . Milady washed her hair and baby's cradles were rocked by Niagara. . . .

The writer and Roycrofter Elbert Hubbard, in urging women to "Do it Electrically," believed that Niagara electricity was "intimately associated with the ease of the housekeeper"; housewives need only press a button and Niagara Power would perform the task.[43]

Although Niagara Falls retained its identity as a symbol of American progress and productivity, that symbolism became increasingly disembodied from the real Niagara landscape. During and after the era of World War I, the unabashedly technological purpose of Niagara Falls led some New Niagara advocates to call for a more honest reckoning with the Falls. Louis Bell, General Electric's chief engineer in 1912, insisted: "Saving Niagara is a sorry joke." Charles Steinmetz, another top engineer for G.E., declared in 1918: "Niagara [is] already spoiled." He questioned why preservationists continued to make so much out of Niagara's natural majesty when "there is no place at or around the cataract where one's sense for nature's wild beauty is not offended." Because Niagara had no remaining intrinsic value as a place of nature, the true significance of the Falls lay solely in the utilitarian realm of technology and productive service to humankind.[44]

This updating of Niagara's image represented a departure in Niagara's history. Until World War I, New Niagara advocates always succeeded in re-creating Niagara anew by bringing Niagara to the cutting edge of progress through the inspiration of nature. The landscape of Niagara Falls was the dramatic stage where Americans played out their expecta-

A *American Sales Book Company*
B *United States Light & Heat Corporation*
C *National Carbon Company, Incorporated*
D *Pittsburgh Metallurgical Company*

E *General Abrasive Company*
F *Republic Carbon Company, Incorporated*
G *United States Ferro Alloys Corporation*
H *Titanium Alloy Manufacturing Company*

I *Shredded Wheat Company*   J *Gilman Fanfold Corporation, Limited*
K *International Paper Company*

Niagara's basic industries, 1927. These views show the contrast between Niagara's harsh industrial zone and the more inviting setting of the Shredded Wheat Company.

tions to remake their world. From bridges, to parks, electric power, utopias, world's fairs, model cities and factories, and a cure-all biscuit, high-profile projects at Niagara Falls synthesized nature and technology and kept the Falls at the forefront of the national consciousness.

After World War I, Niagara Falls no longer seemed so "new" or central to American culture nationalism. The changing dynamics of America's romance for technology and a maturing of tourist culture account for the waning of the New Niagara. As historians have shown, the era of technological enthusiasm persisted until after World War II. Americans continued to lead the world in invention, system-building, and research and development. Nevertheless, engineers, scientists, and industrialists turned their attention from Niagara Falls to other manufacturing and building sites and to alternative technologies.

In part, the New Niagara was a victim of its own success. Niagara's precedent had inspired innumerable electrical projects since its initial harnessing. Once "Niagarics" turned every remote cataract into a practical servant of local or regional communities, Niagara Falls itself ceased to be the nation's primary power source. The pioneering example of Niagara's large-scale power production and alternating current distribution "became so common-place and so numerous," according to Clemons Herschel, "that many men of the present time clearly foresee the day when, scouting state lines and physical obstacles, the whole United States will be able to draw power from a national body of power-houses and power lines." Herschel's words proved prophetic as the nation electrified.[45]

Beyond the pervasiveness of "Niagarics," the very limitations on the harnessing of Niagara power clashed with twentieth-century technological expectations that defied limits. As Niagara's extraordinary power became finite and "ordinary" in the twentieth century, enormous power projects at New York City, at Chicago, at Muscle Shoals, and in California superseded Niagara Falls. These new focal points for the technological sublime combined large building sites, unprecedented capital investment, and direct government involvement; they upgraded technology and rendered the initial turn-of-the-century powerhouse operations at Niagara obsolete. In addition, advances in power production and transmission precluded the need for industrial-power users to relocate to Niagara and diminished the significance of Niagara power transmission throughout the land. As the Smithsonian Institution announced in 1925, "Niagara Falls has a very circumscribed area of use and cannot be transmitted into the middle west to compete with power generated in other plants."[46]

At Niagara itself, the anticipation of a glorious New Niagara in "Electrical America" raised promises and expectations to unrealistic levels. Indeed, the ideal of unbridled technological utopianism, so central to the New Niagara, proved impossible to sustain in the twentieth century. By World War I, hopes that nature and technology could achieve a higher synthesis proved to be naive. Faith in technology to solve society's problems seemed much less plausible after the world witnessed the deadly killing uses of technology in the war. Thanks largely to a vigilant and prolific set of scenic preservationists who defended nature at every turn, the public learned early at Niagara that every human manipulation of the environment takes a toll, often an unforeseeable toll, on the environment.

The immediate area around the Falls never became the thriving, beautiful, park-filled metropolis forecast by the technological romancers. City Beautiful images of the Pan-American Exposition's wondrous and vital "City of Living Light" faded into oblivion once massive, smoke-belching, unaesthetic, and inhuman electrochemical and electrometallurgial plants and drab working-class neighborhoods proliferated throughout the Niagara landscape. On the American side of the cataract, the confined space of the Niagara reservation remained the only breathing spot. Periodic attempts to appropriate more of the gorge-side lands for the reservation or for a national park failed. Thus, as more and more Americans returned to nature in the twentieth century, Niagara lost its associations as a natural retreat. Far from representing the landscape of wilderness restored, anticipated for miles by the roar of the cataract and the freshness of its mist-filled air and lush verdant surroundings, Niagara became a foul industrial environment in the heart of America's rust belt. For many visitors, the defining characteristic of the approach to the Falls was the foul stench emitted by the chemical plants.

The idealistic promise of the New Niagara embodied in the Natural Food Company was a casualty of Niagara's industrial reality. New firms relocated to Niagara Falls in order to maximize profits rather than to promote progressive and utopian ideals. While the Shredded Wheat plant, which was absorbed by Nabisco in 1928, continued to give tours of its facilities, the atmosphere was more quaint than utopian. Increasingly the Shredded Wheat factory became just that—a factory—rather than a "conservatory" or a "home," while the Shredded Wheat Biscuit became just another breakfast cereal, rather than "The wonder of the age." Elsewhere in the country, other industrial firms gave tours of larger and more wondrous production facilities. The social-betterment programs inaugurated by manufacturers like the Natural Food Company spread throughout industry, but the zealous vision of model factories ultimately dimmed and failed to bring industrial harmony. Perhaps it was fitting that the Natural Food Conservatory became rapidly outdated and was finally dismantled in 1952.[47]

The waning of Niagara's technological sublimity held implications for tourism at the cataract as well. By the 1920s, mass use of the automobile and the emergence of an automobile culture greatly increased the number of visitors and honeymooners at the Falls. These tourists came to Niagara Falls for thrilling sensations and a good time and treated it as a commercial commodity. Once again, however, other tourist resorts, parks, and amusements, many of which relied on fantastic technology, reduced Niagara to the commonplace. Olmsted would have been grieved to see the extent to which Niagara became a place of commonplace thrills and mindless escapism. In the twentieth century the only remaining "redeemed" nature spot at Niagara was the diminished cataract. The Niagara landscape itself seemed to lose its sense of purpose and its ability to uplift and inspire; no longer did it retain its symbolic role as an embodiment of American cultural progress.

Indicative of this change, the New York State Reservation at Niagara Falls became a maze of automobile parking lots, roads, souvenir shops, and restaurants. Until the early 1990s, there was even a commercial helicopter service on Goat Island. Ironically, in this disconnected reservation of nature, the most stately additions to Goat Island have been the original Niagara Falls Power Company powerhouse entrance arch with the seal of Frederick Macmonnies and a statue of Nicola Tesla!

This ultimate failure of Niagara Falls as a working symbol for America becomes poignant only if we keep Niagara's history in mind. During the period from 1850 to World War I, no other American landscape matched Niagara's variety of beautiful, sublime, joyous, and instructive attractions. Niagara embodied and symbolized America's cultural progress and romance of development. No other American landscape inspired more reverence, hope, and anticipation among middle-class cultural custodians, technical experts, and visionaries.

Even though the New Niagara always remained perilously close to empty promises and to a desecrated landscape, nonetheless widely disseminated images, testimony, tourist accounts, and mass entertainment stressed its benevolence and its heightened harmony with America's greatest natural spectacle. The idealism that the New Niagara perpetuated for the humane use of technology makes the real industrial, technological, and touristic development of Niagara (and of the United States) appear all the more exploitative and errant. Often the consequences turn out to be worse than anyone could have imagined, as in the Love Canal tragedy. Indeed, as we look on our wayward technologies, hokey tourist attractions, and off-putting urban-industrial landscapes today, the happy synthesis of nature and technology that the New Niagara formerly promised to the nation seems elusive indeed.

Notes

Introduction

1. Rollin Lynde Hartt, "The New Niagara: A City of the Future: 'Exhibit A' of the Pan-American Exposition," *McClure's Magazine* 17 (May 1901), 78–84.

2. Eugene R. White, "Niagarics, the New Force," *Munsey's Magazine* 29 (April 1903), 29–30.

3. Important scholarly assessments of Niagara include Elizabeth McKinsey, *Niagara Falls: Icon of the American Sublime* (Cambridge: Cambridge University Press, 1985); Jeremy Adamson and Elizabeth McKinsey, *Niagara: Two Centuries of Changing Attitudes, 1697–1901* (Washington, D.C.: Corcoran Gallery of Art, 1985); Patrick V. McGreevy, *Imagining Niagara: The Making and Meaning of Niagara Falls* (Amherst: University of Massachusetts Press, 1994); John F. Sears, *Sacred Places: American Tourist Attractions in the Nineteenth Century* (New York: Oxford University Press, 1989), 5–30, 182–89. A fine study of the relationship between culture and public policy at Niagara Falls on both the American side and the Canadian side of the cataract is Gail Edith H. Evans, "Storm over Niagara: A Study of the Interplay of Cultural Values, Resource

Politics, and Environmental Policy in an International Setting, 1670s–1950" (Ph.D. diss., University of California at Santa Barbara, 1991).

4. Before proceeding any further, let me explain that tourism and technology, as I use them, are both broad and inclusive concepts. Tourism involves the traveler's realms of leisure time, transportation, facilities, commerce, images with meaningful associations, entertainment, and education. In nineteenth-century America, tourism revealed cultural values and helped establish an American cultural identity. By *technology* I mean not only machines, structures, and other human constructions, but also the plans, operations, and organization that accompany those constructions and help bring control over the environment. See Sears, *Sacred Places*, 3–4. On the definition of technology, see David P. Billington, *The Tower and the Bridge: The New Art of Structural Engineering* (Princeton: Princeton University Press, 1983), 3–15.

5. See Charles Mason Dow, *Anthology and Bibliography of Niagara Falls* (Albany: State of New York, 1921), vols. 1 and 2, and Adamson and McKinsey, *Niagara: Two Centuries*. Dow's *Anthology* is an invaluable compilation of Niagara source material.

6. McKinsey, *Niagara Falls: Icon*; Sears, *Sacred Places*, 5–30, 182–89.

7. Perry Miller, *The Life of the Mind in America from the Revolution to the Civil War* (New York: Harcourt, Brace & World, 1965), 295–306; Leo Marx, *The Machine in the Garden: Technology and the Pastoral Ideal in America* (New York: Oxford University Press, 1964), 195–207, 230–31; David E. Nye, *American Technological Sublime* (Cambridge: M.I.T. Press, 1994).

8. See Barbara Novak, *Nature and Culture: American Landscape and Painting, 1825–1875* (New York: Oxford University Press, 1980), and Henry Nash Smith, *Virgin Land: The American West as Symbol and Myth* (Cambridge: Harvard University Press, 1950).

9. Novak, *Nature and Culture*; Roderick Nash, *Wilderness and the American Mind* (New Haven: Yale University Press, 1982); Marx, *Machine in the Garden*.

10. John Quincy Adams, "Speech on Niagara Falls," in Dow, *Anthology*, 1:233; Gilbert Haven and Thomas Russell, *Incidents and Anecdotes of the Rev. Edward T. Taylor, for over Forty Years Pastor of the Seamen's Bethel, Boston* (Boston, 1872), 214; George William Curtis, *Lotus-Eating: A Summer Book* (New York, 1852), 137–38.

11. Tench Coxe, quoted in Novak, *Nature and Culture*, 167–68.

12. See Marx, *Machine in the Garden*, 97–144, and John F. Kasson, *Civilizing the Machine: Technology and Republican Values in America, 1776–1900* (New York: Penguin Books, 1976), 3–21.

13. See McKinsey, *Niagara Falls: Icon*.

14. For a discussion of these and other Niagara prints as they relate to the American sublime, see ibid., 98–105. Cole's rendering of Niagara appears in John Howard Hinton, *The History and Topography of the United States of North America, Illustrated with a Series of Views, Drawn on the Spot, and Engraved on Steel, Expressly for This Work*, vol. 2 (Philadelphia, 1832), frontispiece. On p. 484 Hinton wrote a revealing footnote to his treatment of Niagara Falls: "It was our intention to have given a lengthened description of this grand and magnificent scene from a manuscript which we have been presented by a recent traveller, but other matter of a more important though not more interesting character, has left so little room within the limits of our own work, that the description of the beautiful scenery of the lakes, the Hudson, &c. which would require a volume to do it justice must be omitted."

15. Nathaniel Parker Willis, *American Scenery* (Barre, Mass.: Imprint Society, 1971), v, 4. See Novak, *Nature and Culture*.

16. McKinsey, *Niagara Falls: Icon,* 65–85; Virginia Vidler, *Niagara Souvenirs: 100 Years of Souvenirs* (Utica, N.Y.: North Country Books, 1985). Among the more widely circulated prints were the "Hennepin" scene of 1697, drawn after Father Louis Hennepin's first published description of Niagara, and other renderings by Thomas Cole, William H. Bartlett, William J. Bennett, and Jacques Milbert. For the role of Niagara Falls in art, see Adamson and McKinsey, *Niagara.*

17. See, for example, F. W. P. Greenwood, "Falls of the Niagara," in *The Token an Atlantic Souvenir* (Boston, 1832), 317–31; Nicholas A. Woods, *The Prince of Wales in Canada and the United States* (1859; London, 1861) quoted in Dow, *Anthology,* 1:273; Edward Thomas Coke, *A Subaltern's Furlough: Descriptive of Scenes in various parts of the United States, Upper and Lower Canada, New Brunswick, and Nova Scotia, during the summer and autumn of 1832* (New York, 1833), 2:41. Secondary sources on early tourism to Niagara Falls include Darrell A. Norris, "Reaching the Sublime: Niagara Falls Visitor Origins, 1831–1854," *Journal of American Culture* 9 (Spring 1986), 53–59, and Patrick McGreevy, "Niagara as Jerusalem," *Landscape* 28 (1985), 26–32.

18. Frances Milton Trollope, *Domestic Manners of the Americans,* ed. Donald Smalley (New York: Alfred A. Knopf, 1949), 381; Thomas Cole, "Essay on American Scenery, 1835," in John W. McCoubrey, *American Art 1760–1960: Sources and Documents* (Englewood Cliffs, N.J.: Prentice-Hall, 1965), 105; James Faxon, *Niagara Falls Guide, with full Instructions to Direct the Traveler, to All the Points of Interest at the Falls and Vicinity* (Buffalo, 1850), 16.

19. Coke, *Subaltern's Furlough,* 1:37; Andrew Reed and James Matheson, *A Narrative of the Visit to the American Churches by the Deputation from the Congregational Union of England and Wales* (New York, 1835), 1:93.

20. See McKinsey, *Niagara Falls: Icon,* 173–74.

1. *Awakening to Niagara*

1. William Dunlap, *A Trip to Niagara; or, Travellers in America* (New York, 1830), 39 and passim.

2. For American attitudes toward nature, see Hans Huth, *Nature and the Americans: Three Centuries of Changing Attitudes* (Berkeley and Los Angeles: University of California Press, 1957); Perry Miller, *Errand into the Wilderness* (New York: Harper & Row, 1964); Roderick Nash, *Wilderness and the American Mind,* 3d ed. (New Haven: Yale University Press, 1982); Leo Marx, *The Machine in the Garden: Technology and the Pastoral Ideal* (New York: Oxford University Press, 1964). See also Peter Schmitt, *Back to Nature: The Arcadian Myth in Urban America* (New York: Oxford University Press, 1969).

3. Alexander Wilson, *The Foresters; a Poem, Descriptive of a Pedestrian Journey to the Falls of Niagara, in the autumn of 1804* (Newtown, Pa., 1818), 8, 41, 73; Duncan Ingraham, "Description of the Country Between Albany and Niagara in 1792," in E. B. O'Calloghan, *Documentary History of the State of New York* (Albany, N.Y., 1849), 2:1108–10. Spafford's *Gazetteer of the State of New York* reported that exclusive of Forts Niagara and Slosser, only one white family lived in the Niagara region in 1796. Horatio Spafford, *Gazetteer of the State of New York* (Albany, N.Y., 1824), 356.

4. François René de Chateaubriand, *Travels in America*, trans. Richard Switzer (Lexington: University of Kentucky Press, 1969), 35–36; "Sketches of Scenery on Niagara River," *North American Review* 2 (March 1816), 324; Timothy Bigelow, *Journal of a Tour to Niagara Falls in the Year 1805* (Boston, 1876), 60–61.

5. Hector St. John de Crèvecoeur, "Description of Niagara Falls in a Letter to his son under the date of July, 1785," *Magazine of American History* 2, pt. 2 (October 1878): 607, 612; Chateaubriand, *Travels in America*, 35–36.

6. Crèvecoeur, "Description," 607; "The Wonders of Canada: A Letter from a Gentleman to the Antigua Gazette, August 21, 1768," in *Magazine of American History* 1, pt. 1 (1877), 244; Pierre François Xavier de Charlevoix, *Journal of a Voyage to North America, Containing the Geographical Description and Natural History of that Country, particularly Canada* (1744), in Charles Mason Dow, *Anthology and Bibliography of Niagara Falls* (Albany: State of New York, 1921), 1:32.

7. Isaac Weld, *Travels Through the States of North America, and the Provinces of Upper and Lower Canada, during the Years 1795, 1796, and 1797* (London, 1799), 315.

8. Duke de la Rochefoucauld Liancourt, *Travels Through the United States of North America, . . . in the Years 1795, 1796, and 1797* (London, 1799), 397. For a discussion of European picturesque tourism, see John F. Sears, *Sacred Places: American Tourist Attractions in the Nineteenth Century* (New York: Oxford University Press, 1989), 3, and Malcolm Andrews, *The Search for the Picturesque: Landscape, Aesthetics, and Tourism in Britain, 1760–1780* (Aldershot: Scolar, 1989).

9. Jacques Milbert, *Picturesque Itinerary of the Hudson River and the Peripheral Parts of North America*, trans. Constance D. Sherman (Ridgeway, N.J.: Gregg Press, 1968), xxii; Thomas Hamilton, *Men and Manners in America* (1843; reprint ed., New York: Johnson Reprint Corp., 1968), 174. See Marvin Fisher, *Workshops in the Wilderness: The European Response to American Industrialization, 1830–1860* (New York: Oxford University Press, 1967), 61–64.

10. Thomas Cole, "Essay on American Scenery, 1835," in James McCoubrey, *American Art 1760–1960: Sources and Documents* (Englewood Cliffs, N.J.: Prentice-Hall, 1965), 108–9; Frederick Marryat, *Diary in America*, ed. Julius Zanger (Bloomington: Indiana University Press, 1960), 42.

11. On the relationship between the landscape and economic development, see Louis C. Hunter, *Water Power in the Century of the Steam Engine*, vol. 1 of *A History of Industrial Power in the United States, 1780–1930* (Charlottesville: University Press of Virginia, 1979), and Theodore Steinberg, *Nature Incorporated: Industrialization and the Waters of New England* (New York: Cambridge University Press, 1991).

12. Francis Grund, *The Americans in Their Moral, Social, and Political Relations* (Boston, 1837), 150; Frederika Bremer, *The Homes of the New World: Impressions of America*, trans. Mary Howitt, 2 vols. (New York, 1854), 1:48.

13. Hunter, *Water Power*, 114–81.

14. Harriet Martineau, *Retrospect of Western Travel* (New York, 1838), 2:223; Thomas Low Nichols, *Forty Years of American Life, 1821–1861* (1864; reprint, New York: Stackpole Sons, 1937), 61.

15. Frances Trollope, *Domestic Manners of the Americans* (New York: Alfred A. Knopf, 1949), 372–73.

16. Philip Freneau and Hugh Henry Brackenridge, "The Rising Glory of America" (1771), quoted in Henry Nash Smith, *Virgin Land: The American West as Symbol and Myth* (Cambridge: Harvard University Press, 1950), 125.

17. Wilson, *The Foresters*, 74; William W. Campbell, ed., *The Life and Writings of DeWitt Clinton* (New York, 1849), 128; Christian Schultz, *Travels on an Inland Voyage through the States of New York, Pennsylvania, Virginia, Ohio, Kentucky & Tennessee . . . performed in the year 1807–1808* (New York, 1810), 1:143; Michael Aaron Rockland, trans., *Sarmiento's Travels in the United States in 1847* (Princeton: Princeton University Press, 1984), 230. *The Album of the Table Rock*, compiled from the logbook entries of ordinary visitors at the Falls, indicates the pervasiveness of this tendency to interrupt resonant calls of nature with ironic and irreverent calls for utility. Interspersed among odes to Niagara's sublimity and beauty are entries like that of "Jonas": "[Niagara Falls] reminds me of my daddy's *mill pond*, when the gates are hoisted." See *Album of the Table Rock, Niagara Falls, and Sketches of the Falls and Scenery and Adjacent* (Buffalo, N.Y., 1848), 55.

18. William Tatham, *The Political Economy of Inland Navigation, Irrigation, and Drainage, with Thoughts on the Multiplication of Commercial Resources and on Means of Bettering the Condition of Mankind, by the Construction of Canals* (London, 1799), 101–11.

19. Ibid., 102.

20. William Wyckoff, *The Developer's Frontier: The Making of the Western New York Landscape* (New Haven: Yale University Press, 1988).

21. Edward Dean Adams, *Niagara Power: History of the Niagara Falls Power Company, 1886–1918*, 2 vols. (Niagara Falls, N.Y., 1927), 1:58, 63–64.

22. Schultz, *Travels*, 1:79.

23. William Leete Stone, in Dow, *Anthology*, 1:177; broadside, Augustus and Peter B. Porter, "Invitation to Eastern Capitalists and Manufacturers," in Adams, *Niagara Power*, 1:375–76.

24. Ralph Greenhill, *Spanning Niagara: The International Bridges* (Niagara Falls, N.Y.: Niagara University, 1984), 7.

25. John Melish, *Travels in the United States of America, in the Years 1806 & 1807, and 1809, 1810, 1811* (Philadelphia, 1812), 2:347–49; House Committee on Roads and Canals, *Ship Canal Around the Falls of Niagara: Report to Accompany H.R. No. 466*, 25th Cong., 2d sess., January 25, 1838, H. Rept. 463, 1, 2.

26. For general works on the Erie Canal, see Ronald E. Shaw, *Erie Waters West: A History of the Erie Canal, 1792–1854* (Lexington: University of Kentucky Press, 1966), and Patricia A. Anderson, *The Course of Empire: The Erie Canal and the New York Landscape, 1825–1875: July 16–August 12, 1984, The University of Rochester Memorial Art Gallery, Exhibition and Catalogue* (Rochester, N.Y.: The Gallery, 1984).

27. Theodore Dwight, *The Northern Traveller; Containing the Routes to the Springs, Niagara, Quebec, and the Coal Mines . . .* (New York, 1826), 50–90; Lydia Sigourney, *Scenes in My Native Land* (Boston, 1845), 19–20; George William Curtis, *Lotus-Eating: A Summer Book* (New York, 1852), 79. Erie Canal packet boats were typically 60–70 feet long and were the equivalent of a cruise ship to the early-nineteenth-century canal-traveler. They featured sitting rooms, dining rooms, and sleeping compartments. See Dwight, *Northern Traveller*, 50.

28. Theodore Dwight, *Things as They Are; or, Notes of a traveller through some of the middle and northern states* (New York, 1834), 192.

29. Cadwallader D. Colden, *Memoir Prepared at the Request of a Committee of the Common Council of the City of New York, and Presented to the Mayor of the City, at the Celebration of the Completion of the New York Canals* (New York, 1825), 4. The

Reverend Frederick A. Farley called the Erie Canal route "one of the most delightful journeys which our country offers." See Farley, "A Visit to Niagara," *The Rhode Island Book: Selections in Prose and Verse, from the Writings of Rhode-Island Citizens*, ed. Anne C. Lynch (Providence, R.I., 1841), 69–70.

30. Nathaniel Hawthorne, "My Visit to Niagara," *New-England Magazine* 8 (February 1835), 96.

31. Theodore Dwight, *Northern Traveller and Northern Tour with the Routes to Niagara, Quebec, and the Springs . . .* (New York, 1831), 93.

32. House Committee on Roads and Canals, *Ship Canal Around the Falls of Niagara*, 1 and passim; House Committee on Roads and Canals, *Niagara Ship Canal*, 24th Cong., 2d sess., February 14, 1837, H.R. 921.

33. House Committee on Roads and Canals, *Ship Canal*, 16, 18, 21–22.

34. "Proposed Ship Canal Around the Falls of Niagara," hand-colored engraving, Smithsonian Institution, Washington, D.C.

35. Sir Charles Lyell, *Travels in North America, in the years 1841–2; with Geological Observations on the United States, Canada, and Nova Scotia* (New York, 1845), 1:16; Joseph Sturge, *A Visit to the United States in 1841* (New York: Augus M. Killey, 1969), 111.

36. Darrell A. Norris, "Reaching the Sublime: Niagara Visitor Origins, 1831–1854," *Journal of American Culture* 9 (Spring 1986), 53–59; "American Country Life," *The Crayon* 5 (October 1858), 280. According to Grund, "the rates of fares and passages are so low, and so well adapted to the means of the great bulk of the population, that there is scarcely an individual so reduced in circumstances as to be unable to afford his 'dollar or so,' to travel a couple of hundred miles from home 'in order to see the country and the improvements which are going on.'" Grund, *The Americans in Their Morals*, 323.

37. Edward Thomas Coke, *A Subaltern's Furlough: Descriptive of Scenes in various parts of the United States, Upper and Lower Canada, New Brunswick, and Nova Scotia, during the summer and autumn of 1832* (New York, 1833), 2:43; James Faxon, *The Niagara Falls Guide, 1850, with Full Instructions to Direct the Traveler to all the Points of Interest at the Falls and Vicinity* (Buffalo, N.Y., 1850), 7; Horatio Parsons, *A Guide to Travelers Visiting the Falls of Niagara, containing much Interesting and Important Information Respecting the Falls and Vicinity*, 2d ed., greatly enlarged (Buffalo, N.Y., 1835), 82.

38. Faxon, *Niagara Falls Guide*, 24; Harriet Martineau, *Society in America* (New York, 1837), 1:179.

39. Isabella Lucy Bird, *The Englishwoman in America* (1856; reprint, Madison: University of Wisconsin Press, 1966), 229; Sir Richard Henry Bonnycastle, "Canada and the Canadians" (1849), in Dow, *Anthology*, 2:1075.

40. Hawthorne, "My Visit to Niagara," 93.

41. Quoted in Kenneth M. Maddox, *In Search of the Picturesque: Nineteenth-Century Images of Industry Along the Hudson River Valley* (Annandale-on-Hudson, N.Y.: Bard College, 1983), 41.

42. Cole, "Essay on American Scenery," 109; Tocqueville, quoted in George Pierson, *Tocqueville and Beaumont in America* (New York: Oxford University Press, 1938), 310.

43. Curtis, *Lotus-Eating*, 81, 12; Caroline Gilman, *The Poetry of Travelling in the United States* (New York, 1838), 112, 113, 114.

44. Faxon, *Niagara Falls Guide*, 69; Margaret Fuller, *Summer on the Lakes*, ed. Arthur B. Fuller (1844; reprint, New York: Haskell House, 1970), 6. These improvements gave women access to the most favored and sublime vantage points.

45. Captain Basil Hall, *Travels in North America in the Years 1827 and 1828* (Edinburgh, 1829), 1:190–91; Faxon, *Niagara Falls Guide*, 40–41.

46. Caroline Spencer, "Journal: A Trip to New York in 1835," *Magazine of American History* 22 (October 1889), 339; Howells described his first visit during the summer of 1860 in a series of articles for a Cincinnati newspaper. He recalled these initial impressions in "Niagara, First and Last," in *The Niagara Book, A Complete Souvenir of Niagara Falls*, ed. William Dean Howells and Mark Twain (New York, 1901), 265–66; Anthony Trollope, *North America*, ed. Donald Smalley and Bradford Allen Booth (New York: Alfred A. Knopf, 1951), 100. Trollope's book was first published in 1862.

47. Hall, *Travels*, 1:205–7.

48. William Chambers, *Things as They Are in America* (Philadelphia, 1854), 107.

49. Nathaniel P. Willis, *Inklings of Adventure* (New York, 1836), 1:26; Thomas Fowler, *Journal of a Tour Through British America to the Falls of Niagara; written during the summer of 1831* (Aberden, 1832), 214; William Dean Howells, "Niagara Revisited, Twelve Years after Their Wedding Journey," *Atlantic Monthly* 51 (May 1883), 606.

50. Henry Cooke's experience was typical of genteel tourism at Niagara. His hotel bedroom window faced the American Falls, and his favorite way to view the Falls was lying on his bed. "Many an hour have I thus passed gazing there with ceaseless admiration, until sleep has gradually overpowered me." Henry Cooke, "An Excursion to Niagara and Canada in 1849," *Colburn's New Monthly Magazine* (London) 87 (1849), 358. See "Cataract House" (pamphlet), no date, Niagara Falls vertical file, Buffalo and Erie County Historical Society; Norris, "Reaching the Sublime," 53; *Niagara Falls Gazette*, March 10, 1884, and July 21, 1886.

51. Parsons, *Guide to Travelers*, 82.

52. Dwight, *Northern Traveller* (1831), 32. Joseph Gurney averred: "Goat island is no longer the wild resort of adventurous lovers of scenery, but a popular promenade for the gentility of Boston, New York, and Philadelphia." Joseph John Gurney, *A Journey in North American, described in familiar letters to Amelia Opie* (Norwich, 1841), 322. For a discussion of the American Grand Tour, see Sears, *Sacred Places*, 4, 12.

53. Bird, *Englishwoman in America*, 219; Willis, *Inklings of Adventure*, 1:27–36. "Niagara Falls," song lyrics in Elizabeth McKinsey, *Niagara Falls: Icon of the American Sublime* (New York: Cambridge University Press, 1985), 180.

54. Barnett's Museum on the Canadian side was one of the most notable early North American museums. It featured hundreds of specimens of stuffed animals indigenous to the Niagara region, including several eagles. See Parsons, *Guide to Travelers*, 46; "Barnett's Museum" (advertisement), Niagara Falls vertical file, Buffalo and Erie County Historical Society.

55. Dwight, *Northern Traveller* (1831), 88; Parsons, *Guide to Travelers*, 71–72; "Michigan Steamer" broadside, Niagara Falls vertical file, Buffalo and Erie County Historical Society. Dwight reported that only a cat and a goose survived the wreck. Parsons claimed that a crowd of 30,000 saw *The Michigan* in 1827, and 15,000 witnessed a similar spectacle in 1829.

56. William Leete Stone, "From New York to Niagara: Journal of a Tour, in part by the Erie Canal, in the year 1829," in Dow, *Anthology*, 1:176–77; "Notes on America: Niagara Falls," *The Crayon* 6 (August 1859), 245.

57. William Dean Howells, "Niagara, First and Last," William Dean Howells, Mark Twain et al., *The Niagara Book: A Complete Souvenir of Niagara Falls* (Buffalo, N.Y., 1893), 9.

58. Amelia M. Murray, *Letters from the United States, Cuba, and Canada* (New York, 1856), 99; Captain J. W. Oldmixon, *Transatlantic Wanderings; or, A First Look at the United States* (London, 1855), 86–93.

59. Silliman is quoted in John F. Kasson, *Civilizing the Machine: Technology and Republican Values in America, 1776–1900* (New York: Penguin Books, 1976), 58. On pp. 55–58, Kasson gives a fuller discussion of the American reaction to Manchester. See also Robert Fishman, *Bourgeois Utopias: The Rise and Fall of Suburbia* (New York: Basic Books, 1987), 73–102.

60. James Silk Buckingham, *America: Historical, Statistic, and Descriptive* (London, 1841), 2:512; John M. Duncan, *Travels Through Part of the United States and Canada in 1818 and 1819* (Glasgow, 1823), 1:33–34; Parsons, *Guide to Travelers* (1834), 9, quoted in McKinsey, *Niagara Falls: Icon*, 134. Although travelers continued to refer to the village at Niagara Falls as Manchester, town fathers forsook the name when it created confusion with New York State's other Manchesters.

61. Coke, *Subaltern's Furlough*, 2:36–37; Anna Jameson, *Winter Studies and Summer Rambles in Canada* (New York, 1839), 1:269–70.

62. William Chambers reported: "There is a proposition before the world to turn the whole force of the river to profitable account in some kind of mechanical processes." Chambers, *Things as They Are*, 111. The power estimate from *Silliman's Journal* was cited in Faxon, *Niagara Falls Guide*, 33.

63. *Sarmiento's Travels*, 229.

64. Nichols, *Forty Years of American Life*, 104.

65. J. W. Orr, *Pictorial Guide to the Falls of Niagara; A Manual for Visiters Giving an Account of this Stupendous Natural Wonder and All the Objects of Curiosity in its Vicinity...* (Buffalo, N.Y., 1842), 57, 57–58.

66. Ibid., 59.

67. Jameson, *Winter Studies*, 1:269.

68. Faxon, *Niagara Falls Guide*, 33; Buckingham, *America*, 2:512, 511; Curtis, *Lotus-Eating*, 93.

69. Fuller, *Summer on the Lakes*, 6; Charles Mackay, *Life and Liberty in America; or, Sketches of a Tour in the United States and Canada in 1857–1858* (New York, 1859), 58–59.

2. Bridge to a New Niagara

1. The seven bridges included Charles Ellet's Niagara Suspension Bridge (1848), Roebling's Niagara Railway Suspension Bridge, Samuel Keefer's Clifton Suspension Bridge (1868–1869), the Niagara Cantilever Bridge (1883), a rebuilt suspension bridge on the site of Keefer's bridge (1889), and the Lower and Upper Steel Arch Bridges (1897), which replaced the suspension bridges. The succession of bridges at Niagara rendered the site "an epitome of American bridge building." See Frank W. Skinner, "Great Achievements in Modern Bridge Building," *McClure's Magazine* 16 (January

1901), 256; and Gebhard Napier, "Bridges and Bridge Building," *Munsey's Magazine* 25 (June 1901), 352. The Falls continued as a significant bridge center into the twentieth century. See Ralph Greenhill, *Spanning Niagara: The International Bridges, 1848–1962* (Niagara Falls, N.Y.: Niagara University, 1984).

2. Thomas Pope, *A Treatise on Bridge Architecture, in Which the Superior Advantages of the Flying Pendant Lever Bridge Are Fully Proved* (New York, 1811). For a history of bridge-building and of bridge-builders, see David Plowden, *Bridges: The Spans of North America* (New York: Viking Press, 1974); Joseph Gies, *Bridges and Men* (New York: Doubleday, 1963); David McCullough, *The Great Bridge* (New York, 1972); David B. Steinman and Sara Ruth Watson, *Bridges and Their Builders*, 2d rev. ed. (New York: Dover Publications, 1957); David P. Billington, *The Tower and the Bridge: The New Art of Structural Engineering* (Princeton: Princeton University Press, 1983).

3. Greenhill, *Spanning Niagara*, 7–8; Charles Ellet Jr. to Charles B. Stuart, October 12, 1845, in Charles B. Stuart, *Lives and Works of Civil and Military Engineering in America* (New York, 1871), 270–71; Charles Ellet, *A Popular Notice of Suspension Bridges with a Brief Description of the Wire Bridge Across the Schuylkill, at Fairmount* (Philadelphia, 1843), 8.

4. *Appendix to the Journal of the House of Assembly of Upper Canada . . .* , Session 1836, III, no. 135, 7, quoted in Greenhill, *Spanning Niagara*, 7.

5. W. Hamilton Merritt, "Niagara and Detroit Railroad: Prospectus," in *American Railroad Journal* 18 (September 4, 1845), 571. Charles Ellet Jr. to George S. Tiffany, Esq., Chairman of the Great Western Railroad Company, and Washington Hunt, Esq., President of the Niagara Falls & Lockport Railroad Company, November 27, 1845, in *American Railroad Journal* 19 (January 17, 1846), 36.

6. Stuart, *Lives and Works,* 270. Each of these engineers eventually erected a suspension bridge across the Niagara gorge. Serrell built the first permanent bridge in the gorge at Lewiston in 1850–51. The Lewiston Suspension Bridge (1850) was six miles from the Falls. Keefer built the Clifton Suspension Bridge in front of the cataract in 1868–69.

7. Billington, *The Tower and the Bridge*, 35–37; David E. Nye, *American Technological Sublime* (Cambridge: M.I.T. Press, 1994), 78–79.

8. Stuart, *Lives and Works,* 270; Ellet to Tiffany, November 27, 1845; Ellet attached an angry postscript to his 1848 proposal for a railroad suspension bridge at Middletown, Connecticut, to dispute the accusations that his plans to include railroad traffic on his Niagara bridge then under construction were "chimerical." See Charles Ellet, *Report on a Suspension Bridge Across the Connecticut at Middletown . . . with a Proposal for its Construction* (Philadelphia, 1848), 58. Roebling lamented: "Suspension bridges have generally been looked upon as loose fabric hanging up in the air, as if for the very purpose of swinging. Repeated failures of such works have strengthened this belief." John A. Roebling, "Memoir of the Niagara Falls Suspension and Niagara Falls International Bridge Companies," in *Papers and Practical Illustrations of Public Works of Recent Construction Both British and American* (London, 1856), 3–4.

9. Billington, *The Tower and the Bridge,* 47–49; Roebling sent a letter to Charles Stuart dated January 7, 1847, in which he rebutted Stephenson's assertion that railway suspension bridges were impractical. See Stuart, *Lives and Works,* 306–9.

10. "Suspension Bridge over the Niagara River," *American Railroad Journal* 19 (January 17, 1846), 41.

11. Stuart, *Lives and Works,* 272; Charles Ellet to Charles B. Stuart, February 13, 1847, in ibid., 271–72.

12. Stuart, *Lives and Works*, 273; James Faxon, *Niagara Falls Guide, With Full Instructions to Direct the Traveler, to All the Points of Interest at the Falls and Vicinity* (Buffalo, N.Y., 1850), 86–90.

13. *Burke's Descriptive Guide; or, The Visitors' Companion to Niagara Falls, its Strange and Wonderful Localities* (Buffalo, N.Y., 1853), 85–86; Faxon, *Niagara Falls Guide*, 89–90.

14. Some travelers, like Nathaniel Hawthorne, lamented that transportation improvements and the rise of tourism diminished the sublimity of the Falls. See Nathaniel Hawthorne, "My Visit to Niagara," *New-England Magazine* 8 (February 1835), 93. Similarly, in an 1830 play by William Dunlap, the rough-hewn American character Leatherstocking decried the tourist improvements at Niagara Falls: "What has houses and bridges to do among the wonders of heaven? They spoil all. They spoil all." See William Dunlap, *A Trip to Niagara; or, Travellers in America* (New York, 1830), 39.

15. *Burke's Descriptive Guide*, 83, 83–85; Susanna Moodie, *Life in the Clearings* (Toronto: Macmillan, 1959), 256; Alexander Marjoribanks, *Travels in South and North America* (London, 1853), 273.

16. Marjoribanks, *Travels*, 273–74. Marjoribanks admitted that when he started walking across the bridge his courage gave out and he had to turn back. For a thorough account of the sentimentalization of Niagara and the waning natural sublimity of Niagara Falls, see Elizabeth McKinsey, *Niagara Falls: Icon of the American Sublime* (New York: Cambridge University Press, 1985).

17. *The Journal of Prince Alexander Liholiho: The Voyages Made to the United States, England, and France in 1849–1850*, ed. Jacob Adler (Hawaii: University of Hawaii Press, 1967), 114.

18. Plowden, *Bridges: The Spans of North America*, 79.

19. John A. Roebling, *Report . . . to the Presidents and Directors of the Niagara Falls International and Suspension Bridge Companies* (Buffalo, N.Y., 1852), 12.

20. See Richard G. Carrott, *The Egyptian Revival: Its Sources, Monuments, and Meaning, 1808–1858* (Berkeley and Los Angeles: University of California Press, 1978), 47–105. Ellet's plans also had called for Egyptian towers and Edward W. Serrell's Lewiston Suspension Bridge (1850–51) established the Egyptian style across the Niagara gorge.

21. Roebling, *Report*, 12.

22. The correspondent assumed that rail tracks on the bridge would allow horse-pulled passenger and freight cars to pass, but not locomotives. "A Convention of Railroad Directors," *Scientific American* 7 (June 5, 1852), 297.

23. Roebling, *Memoir of the Niagara Falls Suspension Bridge*, 26.

24. *Niagara Falls Gazette*, June 14 and 21, 1854; "Railway-Engineering in the United States," *Atlantic Monthly* 2 (November 1858), 655. On the engineering profession in the nineteenth century, see Raymond A. Merritt, *Engineering in American Society, 1850–1875* (Lexington: University Press of Kentucky, 1969), 1–26.

25. *Niagara Falls Gazette*, June 14, 1854; Billington, *The Tower and the Bridge*, 77–78; Peter W. Barlow, "Observations on the Niagara Railway Suspension Bridge," *Journal of the Franklin Institute* 71 (January 1861), 16–22.

26. Roebling, "Memoir of the Niagara Falls Suspension Bridge," 3–6. The corrosive properties of iron left its longevity in the Niagara climate open to debate.

27. Barlow, "Observations," 16–22, 160–65; Stephenson, quoted in John Bogart, "Feats of Railway Engineering," *Scribner's* 4 (July 1888), 29. Barlow noted that skepti-

cism over the Niagara bridge mounted because trains crossed it at a walker's pace of four or five miles an hour. He pointed out that although Roebling set the speed limit, five miles an hour was the standard speed limit on all types of bridges throughout America. Barlow, "Observations," 17–18.

28. Barlow found that the primary danger of trains leaving the track at high speeds was not from vibration and deflection caused by the train but from imperfections in the track. Because no bridge would have been safe if a train left the track traveling at fifty miles an hour, prudence dictated that, when faced with the prospect of a 240-foot descent into the gorge, it was wise for trains to go slowly. Moreover, nothing was gained by traveling at high speeds, since there were train stations at each end of the bridge. See Barlow, "Observations," 18, 22, 89–92, 160–163.

29. Roebling, *Report of John A. Roebling, Civil Engineer, to President and Board of Directors of the Covington and Cincinnati Bridge Company*, April 1, 1867, 77; Roebling, "Memoir of the Niagara Falls Suspension Bridge," 1, 2.

30. Roebling, "Long and Short Span Railway Bridges," *Van Nostrand's Eclectic Engineering Magazine* 2 (September 1, 1868), 78–80.

31. William Chambers, *Things as They Are in America* (London, 1854), 110; Walt Whitman, "Seeing Niagara to Advantage," in Charles Mason Dow, *Anthology and Bibliography of Niagara Falls* (Albany: State of New York, 1921), 1:341.

32. William Howard Russell, *Canada: Its Defences, Condition, and Resources* (London, 1865), 32; Mark Twain, *Mark Twain's Sketches, New and Old* (Hartford, Conn., 1875), 64.

33. Russell, *Canada*, 35; Charles Mackay, *Life and Liberty in America; or, Sketches of a Tour in the United States and Canada in 1857–1858* (New York: Johnson Reprint Corp., 1971), 87.

34. George W. Holley, *Niagara: Its History, Geology, Incidents, and Poetry* (New York, 1872), 138; Amelia M. Murray, *Letters from the United States, Cuba, and Canada* (New York, 1856), 109.

35. Roebling, "Long and Short Span Railway Bridges," 79; Merritt, *Engineering in American Society*, 145–46; David P. Billington, *The Tower and the Bridge*, 74–77.

36. For the story of the kite and the genesis of the bridge, see Orrin Dunlap, "Romance of Niagara's Bridges," *Strand Magazine* 18 (November 1899), 425–26; *Burke's Descriptive Guide*, 83–84; Holley, *Niagara*, 137.

37. See McKinsey, *Niagara Falls: Icon*, 253–56.

38. John A. Roebling, "Passage of the First Locomotive over the Suspension Bridge over the Falls of Niagara," *Journal of the Franklin Institute* 59 (April 1855), 233.

39. Dow reprinted several reviews of Church's masterpiece in his *Anthology*. The *New York Daily News* insisted: "It is the great painting of the grandest subject of nature! It is the chef d'oeuvre of Niagaras upon any canvas and must give to its painter a fame as imperishable as his subject." The *Boston Weekly Traveller* reported: "When you see this, you feel at once, this is Niagara." See Dow, *Anthology*, 2:909, 910.

40. Church further intensified this effect by cutting off the left edge of the cataract and shrouding the extent of the drop in his rendering of the water and the rising cloud of mist.

41. "Niagara and Its Wonders: Niagara Suspension Bridge" (1856), lithograph with hand-coloring, is part of the Buffalo Bookstore Collection, Buffalo, New York. Another version of the print is in the Rare Book Room, Buffalo and Erie County Public Library, Buffalo, New York.

42. Merritt, *Engineering in American Society*, 2–4; "Railway Engineering in the United States," 641.

43. "Railway Engineering in the United States," 641, 648.

44. American Society of Civil Engineers (ASCE) President Ashbel Welch is quoted in John Bogart, "Feats of Railway Engineering," *Scribner's* 4 (July 1888), 13. See also Roebling, "Memoir of the Niagara Falls Suspension Bridge," 2; and Billington, *The Tower and the Bridge*, 17.

45. Based on his observations of Roebling's bridge, Peter Barlow hoped the example of the Niagara bridge could solve London's traffic congestion. Barlow, "Observations," 164–65.

46. For more on Roebling's career and the cultural history of the Brooklyn Bridge, see Alan Trachtenberg, *The Brooklyn Bridge: Fact and Symbol* (Chicago: University of Chicago Press, 1979). See also McCullough, *The Great Bridge*, and Billington, *The Tower and the Bridge*, 72–82.

47. Bogart, "Feats of Railroad Engineering," 3–34; Montgomery Schuyler, "The Bridge as Monument," *Harper's Weekly* 27, pt. 1 (May 26, 1883), 326.

48. Charles C. Woodman, *Argument in Favor of a Marine Railway around the Falls of Niagara. Addressed to the Committee on Military Affairs of the Senate of the United States* (Washington, D.C., 1865), 1.

49. Bogart, "Feats of Railway Engineering," 3.

50. Thomas Parke Hughes uses this term to describe the prevailing American cultural climate of the late nineteenth century and twentieth century. See Thomas Parke Hughes, *American Genesis: A Century of Invention and Technological Enthusiasm, 1870–1970* (New York: Viking Press, 1989).

51. Bogart, "Feats of Railway Engineering," 3–34; Montgomery Schuyler, "The Bridge as Monument," 326. David E. Nye argues that the public embraced bridges as the foremost object of the technological sublime when the novelty of the railroad wore off after the Civil War. See Nye, *American Technological Sublime*, 78.

52. *Niagara Falls Gazette*, May 14, May 17, and June 21, 1854.

53. J. Disturnell, *A Trip Through the Lakes of North America* (New York, 1857), 215–16.

54. Theodore D. Judah's "Engineering" broadside is located in the Rare Book Room of the Buffalo and Erie County Public Library. The "Proposed Tubular Bridge for Crossing the Niagara Gorge" (1860), chromolithograph, is located in the Local History Department, Niagara Falls Public Library, Niagara Falls, New York.

55. Anthony Trollope, *North America,* ed. Donald Smalley and Bradford Allen Booth (New York: Alfred A. Knopf, 1951), 97.

56. Keefer's romance with Niagara extended back to his failed entry in the competition to build the railway suspension bridge. In the intervening years, he earned his engineering reputation as the designer of Canada's first great suspension span at Chaudière Falls in Quebec.

57. William Dean Howells, *Their Wedding Journey* (Boston, 1872), 127.

58. "The Bridges of Niagara Gorge," *Scientific American* 80 (June 17, 1899), 396.

59. Charles Davis Jameson, "The Evolution of the Modern Railway Bridge," *Popular Science Monthly* 36 (February 1890), 476–79, quotation on 476.

60. "The Great Cantilever Bridge over Niagara," *Scientific American* 49 (December 1, 1883), 335, 340. See also Thomas Tugby, *Tugby's Guide to Niagara Falls being a*

Complete guide to all points of interest around and in the immediate vicinity (Niagara Falls, N.Y., 1890), 20.

61. *Niagara Falls Gazette,* November 10, 1883; Bogart, "Feats of Railway Engineering," 32.

62. Civil Engineer Carl Gayler is quoted in "The Cantilever Bridge at Niagara Falls, with Discussion," *Transactions of the American Society of Civil Engineering* 14 (November 1885), 549; Charles E. Greene, "The Cantilever Bridge at Niagara," *Science* 3 (May 9, 1884), 572–74.

63. See the official invitation to the opening of the bridge and several photographs of the bridge in "Bridges" and "Niagara Falls" vertical files, Buffalo and Erie County Historical Society. The American romance of modern machines and materials such as gears and girders is detailed in Cecelia Tichi, *Shifting Gears: Technology, Literature, Culture in Modernist America* (Chapel Hill: University of North Carolina Press, 1987).

64. Rollin Lynde Hartt, "The New Niagara: A City of the Future and 'Exhibit A' of the Pan-American Exposition," *McClure's Magazine* 17 (May 1901), 81; Skinner, "Great Achievements," 256.

65. Dunlap, "Romance of Niagara's Bridges," 427; Skinner, "Great Achievements," 256. For the weights of locomotives, see "The Bridges of Niagara Gorge," 396, and Roebling, "Passage of the First Locomotive," 233.

66. Dunlap, "Romance of Niagara's Bridges," 433; Billington, *The Tower and the Bridge,* 127–28.

67. Niagara Falls Chamber of Commerce, *Niagara Falls, the Greatest Electric and Power City of the World* (Niagara Falls, N.Y., 1897), 5–7, 63.

68. Niagara Falls & Lewiston R.R., *Through the Gorge of Niagara: Photo-gravures* (Buffalo, N.Y., 1896); *The Niagara Great Gorge Railroad: The Most Magnificent Scenic Route in the World* (Niagara Falls, N.Y., 1899); Niagara Falls Park & River Railway, *The Niagara River from the Rapids above the Falls to Lake Ontario* (Buffalo, N.Y., n.d.), 8.

69. New York Central Railroad, *Four Track Series: The Luxury of Modern Railway Travel* (New York, 1893), back cover; New York Central Railroad, *Two Days at Niagara Falls* (New York, c.1892), back cover.

70. *Niagara Falls Gazette,* March 29, 1884. A typical ad for the Michigan Central showed two of its trains heading in opposite directions on the Cantilever Bridge. "All Michigan Central express trains with through cars to Detroit, Toledo, Chicago, St. Louis, etc., cross the great Cantilever Bridge below and in front of the Falls, as is shown in this cut, thence along the West Bank of the Niagara River to Falls View, where passengers are afforded the grandest view of the cataract." See advertisement in James W. Greene, *Free Niagara: Nature's Grandest Wonder* (Buffalo, N.Y., 1885).

71. New York Central Railroad, *Two Days at Niagara; Four Track News* 1 (November 1901), 21; "Traveling by Telegraphy—Northward to Niagara," *Scribner's Monthly* 4 (May 1872), 20. Another example of this railroad line emphasis on built wonders may be seen in the Michigan Central's proposal to build a "Crystal Palace-like" structure on its "Falls View" platform. See *Niagara Falls Gazette,* July 20, 1885.

72. Dunlap, "Romance of Niagara Bridges," 428–29; *Across Niagara's Gorge: Grand Trunk Railway System* (Battle Creek, Mich., 1897), 2–3. The Grand Trunk Line announced that the Lower Steel Arch Bridge represented another "one of a series of achievements which have marked the history of the Grand Trunk Line" (ibid., 15–16).

73. Gebhard Napier, "Bridges and Bridge Building," *Munsey's Magazine* 25 (June 1901), 352.

3. Preserving Niagara and Creating the State Reservation

1. For a comprehensive analysis of the Niagara Falls Preservation Movement on each side of the cataract, see Gail Edith H. Evans, "Storm over Niagara: A Study of the Interplay of Cultural Values, Resource Politics, and Environmental Policy in an International Setting, 1670s–1950" (Ph.D. diss., University of California at Santa Barbara, 1991). The story of the creation of the reservation is told in Alfred Runte, "Beyond the Spectacular: The Niagara Falls Reservation Campaign," *New York Historical Society Quarterly* 57 (January 1973), 30–50; Charles E. Beveridge, *The Distinctive Charms of Niagara Scenery: Frederick Law Olmsted and the Niagara Reservation* (Niagara Falls, N.Y.: Niagara University, 1985).

2. *Niagara Falls Gazette*, July 30, 1884. See advertisements throughout the issues of the *Gazette*.

3. Thomas Holder, *A Complete Record of Niagara Falls and Vicinage, being Descriptive, Historical and Industrial* (Niagara Falls, N.Y., 1882), 58; advertisements in the *Niagara Falls Gazette*, on May 31, 1883, and June 6, 1883; William Dean Howells, "Niagara Revisited, Twelve Years After Their Wedding Journey," *Atlantic Monthly* 51 (May 1883), 604. Frederick Law Olmsted and Calvert Vaux discussed the displacement of natural vegetation in *General Plan for the Improvement of the Niagara Reservation* (New York, 1887), 10. See also *Niagara Falls Gazette*, August 6, 1884.

4. *Niagara Falls Gazette*, "Daily Edition Supplement," May 21, 1884; ads in the *Gazette* on May 31, 1883, and June 6, 1883; *Guide to Niagara Falls* (Niagara Falls, [1870s]), 9–12; *The Complete Illustrated Guide to Niagara Falls and Vicinity* (Niagara Falls, N.Y.: 1883), 47. The Brush illuminating machines created a popular sensation wherever they appeared when they were first introduced. See David E. Nye, *American Technological Sublime* (Cambridge: M.I.T. Press, 1994), 176.

5. John Baxter Harrison, *The Condition of Niagara Falls and the Measures Needed to Preserve Them, Eight Letters Published in the New York Evening Post, the New York Tribune, and the Boston Daily Advertiser During the Summer of 1882* (New York, 1882), 11; Olmsted and Vaux, *General Plan*, 10; Henry Norman, *The Preservation of Niagara: Letters to the Boston Daily Advertiser, the New York Evening Post, . . . in August & September, 1881* (New York, 1881), 6, 14.

6. Harrison, *Condition of Niagara Falls*, 48; Norman, *The Preservation of Niagara*, 34–35.

7. Harrison, *Condition of Niagara Falls*, 23, 32.

8. See, for example, Sir Lepel Henry Griffin, *The Great Republic* (New York, 1884), 23–27.

9. William Cullen Bryant, ed., *Picturesque America; or, The Land We Live In. A Delineation by Pen and Pencil of Mountains, Rivers, Lakes, Forests, Waterfalls, Shores, Cañons, Valleys, Cuts, and Other Picturesque Features of Our Environment* (New York,

1872), 438. See also Norman, *Preservation of Niagara,* 6; and "Taking the Stranger in at Niagara," *Brotherhood of Locomotive Engineers Monthly Journal* 18 (1884), 74.

10. Howells, "Niagara Revisited," 604–8. For the hoteliers' views on the Niagara tourist trade, see Norman, *Preservation of Niagara,* 12–13; Harrison, *Condition of Niagara Falls,* 25, 34; *Niagara Falls Gazette,* July 16, 23, 30, 1884, and June 10, 1885, for testimony of John M. Bush, owner of Clifton Hotel and testimony of Mr. Ellsworth, father-in-law of Peter A. Porter; *Niagara Falls Gazette,* August 6, 1884, for testimony of Frank R. Delano, president of Cataract Bank and part owner of International Hotel. Henry Norman consistently denounced excursionists and believed these "second class tourists" drove the "best people" away. See Norman, *Preservation of Niagara,* 12–13.

11. *Picturesque America,* 453 and passim.

12. Samuel Bowles, *Our New West. Records of Travel between The Mississippi River and the Pacific Ocean* (Hartford, Conn., 1869), v. After the Civil War, the West superseded Niagara as the realm of American nature. See Alfred Runte, *National Parks: The American Experience* (Lincoln: University of Nebraska Press, 1987), 11–32.

13. Bowles, *Our New West,* vii; *Picturesque America,* 298, 434. One such adventurous traveler's account is W. H. C. Kingston, *The Western World: Picturesque sketches of Nature and Natural History in Northern and Central America* (London, 1884), 48.

14. Greenwood is quoted in Runte, *National Parks,* 162–63; U.S. Congress, Committee on Public Lands, *The Yellowstone Park,* H. Rept. 26 to accompany H.R. 764, 42d Cong., 2d sess., February 27, 1872, p. 1.

15. See Frank Graham Jr., *The Adirondack Park: A Political History* (Syracuse, N.Y.: Syracuse University Press, 1978).

16. Frederick Law Olmsted to Thomas V. Welch, February 16, 1889, Frederick Law Olmsted Papers, The Library of Congress, Washington, D.C. (hereafter, FLO Papers). Olmstead said he first raised the topic of a Niagara reservation during a tour of Goat Island in 1869. See excerpt of Olmsted's letter to Thomas V. Welch in Charles Mason Dow, *The State Reservation at Niagara: A History* (Albany, N.Y.: J. B. Lyon Co., 1914), 10–11.

17. Governor Robinson's message of January 9, 1879, appears in Niagara Falls Association, *Report of the Executive Committee of the Niagara Falls Association, January, 1885* (New York, 1885), 4; *State Survey: Special Report on the Preservation of Niagara Falls, and Fourth Annual Report on the Triangulation of the State for the Year 1879. James T. Gardner, Director* (Albany, N.Y., 1880), 7.

18. *State Survey,* 11–12, 23. J. B. Harrison later insisted that "after twice canvassing the state it was plain to all who were engaged in the work that a plan even slightly more ambitious would have insured the defeat of the enterprise." John Baxter Harrison, "The Movement for the Redemption of Niagara," *Princeton Review* 1 (March 1886), 244.

19. Thomas V. Welch, "How Niagara Was Made Free: The Passage of the Niagara Reservation Act in 1885," *Publications of the Buffalo Historical Society* 5 (Buffalo, N.Y.: Buffalo Historical Society, 1902), 326, 344.

20. *Niagara Falls Gazette,* April 15, 1885.

21. Niagara Falls Association, *Report of the Executive Committee,* 6–10, 31–43. See also Welch, "How Niagara Was Made Free," 326–27.

22. Niagara Falls Association, *Report of the Executive Committee,* 6, 9; Welch, "How Niagara Was Made Free," 328, 332, 335–36.

23. Welch, "How Niagara Was Made Free," 350–59; Dow, *State Reservation,* 31–34.

24. *State Survey*, 15; "The Attempt to Save Niagara," *Century Magazine* 29 (November 1884), 954–55.

25. Niagara Falls Association, *Report of the Executive Committee*, 15; "Attempt to Save Niagara," 954–55; *The State Reservation at Niagara, Speech of the Honorable Thomas V. Welch in the Assembly of the State of New York, March 2, 1883* (Niagara Falls, N.Y., 1885), 12–13; Norman, *Preservation of Niagara*, 9.

26. *State Survey*, 15; Niagara Falls Association, *Report of the Executive Committee*, 16–17.

27. See "The Love of Nature," *Garden and Forest* 5 (April 27, 1892), 193–94. A most helpful discussion of the ideology of nature and landscape design is Geoffrey Blodgett, "Landscape Design as Conservative Reform," in Bruce Kelly et al., *Art of the Olmsted Landscape* (New York: New York City Landmarks Preservation Commission, 1981), 111–39.

28. For example, see the guidebook by P. E. Dunlap, *Sheldon and Hawley's Illustrated Guide to Niagara Falls and Points of Interest* (Niagara Falls, N.Y., 1890), 7.

29. Quoted from the *Detroit Free Press* in *Niagara Falls Gazette*, June 17, 1885.

30. Harrison, *Condition of Niagara Falls*, 22.

31. Ibid., 34–38; *State Survey*, 14.

32. Harrison, *Condition of Niagara Falls*, 35–38; Holder, *Complete Record of Niagara Falls*, 5.

33. Harrison, *Condition of Niagara Falls*, 25, 58.

34. James W. Greene, *Free Niagara: Nature's Grandest Wonder* (Buffalo, N.Y., 1885). For the role of parades and pageants in nineteenth-century America, see Nye, *Technological Sublime in America*, 34–36, 65–67.

35. "Memorial of Lord Dufferin," in FLO Papers; *Niagara Falls Gazette*, July 15, 1885. Dufferin's address to the Toronto Society of Artists (September 26, 1878) is reprinted in Dow, *State Reservation*, 13–14.

36. Welch, "Speech," 8.

37. "National Parks," *Garden and Forest* 3 (August 6, 1890), 377; Welch, "Speech," 8–10. Any park designed by a landscape gardener was likely to face severe criticism. Lord Dufferin protested against having Niagara "desecrated or in any way sophisticated by the penny arts of the landscape gardener" (Memorial, Lord Dufferin); Dufferin quoted in Dow, *State Reservation*, 14. Another objection to the appointment of a landscape architect raised issues of the reservation's cost and potential for corruption. See *Niagara Falls Gazette*, March 24, 1886 (reprint of article from *Rochester Post-Express*).

38. *General Plan*, 9–12, 16; "The Attack on the Niagara Reservation," *Garden and Forest* 2 (May 22, 1889), 241; bound letters "To J. B. Harrison, General Secretary of the Niagara Falls Association." See letter from the Hon. Joseph H. Stroms, Hopewell Junction, March 4, 1885, and from George F. Morse, in *Letters to the Niagara Falls Association*, unpublished notebooks, Local History Room, Niagara Falls Public Library, Niagara Falls, New York.

39. *Niagara Falls Gazette*, June 1, 1886; "Niagara Falls—Points of Interest," *Niagara Falls Gazette* Summer 1886 supplement.

40. *Niagara Falls Gazette*, July 7 and 29, 1886.

41. *Niagara Falls Gazette*, March 10 and 17, 1886, reprinted from the *New York Tribune; Niagara Falls Gazette*, March 24, 1886, reprinted from the *New York Sun*.

42. *State Survey*.

43. *Niagara Falls Gazette*, November 24, 1886, reprinted from the *New York Tribune*.

44. Andrew H. Green to William Dorsheimer, July 21, 1886, in FLO Papers; *Niagara Falls Gazette,* March 24, 1886, reprinted from the *New York Sun;* Frederick Law Olmsted to Governor David B. Hill, July 21, 1886, FLO Papers.

45. Frederick Law Olmsted to Governor Hill, July 21, 1886, FLO Papers.

46. *General Plan,* 3–4.

47. Ibid., 15.

48. Ibid., 15–16.

49. Frederick Law Olmsted to William Dorsheimer, February 26, 1886; C. Vaux to Olmsted, December 24, 1886, FLO Papers. For the history of the "building" of Central Park, see Roy Rosenzweig and Elizabeth Blackmar, *The Park and the People: A History of Central Park* (Ithaca: Cornell University Press, 1992). For a discussion of Frederick Law Olmsted's landscape tenets, see Bruce Kelly, "Art of the Olmsted Landscape," in Kelly et al., *Art of the Olmsted Landscape,* 5–70. Olmsted's plans for Delaware Park in Buffalo, N.Y., are discussed in Francis R. Kowsky, ed., *The Best Planned City: The Olmsted Legacy in Buffalo* (Buffalo, N.Y.: Buffalo State College Foundation, 1991).

50. Thomas V. Welch, "Annual Report of the Superintendent," in *Report of the Commissioners of the State Reservation at Niagara for the Year 1885* (Albany, N.Y., 1886), 9–11; *General Plan,* 23.

51. See Olmsted's remarks in *State Survey,* 30.

52. After describing Niagara's distinctive scenery, Olmsted said: "If it were possible to have the same conditions detached from the falls (and it is not . . .), Niagara would still be a place of singular fascination; possibly to some, upon whom the falls have a terrifying effect, even more so than it is now." Ibid., 29.

53. Ibid., 9, 21. Ironically, this neglect of the cataract and early assurance that "the Falls themselves man cannot touch" would haunt the reservation commissioners once the power developers gained water-diversion charters.

54. Ibid., 29; Harrison, *Condition of Niagara Falls,* 7.

55. *General Plan,* 27, 34–36, 38–41.

56. Ibid., 10, 26–28.

57. Ibid., 40–41.

58. Ibid., 20–21.

59. Ibid., 18–20.

60. Francis Parkman to Frederick Law Olmsted, March 7, 1887, FLO Papers.

61. Frederick Law Olmsted to Colonel Casimir S. Gzowski, August 15, 1887, FLO Papers; *General Plan,* 22. Gzowski was president of the commissioners of the Canadian park. For a detailed analysis of the formation and administration of Queen Victoria Park, see Evans, "Storm over Niagara," 167–85, 200–204.

62. Governor Hill is quoted in *Niagara Falls Gazette,* July 22, 1885.

63. Dunlap, *Sheldon and Hawley's Illustrated Guide,* 7; Harrison, "Movement for Redemption," 244. See also "Attacks on Civilization," *Garden and Forest* 2 (October 23, 1889), 505.

64. Erastus Brooks quoted in *Niagara Falls Gazette,* July 15, 1885.

65. "The Preservation of Natural Scenery," *Garden and Forest* 3 (July 23, 1890), 354. See also Mary Caroline Robbins, "Park-Making as a National Art," *Atlantic Monthly* 79 (January 1887), 86.

66. *Sixteenth Annual Report of the Commissioners of the New York State Reservation at Niagara, From October 1, 1898, to September 30, 1899* (Albany, N.Y., 1900), 15.

67. *Wonders of Niagara, Scenic and Industrial* (Niagara Falls, N.Y.: Shredded Wheat Company, 1914); "A Day at Niagara," *Demorest's Family Magazine* 29 (August 1893), 584.

68. *Tenth Annual Report of the Commissioners of the State Reservation of New York at Niagara Falls, From October 1, 1892, to September 30, 1893* (Albany, N.Y., 1894), 5–16; *Eighteenth Annual Report of the Commissioners of the State Reservation at Niagara, October 1, 1900, to September 30, 1901* (Albany, N.Y., 1902), 5–7.

69. *Niagara Falls Gazette*, June 3, 1885.

70. *Niagara Falls Gazette*, May 13, 1885; *Niagara Falls Gazette*, June 2, 1886.

71. See especially Samuel P. Hays, *Conservation and the Gospel of Efficiency: The Progressive Conservation Movement, 1890–1920* (Cambridge: Harvard University Press, 1959), and Runte, *National Parks*, 44–45, 83–105.

72. E. T. Williams, *Niagara Falls: Power City of the World* (Niagara Falls, N.Y., 1914). *Garden and Forest* labeled the power-harnessing schemes "Attacks on Civilization." See "Attacks on Civilization," 505.

4. Capturing the Falls: Power, Powerhouses, and the Electricity Age

1. Sir William Thomson, "On the Sources of Energy in Nature Available to Man for the Production of Mechanical Effect," *Nature* 24 (September 8, 1881), 434–35; Archibald Williams, *The Romance of Modern Engineering* (Philadelphia: J. B. Lippincott, 1904), 11–13. See also Thomas Park Hughes, *American Genesis: A Century of Invention and Technological Enthusiasm, 1870–1970* (New York: Viking Press, 1989), 6–17.

2. E. Jay Edwards, "The Capture of Niagara," *McClure's Magazine* 3 (October 1894), 423–25; Ernest La Sueur, "Commercial Power Development at Niagara," *Popular Science Monthly* 45 (September 1894), 611. See *Niagara Falls, the Great Manufacturing Village of the West; Being a Statement of the Operations of the Niagara Falls Hydraulic Company* (Boston, 1853), 3–16. As discussed in Chapter 2 above, estimates of Niagara's millions of horsepower predated the 1850s.

3. Arthur Vaughan Abbott, "Industrial Niagara," *Review of Reviews* 12 (September 1895), 295.

4. A review of the power charters is contained in John L. Harper and J. A. Johnson, "Hydroelectric Development at Niagara Falls," *Journal of the American Institute of Electrical Engineers* 40 (July 1921), 561, 563. For a study of American and Canadian public policy at Niagara Falls, see Gail Edith H. Evans, "Storm over Niagara: A Study of the Interplay of Cultural Values, Resource Politics, and Environmental Policy in an International Setting, 1670s–1950" (Ph.D. diss., University of California at Santa Barbara, 1991).

5. Williams, *Romance of Modern Engineering*, 11–16. On the technological sublime and religious feeling, see David E. Nye, *American Technological Sublime* (Cambridge: M.I.T. Press, 1994), 28–29. See also Leo Marx, *The Machine in the Garden: Technology and the Pastoral Idea in America* (New York: Oxford University Press, 1965), 195–207.

6. Hughes, *American Genesis*, 13–40, 83–93; Nye, *American Technological Sublime*, 77–79.

7. Wyn Wachhorst, *Thomas Alva Edison: An American Myth* (Cambridge: M.I.T. Press, 1981), 39–40; Thomas Parke Hughes, *Networks of Power: Electrification in Western Society, 1880–1930* (Baltimore: Johns Hopkins University Press, 1983), 41–42. Tourists who were curious about Edison and his latest magical inventions continued to make pilgrimages to Menlo Park.

8. Hughes, *Networks of Power*, 50–52, 129–39; Nye, *Electrifying America: Social Meanings of a New Technology, 1880–1940* (Cambridge: M.I.T. Press, 1990), 33–37.

9. The *New York Sun* article appeared on October 20, 1878. See Robert Friedel and Paul Israel, *Edison's Electric Light: A Biography of Invention* (New Brunswick, N.J.: Rutgers University Press, 1986), 7; Hughes, *American Genesis*, 17–18, 36, 85–89. See also John J. O'Neill, *Prodigal Genius: The Life of Nicola Tesla* (New York: Ives Washburn, 1944).

10. An example of this tendency to label other waterfalls "miniature Niagaras" is found in John Leng, *America in 1876: Pencillings During a Tour in the Centennial Year* (Dundee, 1887), 131. On waterpower in early-nineteenth-century America, see Louis C. Hunter, *The Transmission of Power*, vol. 1 of *A History of Industrial Power in the United States, 1780–1930* (Charlottesville: University Press of Virginia, 1979).

11. W. C. Johnson, "The Hydraulic Canal," in William Dean Howells and Mark Twain, eds., *The Niagara Book: A Complete Souvenir of Niagara Falls* (Buffalo, N.Y., 1893), 222–25.

12. "The Milling District" (photo), in *Niagara Falls in Summer and Winter* (Buffalo, N.Y.: Nicklis Co., 1905); "Niagara Falls Industrial Number," *Scientific American Supplement* 49 (May 3, 1900), 20216; J. Munro, "Electricity from Niagara," *Littell's Living Age* 197 (May 27, 1893), 567–68. See also Edward Dean Adams, *Niagara Power: History of the Niagara Falls Power Company, 1886 to 1918* (Niagara Falls, N.Y., 1927), 1:70–71, 77, 80.

13. Gilmer Speed, "Harnessing Niagara," *Harper's Weekly* 35 (December 26, 1891), 1042; Adams, *Niagara Power*, 1:114–19.

14. Adams, *Niagara Power*, 1:115.

15. *Niagara Falls Electrical Handbook: Being a Guide for Visitors from Abroad attending the International Electrical Congress, St. Louis, Missouri, September, 1904* (Niagara Falls, N.Y.: American Institute of Electrical Engineers, 1904), 168. The text continued: "So difficult and varied are the many problems connected with the installation of the plants necessary for the utilizing of the power that it has taken the combined efforts of the best engineers in the world to devise apparatus and plants which have made possible the development of thousands of horsepower within comparatively small limits, and the transmission of the power to cities many miles distant." See also Lewis Buckley Stillwell, "Electric Power Generation at Niagara," *Cassier's Magazine* 8 (July 1895), 255, and Coleman Sellers, "Utilization of Niagara's Power," in Howells and Twain, *Niagara Book* (1901), 182–84.

16. Adams, *Niagara Power*, 1:141–44, 2:8–11; Abbott, "Industrial Niagara," 295, 299.

17. For a discussion of central stations, see John R. Stilgoe, *Metropolitan Corridor: Railroads and the American Scene* (New Haven: Yale University Press, 1983), 111–14. Thomas Parke Hughes, *Networks of Power*, 79–139, discusses the attempts to resolve the critical problem of power transmission and distribution.

18. Adams, *Niagara Power*, 1:128, 2:100. See also Louis C. Hunter and Lynwood Bryant, *The Transmission of Power*, vol. 3 of *A History of Industrial Power in the United States, 1780–1930* (Cambridge: M.I.T. Press, 1991), 254–57.

19. Adams, *Niagara Power*, 1:234–36, 129–32, 144, 234, De Lancey Rankine, *Memorabilia of William Burch Rankine of Niagara Falls, New York* (Niagara Falls, N.Y.: Power City Press, 1926), 34–35; Hughes, *Networks of Power*, 139; Sellers, "Utilization" (1901), 182–84.

20. *Niagara Falls Gazette*, April 2 and 5, 1890; S. Dana Greene, "Distribution of the Electrical Energy from Niagara Falls," *Cassier's Magazine* 8 (July 1895), 336–37.

21. Adams, *Niagara Power*, 1:171; Hunter and Bryant, *Transmission of Power*, 254–55; *Niagara Falls Gazette*, September 12, 1890. On September 28, 1889, Edison cabled Adams, insisting: "No difficulty transferring unlimited power. Will assist." Adams, *Niagara Power*, 1:144.

22. Hughes, *Networks of Power*, 81–86.

23. John Trowbridge, "Niagara the Motor for the World's Fair," *The Chautauquan* 14 (January 1892), 441–45. See also Hughes, *Networks of Power*, 106–8. The textbook was *The Electric Transmission of Energy*, by Gisbert Kapp. See Adams, *Niagara Power*, 1:144–47, 2:173, 176.

24. Francis Lynde Stetson, "The Use of Niagara Waterpower," *Cassier's Magazine*, 8 (July 1895), 186; Adams, *Niagara Power*, 2:74.

25. Adams, *Niagara Power*, 1:130.

26. Report of Coleman Sellers, quoted in ibid., 1:192; see also ibid., 1:181–92.

27. Ibid., 1:187–90; Speed, "Harnessing Niagara," 1047.

28. Hughes, *Networks of Power*, 133, 129–135; Adams, *Niagara Power*, 2:233–34.

29. "Niagara and Lord Kelvin," *Literary Digest* 15 (September 18, 1897), 675; "Is Niagara Doomed," *Literary Digest* 15 (October 2, 1897), 614.

30. Aricles in *Scientific American* included "Utilizing Niagara Falls Water Power," 63 (November 22, 1890), 328; "Great Power House at Niagara," 78 (June 18, 1898), 393–94; "Niagara Falls Electric Power Plant," 74 (January 15, 1896); "Utilizing the Water Power of Niagara Falls," 71 (October 20, 1892), 245–46. Some of the articles in the "Niagara Power Number" of *Cassier's Magazine* 8 (July 1895), included Albert H. Porter, "Some Details of the Niagara Tunnel," 203–10; Lewis Buckley Stickwell, "Electric Power Generation at Niagara Falls," 253–304; S. D. Greene, "Distribution of Electric Power," 333–62; Francis Lynde Stetson, "The Use of the Niagara Waterpower," 173–92; and Clemons Herschel, "Niagara Mill Sites, Water Connections, and Turbines," 227–50. See also F. L. Pope, "Distribution of Niagara Falls Electrical Power," *Engineering Magazine* 10 (1895), 407.

31. Williams, *Romance of Modern Engineering*, 15. See also Hughes, *American Genesis*, 36. Some of these articles included L. Abbott, "Niagara Falls in Harness," *Outlook* 52 (November 16, 1895), 788–91; Orrin E. Dunlap, "The Wonderful Story of the Chaining of Niagara Power," *World's Work* 2 (July 1901), 1161; Francis L. Stetson, "Niagara in Chains: Electric Power Projects," *Review of Reviews* 12 (August 1895), 208–9; Rollin Lynde Hartt, "The New Niagara," *McClure's Magazine* 17 (May 1901), 78–84; J. Munro, "Electricity from Niagara," *Littell's Living Age* 197 (May 27, 1893), 567–71; F. L. Blanchard, "Niagara Power at Buffalo," *Harper's Weekly* 41 (June 5, 1897), 569; "Niagara Harnessed," *Harper's Weekly* 39 (April 6, 1895), 330–33; Curtis Brown, "Diversion of Niagara," *Cosmopolitan* 17 (September 1894), 526–45; E. Jay Edwards, "The Capture of Niagara," *McClure's Magazine* 3 (October 1894), 423–35.

32. Peter A. Porter, *Official Guide: Niagara Falls–River–Frontier–Scenic–Botanical–Electric–Historic–Geologic–Hydraulic* (Niagara Falls, N.Y., 1901), 271; Brown, "Diversion of Niagara," 530.

33. Peter A. Porter, "The Niagara Region in History," *Cassier's Magazine* 8 (July 1895), 384; Peter A. Porter, *Niagara, an Aboriginal Center of Trade* (Niagara Falls, N.Y., 1906), 73–74, 3.

34. Williams, *Romance of Modern Engineering*, 11–33; Brown, "Diversion of Niagara," 528.

35. Brown, "Diversion of Niagara," 528.

36. Ibid., 536, 537, 540, 542.

37. Ibid., 528.

38. See, for example, Sellers, "Utilization" (1893), 200. Cecelia Tichi discusses the integration of the mechanical world into the natural realm in *Shifting Gears: Technology, Literature, Culture in Modernist America* (Chapel Hill: University of North Carolina Press, 1987), 17–19.

39. Adams, *Niagara Power*, 1:108. Francis Lynde Stetson insisted: "This protection of the natural beauty of Niagara was the underlying idea in [Evershed's] conception and [in the] development of his plan." See Stetson, "Use of the Niagara Water Power," 178.

40. Sellers, "Utilization" (1893), 193; *Paul's Dictionary of Buffalo, Niagara Falls, Tonawanda & Vicinity* (Buffalo, N.Y., 1896), 240.

41. Edwards, "Capture of Niagara," 430. See also "*Maid of the Mist* Steamboat Co: A Most Novel and Charming Water Trip: the Only Way to Fully Realize the Grandeur and Height of the Great Falls of Niagara" (leaflet), n.d., in Niagara Falls Vertical File, Buffalo and Erie County Historical Society; James N. Granger and Banker R. Paine, *The Great Tunnel at Niagara Falls: A Story of a Bore That Is Not a Bore* (Rochester, N.Y., 1893), 7; New York Central & Hudson River Railway, *2 Days at Niagara Falls* (New York, c. 1892), 21–24; "The Cataract House: The Best and Best-Known Hotel at Niagara," in *Niagara Falls Gazette*, "Special Edition," n.d., Vertical File, Buffalo and Erie County Historical Society.

42. Edwards, "Capture of Niagara," 430; Michigan Central Railroad, *Niagara Falls in Miniature* (Chicago, 1896); Brown, "Diversion of Niagara," 530.

43. Adams, *Niagara Power*, 2:331.

44. Ibid., 2:65–66.

45. Stilgoe, *Metropolitan Corridor*, 122–23. The original powerhouse of the Niagara Falls Hydraulic Manufacturing Company proved the point. H. G. Wells believed that this power plant was nothing more than a hideously defiling shed. See H. G. Wells, "The Future in America: A Search of Its Realities—The End of Niagara," *Harper's Weekly* 50 (July 21, 1906), 1019.

46. Studies on McKim, Mead & White include: Leland Roth, *McKim, Mead & White, Architects* (New York: Harper & Row, 1983); and Richard Guy Wilson, *McKim, Mead & White, Architects* (New York: Rizzoli, 1983). See also Leland Roth, *The Architecture of McKim, Mead, and White, 1870–1920: A Building List* (New York: Garland, 1978).

47. Adams, *Niagara Power*, 2:66; Edwards, "Capture of Niagara," 429.

48. Sellers, "Utilization" (1893), 200. Powerhouse Number Two used the same local limestone stone-brickwork, as did later powerhouses on the Canadian side.

49. Roth, *McKim, Mead & White, Architects*, 204. See also Nye, *American Technological Sublime*, 134–36.

50. Adams, *Niagara Power*, 2:344.

51. Ibid.; Sellers, "Utilization" (1901), 189.

52. The Canadian Niagara Power Company was a subsidiary of the Niagara Falls Power Company, and the Ontario Power Company was funded by capital from Buffalo.

53. P. N. Nunn, *The Power Development of the Ontario Power Company* (Niagara Falls, Ont.: Ontario Power Company, 1905), 5. J. Horace McFarland, secretary of the American Civic Association, disputed the benevolent claims of the power companies. He noted that power companies "white washed" their powerhouses in order to obscure the fact that they were blots on the Niagara landscape. He dismissed the companies' pretensions to high architecture: "Ye Gods, Niagara has waited all these years to have an Italian Renaissance adornment added to her majesty!" McFarland's testimony, in U.S. Congress, House Committee on Rivers and Harbors, *Preservation of Niagara Falls (H.R. 18024), Hearings,* 59th Cong., 1st sess., April 1906, 159.

54. Francis V. Greene, *Niagara Falls in 1907* (Niagara Falls, Ont.: Ontario Power Company, 1907), 34.

55. Ibid., 5–7, 31–40, and passim.

56. Stephen M. Dale, "Seeing Niagara Falls for the First Time," *Ladies' Home Journal* 21 (June 1904), 9–10.

57. Henry Adams, *The Education of Henry Adams* (Boston: Houghton Mifflin, 1973), 380–413; Wells, "Future in America," 1019.

58. Wells, "Future in America," 1019; Sellers, "Utilization" (1893), 201–2.

59. Stilgoe, *Metropolitan Corridor,* 111; William C. Andrews, "How Niagara Has Been Harnessed," *Review of Reviews* 23 (June 1901), 696.

60. Coleman Sellers described the tourist facilities of the plant in detail: "Through the office doors at the left of the entrance, visitors have access, by a flight of stairs to a platform at the level of the second story, from which a second short flight of steps leads to a bridge that crosses the main room of the power station. From this bridge a view can be obtained of the electric generators and machinery which occupy the general floor of the building." Sellers, "Utilization" (1901), 190.

61. Andrews, "How Niagara Has Been Harnessed," 696; Wells, "Future in America," 1019; Greene, *Niagara Falls in 1907,* 44.

62. Williams, *Romance of Modern Engineering,* 25.

63. *Industrial Niagara: Niagara Falls City Guide—The Falls and Scenery Illustrated* (Niagara Falls, N.Y., 1913), 20; *The Niagara Falls Electrical Handbook* (Niagara Falls, N.Y.: American Institute of Electrical Engineers, 1904), 74–81.

64. "Some Information Regarding the Pan-American Exposition [1901]," in Buffalo and Erie County Historical Society, "Pan-American Exposition" Vertical File, "Duplicate Material Only" box.

65. Dale, "Seeing Niagara for the First Time," 9–10; "The Niagara Gorge," *Travel and Recreation* 1 (August 1897), 5–6. See John Kasson, *Amusing the Million: Coney Island at the Turn of the Century* (New York: Hill & Wang, 1976), 73–82. Kasson notes that the amusement-park roller coasters and rides borrowed heavily from electric and steam trains.

66. Adams, *Niagara Power,* 2:331–32.

67. Ibid., 2:331–43; Francis Lynde Stetson, testimony, Secretary of War, in *Hearings Upon Applications for Permits for the Diversion of Water from Niagara River . . . before the Secretary of War at Niagara Falls, N.Y., July 12, 1906* (Washington, D.C., 1906), 23.

68. Adams, *Niagara Power,* 2:336, 65.

69. Dale, "Seeing Niagara for the First Time," 9; Fred Atherton Fernald, *The Index Guide to Buffalo and Niagara Falls* (Buffalo, N.Y.: Frederik A. Fernald, 1910), 130. Stephen M. Dale wrote a series of articles for the *Ladies' Home Journal* entitled "What Folks Do" at favorite tourist attractions.

70. Sellers, "Utilization" (1901), 212.

71. Adams, *Niagara Power*, 1:109.

72. Hughes, *American Genesis*, 2, 8–11; Arnold Bennett, *Your United States: Impressions of a First Visit* (New York: Harper & Brothers, 1912), 82–83.

5. Electricity's Throne: Niagara Falls and the Utopian Impulse

1. The name "Electricity's throne" comes from an 1895 promotional booklet for a utopian real-estate venture, *Electricity's Throne* (Buffalo, N.Y., 1895).

2. *Niagara Falls Gazette*, April 2 and 5, 1890.

3. Thomas Park Hughes, *American Genesis: A Century of Invention and Technological Enthusiasm, 1870–1970* (New York: Viking Press, 1989), 1–5, 13–16.

4. Howard P. Segal, *Technological Utopianism in American Culture* (Chicago: University of Chicago Press, 1985), 78 and passim. See also Kenneth Roemer, *The Obsolete Necessity: America in Utopian Writings, 1888–1900* (Kent, Ohio: Kent State University Press, 1976).

5. Segal, *Technological Utopianism*, 98–128; Roemer, *The Obsolete Necessity*. For a survey of nineteenth-century reform, see Ronald Walters, *American Reformers, 1815–1860* (New York: Hill & Wang, 1978), and Robert Crunden, *Ministers of Reform: The Progressives' Achievement in American Civilization, 1889–1920* (Chicago: University of Illinois Press, 1982). Roderick Nash, *Wilderness and the American Mind* (New Haven: Yale University Press, 1973), examines the history of the American conservation movement.

6. See John F. Kasson, *Civilizing the Machine: Technology and Republican Values in America, 1776–1900* (New York: Penguin, 1977), 183–234; Kenneth Roemer, *The Obsolete Necessity*, 172–76. Two analyses of the turn-of-the-century cultural crisis are Robert H. Weibe, *The Search for Order, 1877–1900* (New York: Hill & Wang, 1967), and T. J. Jackson Lears, *No Place of Grace: Antimodernism and the Transformation of American Culture, 1880–1920* (New York: Pantheon, 1981).

7. Niagara Falls Chamber of Commerce, *Niagara Falls: The Greatest Electric and Power City of the World* (Niagara Falls, N.Y., 1897), 62. The engineer Clemons Herschel subscribed to the same prediction. See Clemons Herschel, "Niagara Mill Sites, Water Connections, and Turbines," *Cassier's Magazine* 8 (July 1895), 249–50.

8. *Niagara Falls Gazette*, November 10, 1898; Adams, *Niagara Power*, 2:168.

9. Herschel, "Niagara Mill Sites, Water Connections, and Turbines," 250.

10. *Niagara Falls Gazette*, October 8, 1890.

11. These conditions were vividly portrayed in Edward Bellamy's *Looking Backward*. See also Weibe, *Search for Order*, 11–43.

12. The New Niagara embodied the ideals of the City Beautiful Movement. See William H. Wilson, *The City Beautiful Movement* (Baltimore: Johns Hopkins University Press, 1989), 35–95.

13. For another account of the utopian schemes of Henkle, Gillette, and Love, see Patrick V. McGreevy, *Imagining Niagara: The Meaning and Making of Niagara Falls* (Amherst: University of Massachusetts Press, 1994), 120–36.

14. "Alladin Quite Outdone: Giant Palace to Span the Mighty Niagara," *The World*, February 9, 1896, mentioned in McGreevy, *Imagining Niagara*, 135; Leonard Henkle, "The Great Dynamic Palace and International Hall for Niagara Falls" (broadside), in "Niagara Falls Power" Vertical File, Buffalo and Erie County Historical Society.

15. Henkle, "Great Dynamic Palace."

16. For biographical information on Gillette, see Segal, *Technological Utopianism*, 48–49, 52, 168; and Russell B. Adams Jr., *King C. Gillette: The Man and His Wonderful Shaving Device* (Boston: Little, Brown, 1978).

17. Segal, *Technological Utopianism*, 1–9; King C. Gillette, *The Human Drift* (Boston, 1894), 36.

18. Gillette, *Human Drift*, 44–46.

19. Ibid., v; *The World Corporation* (Boston: New England News Corp., 1910).

20. Gillette, *Human Drift*, 4–6, 14–16, 22–29.

21. Ibid., 84, 24, 87.

22. Ibid., 24–29, 115.

23. Ibid., 63, 89, 112.

24. Ibid., 95, 97.

25. Ibid., 90–93, 93.

26. William T. Love, *Model City: The New Manufacturing Center of America* (Buffalo, N.Y.: Niagara Power & Development Co., n.d. [1901]), 11, 7; *Description and Plan of the Model City Located at Lewistown, Niagara County, N.Y. Chartered by Special Act of the New York Legislature. Designed to be the most Perfect City in Existence* (Lewiston, N.Y., 1893).

27. Love, *Model City*, 5–7, 11.

28. Ibid., 9; *Description and Plan of the Model City*, 7.

29. *Model City*, 14; *Description and Plan of the Model City*, 22–23, 12–13.

30. *Model City*, 14, 13; *Description and Plan of the Model City*, 13.

31. *Description and Plan of the Model City*, 22–23, 20–21, 24.

32. McGreevy, *Imagining Niagara*, 122; *Model City*, 6.

33. Ironically, as Niagara civic boosters and tourist promoters contemplated the future, they were in an ambivalent position regarding the refinement of electrical science. After the harnessing of Niagara, experts anticipated little Niagaras of electrical production to spring up wherever falling water was available. Harnessed waterpower everywhere was known as "Niagarics." This meant that, in order for Niagara Falls itself to keep its reputation as a waterpower site, "the New Niagara, then, must outvie innumerable still newer little Niagaras." Yet, even if Niagara surpassed all these little Niagaras, development of an efficient and inexpensive method of long-distance power transmission would probably arrest the rising metropolis at Niagara before it began. See William C. Andrews, "How Niagara Has Been Harnessed," *Review of Reviews* 23 (June 1901), 697; Eugene R. White, "Niagarics, the New Force," *Munsey's Magazine* 29 (April 1903), 29–30. Rollin Lynde Hartt, "The New Niagara: A City of the Future—'Exhibit A' of the Pan-American Exposition," *McClure's Magazine* 17 (May 1901), 83.

34. "Niagara Falls as an Electro-Chemical Center," *Current Literature* 87 (October 11, 1902), 728. For Niagara's role in the electrochemical industry, see Martha M. Trescott, *The Rise of the American Electrochemicals Industry, 1880–1910* (Westport, Conn.: Greenwood Press, 1981), 34–91.

35. E. T. Williams, *Niagara Falls: Power City of the World* (Niagara Falls, N.Y., 1914).

36. Mary Bronson Hartt, "The Passing of Niagara," *Outlook* 68 (May 4, 1901), 1–24, 24, 23. John R. Stilgoe's chapter "Zone," in *Metropolitan Corridor: Railroads and the American Scene* (New Haven: Yale University Press, 1983), 77–103, offers an account of the lurid fascination of late-nineteenth-century industrial zones.

37. The *Niagara Falls Gazette*, April 20, May 19, and June 25, 1900, exposed these conditions with such headlines as "The Notorious Tunnel District" and "Hotbed of Diseases in Heart of City."

38. *Niagara Falls, the Greatest Electric and Power City*, 61. See also *Niagara Falls as a Resort, as a Place of Residence, and as an Industrial and Power Producing Center* (Buffalo, N.Y., 1898).

39. Archibald Williams, *The Romance of Modern Engineering* (Philadelphia: J. B. Lippincott, 1904), 31–32; Arthur Vaughn Abbott, "Industrial Niagara," *Review of Reviews* 12 (September 1895), 296. See also Leland Roth, "Three Industrial Towns by McKim, Mead, and White," *Journal of the Society of Architectural Historians* 38 (December 1979), 324–32; Adams, *Niagara Power*, 1:329; and *Niagara Falls Power—Its application and use on the Niagara Frontier* (Niagara Falls, N.Y.: Niagara Falls Power Company, 1901). Although most Echota dwellings were rented "at very modest rates," the company allowed workers to purchase their houses at fair prices, thus enabling the town to avoid the stigma of other company towns that seemed to prey on captive workers. Abbott, "Industrial Niagara," 296.

40. Abbott, "Industrial Niagara," 296; Williams, *Romance of Modern Engineering*, 31. See also *Paul's Dictionary of Buffalo, Niagara Falls, Tonawanda, & Vicinity* (Buffalo, N.Y., 1896), 51.

41. Michigan Central Railroad, *Niagara Falls in Miniature* (Chicago, 1896); Budgett Meakin, *Model Factories and Villages: Ideal Conditions of Labor and Housing* (1905; reprint, New York: Garland Publishing, 1985), 411.

42. Williams, *Romance of Modern Engineering*, 31; Rollin Lynde Hartt, "The New Niagara," 80; "Progressive American Cities: Niagara Falls, the City," *National Magazine* 19 (October 1903), 129.

43. *Niagara Falls of Today: Electricity the Power, Niagara the Source, Domestic and Industrial* (Niagara Falls: Board of Trade, 1907).

6. *The Spirit of Niagara: Niagara Falls and the Pan-American Exposition of 1901*

1. Mabel E. Barnes, "Peeps at the Pan-American" (unpublished notebook), Buffalo and Erie County Historical Society, 1:164–65.

2. See John Cawelti, "America on Display, 1876, 1893, 1933," in *America in the Age of Industrialization*, ed. Frederick C. Jaher (New York: Free Press, 1968), 317–63; Robert W. Rydell, *All the World's a Fair: Visions of Empire at American International Expositions, 1876–1916* (Chicago: University of Chicago Press, 1984); David F. Burg, *Chicago's White City of 1893* (Lexington: University of Kentucky Press, 1976); Reid Badger, *The Great American Fair: The World's Columbian Exposition and American Culture* (Chicago: Nelson Hall, 1979); William H. Wilson, *The City Beautiful Movement* (Baltimore: Johns Hopkins University Press, 1989), 53–74.

3. Howard Segal points out that "these popular exhibitions represent the emergence of another expression of American utopianism." See his *Technological Utopianism in American Culture* (Chicago: University of Chicago Press, 1985), 125. David Nye sees world's fairs as a central aspect of the technological sublime in America. See Nye, *American Technological Sublime* (Cambridge: M.I.T. Press, 1994), 151.

4. *Niagara Falls Gazette*, August 27, 1897. The *Gazette* reported that the grand exhibition halls would become permanent factories after the exposition.

5. *Niagara Falls Gazette*, October 15, 1897; Niagara Falls Chamber of Commerce, *Niagara Falls, the Greatest Electric and Power City of the World* (Niagara Falls, N.Y., 1897).

6. *Niagara Falls Gazette*, May 15, 1899; *Buffalo Finite*, January 19, 1899. Detroit's bid for the exposition coincided with its desire to celebrate its centennial year as a city. Herbert P. Bissell, a director of the Pan-American Exposition, quoted in *Buffalo Finite*, January 19, 1899, in Pan-American Newspaper Clippings, microfilm, Reel 1, Buffalo and Erie County Historical Society.

7. Carleton Sprague, "Some Phases of Exposition Making," *American Architect and Building News* 74 (October 19, 1901), 19.

8. Herbert Croly, "Some Novel Features of the Pan-American Exposition," *Architectural Record* 11 (October 1901), 591.

9. Ibid., 590–92, 594.

10. "How the Exposition Was Advertised," *Profitable Advertising* 11 (June 1901), 51; *Pan-American Exposition: Its Purpose and Plan* (Buffalo, N.Y.: Pan-American Exposition Co., 1901); *Niagara Falls Gazette*, December 8, 1900.

11. *Pan-American Exposition: Its Purpose and Plan; Pan-American Exposition: Thirty Minutes from Niagara Falls* (Buffalo, N.Y., 1901); "Publicity and the Exposition," *Pan-American Magazine* 2 (October 1900), 13; "What the Railroads Are Doing," *Profitable Advertising* 11 (June 1901), 96.

12. "How the Exposition Was Advertised," 45.

13. "Publicity and the Exposition," 13–14; "How the Exposition Was Advertised," 48.

14. For an alternative interpretation of the "Spirit of Niagara," see K. Porter Aichele, "The 'Spirit of Niagara': Success or Failure?" in *Art Journal* 44 (September 1984), 46–49.

15. *Pan-American Exposition* (green pamphlet) (Buffalo, N.Y., 1901) in Pan-American Exposition Vertical File, Box 2, Buffalo and Erie County Historical Society. *Profitable Advertising* called this booklet "the first pretentious booklet issued." See "How the Exposition Was Advertised," 49.

16. Gas and steam were allowed only in the Machinery and Transportation Building. "Rules Regarding the Supply of Electricity at the Pan-American Exposition," Pan-American Exposition Vertical File, Box 5, Buffalo and Erie County Historical Society.

17. John Trowbridge, "Niagara the Motor for the World's Fair," *The Chautauquan* 14 (January 1892), 441–45; Michael Idvorsky Pupin, "Electrical Progress During the Last Decade," *Cosmopolitan* 31 (September 1901), 523.

18. Orrin E. Dunlap, "The Wonderful Story of the Chaining of Niagara," *World's Work* 2 (August 1901), 1052–54; *Pan-American Exposition* (green pamphlet); Rollin Lynde Hartt, "The New Niagara: A City of the Future—'Exhibit A' of the Pan-American Exposition," *McClure's Magazine* 17 (June 1901), 84; Pupin, "Electrical Progress," 523.

19. Sprague, "Some Phases of Exposition Making," 20.

20. Robert Grant, "Notes on the Pan-American Exposition," *Cosmopolitan* 31 (September 1901), 452.

21. Arthur Goodrich, "Short Stories of Interesting Exhibits," *World's Work* 2 (August 1901), 1083–89; Mary Bronson Hartt, "How to See the Pan-American Exposition," *Everybody's Magazine* 5 (October 1901), 489; Finley Peter Dunne's fictitious character Mr. Dooley offered another viewpoint: "I niver see Niag'ra Falls, but I don't like to think iv it as a lamp-lighter tearin' round with a ladder an' a little torch. I don't believe in makin' light iv th' falls." See F. P Dunne, "Mr. Dooley at the Midway," *Cosmopolitan* 31 (September 1901), 478.

22. Arthur Brisbane, "The Incubator Baby and Niagara Falls," *Cosmopolitan* 31 (September 1901), 509, 510, 513.

23. Julian Hawthorne, "Some Novelties at Buffalo Fair," *Cosmopolitan* 31 (September 1901), 485. See also Cecelia Tichi, *Shifting Gears: Technology, Literature, Culture in Modernist America* (Chapel Hill: University of North Carolina Press, 1987), 17–19.

24. "How the Exposition Was Advertised," 48; *Bennitt's Illustrated Souvenir Guide to the Pan-American Exposition: A Complete Souvenir with Condensed Guide to Buffalo and Niagara Falls*, ed. Mark Bennitt (Buffalo, N.Y., 1901); Mary Bronson Hartt, "The Play Side of the Fair," *World's Work* 2 (August 1901), 1098.

25. M. B. Hartt, "The Play Side of the Fair," 1100.

26. M. B. Hartt, "How to See the Pan-American Exposition," 489.

27. Goodrich, "Short Stories," 1054; Grant, "Notes," 456.

28. W. Maurice Newton, "Pan-American Exposition—Architectural Scheme," *American Architect and Building News* 70 (December 15, 1900), 83.

29. "Some Information Regarding the Pan-American Exposition, to be held at Buffalo, New York, from May 1 to November 1, 1901" (leaflet), in Pan-American Exposition Vertical File. See also the booklet "Electricity and Electrical Exhibits" (Buffalo, N.Y.: Pan-American Exposition Company, 1900).

30. Edward Hale Brush, "Artistic Side of the Pan-American Exposition," *The Architectural Review: For the Artist and Craftsman* 9 (London, 1901), 103.

31. Dunlap, "Wonderful Story," 1053; Goodrich, "Short Stories," 1082.

32. Grant, "Notes," 453.

33. Ibid.; Walter Hines Page, "The Pan-American Exposition," *World's Work* 2 (August 1901), 1017.

34. F. Maurice Newton, "Sculpture at the Exposition," *American Architect and Building News* 71 (February 2, 1901), 35–38.

35. C. Y. Turner, "Organization as Applied to Art," *Cosmopolitan* 31 (September 1901), 494–95.

36. Ibid.; Turner, "The Pan-American Color Scheme," *Independent* 53 (April 25, 1901), 948–49.

37. Turner, "Organization as Applied to Art," 495.

38. Page, "Pan-American Exposition," 1019.

39. Claude Bragdon, "Some Pan-American Impressions," *American Architect and Building News* 72 (May 11, 1901), 43.

40. W. Maurice Newton, "The Pan-American Exposition," *American Architect and Building News* 71 (December 15, 1900), 85. For the history of the skyscraper in America, see Paul Goldberger, *Skyscraper* (New York: Alfred A. Knopf, 1981).

41. Like the pavilions at the fair, Howard's Electric Tower was an impermanent structure made of steel and staff. However, after the Pan-American, the Buffalo General Electric Company adapted the design of the tower for its new company headquarters.

42. Turner, "Organization as Applied to Art," 495; Hawthorne, "Some Novelties," 487.

43. Rydell, *All the World's a Fair*, 2–8.

44. Hawthorne, "Some Novelties," 484.

45. Croly, "Some Novel Features," 592.

46. Hartley Davis, "The City of Living Light," *Munsey's Magazine* 26 (October 1901), 116, 116–29; Newton, "The Pan-American Exposition," 85.

47. Page, "Pan-American Exposition," 1023. For the ideology of the City Beautiful Movement as it relates to world's fairs, see Wilson, *City Beautiful Movement*, 91, 78–95.

48. Nicholas Murray Butler, "The Educational Influence of the Exposition," *Cosmopolitan* 31 (September 1901), 538–40.

49. Croly, "Some Novel Features," 611.

50. Ibid., 608–14.

51. Alan Trachtenberg, *The Incorporation of America: Culture and Society in the Gilded Age* (New York: Hill & Wang, 1982), 226–30.

52. Grant, "Notes," 454.

53. Albert Shaw, "The Real Value of the Exposition," *Cosmopolitan* 31 (September 1901), 466; John Brisben Walker, "City of the Future—A Prophecy," *Cosmopolitan* 31 (September 1901), 474.

54. Wilson, *City Beautiful Movement*, 75–77, 37–39.

55. Bragdon, "Some Pan-American Impressions," 44; Charles Mulford Robinson, "Echota: A Village Color Scheme," *Architects' and Builders' Magazine* 3 (April 1902), 241–43.

56. Croly, "Some Novel Features," 604.

57. Robinson, "Echota," 242–43; *Niagara Falls Gazette*, December 4 and 11, 1901.

58. Robinson, "Echota," 243, 242.

59. Bragdon, "Some Pan-American Impressions," 44; Hawthorne, "Some Novelties," 484; Walker, "City of the Future," 473.

60. Walker, "City of the Future," 475.

61. Sprague, "Some Phases of Exhibition Making," 22.

62. Walker, "City of the Future," 473–75; Shaw, "Real Value of the Exposition," 463–72; Croly, "Some Novel Features," 608–14; Hawthorne, "Some Novelties," 483.

63. R. L. Hartt, "The New Niagara," 78–84; Grant, "Notes," 454; Hawthorne, "Some Novelties," 484.

64. *Pan-American Exposition: Its Purpose and Its Plan*.

7. "The Wonder of the Age": Shredded Wheat and the Natural Food Company's Model Factory

1. Charles W. Hurd, "Color Display in the Dealer's Window and How It Pays," *Printer's Ink: A Journal for Advertisers* 87 (May 28, 1914), 23–24; *The Vital Question*,

Devoted to Natural Food (Niagara Falls, N.Y.: Natural Food Company, 1901), 1–8; *Niagara Falls Gazette*, December 22, 1900.

2. *Niagara Falls Gazette*, December 14 and 22, 1900; January 22, 1901. Perky also wrote *A Series of Lectures on the Food Subjects as Delivered at the Oread Institute* (Worcester, Mass., 1903) and *Wisdom and Foolishness* (Worcester, Mass., 1902).

3. David Armstrong and Elizabeth Metzger Armstrong, *The Great American Medicine Show: Being an Illustrated History of Hucksters, Healers, Health Evangelists, and Heroes from Plymouth Rock to the Present* (New York: Simon & Schuster, 1991), 107–16. For background on Charles W. Post, see William Cahn, *Out of the Cracker Barrel: The Nabisco Story, from Animal Crackers to Zuzus* (New York: Simon & Schuster, 1969), 208; Harvey Green, *Fit for America: Health, Fitness, and Sport in American Society* (New York: Pantheon Books, 1986), 307, 311. For background on John Harvey Kellogg, see the biography of his brother by Horace B. Powell, *The Original Has His Signature: W. K. Kellogg* (Englewood, N.J.: Prentice-Hall, 1956); Gerald Carson, *Cornflake Crusade* (New York: Rinehart, 1957).

4. *Vital Question*, 4–8; *The Happy Way to Health: A Little Book on How to Live in Harmony with Natural Law* (Niagara Falls, N.Y.: Shredded Wheat Company, 1917).

5. *Niagara Falls Gazette*, December 14 and 22, 1900; January 22, 1901.

6. *Wonders of Niagara Falls* (Niagara Falls, N.Y.: Shredded Wheat Company, 1914).

7. *Triscuit: The Electric Baked Food* (Niagara Falls, N.Y.: Natural Food Company, n.d.), in the *Collection of Advertising History*, Archives Center, National Museum of American History, Smithsonian Institution, Washington, D.C.

8. Natural Food Company postcards and advertising cards are held in the collections of the Local History Room of the Niagara Falls Public Library and the Buffalo and Erie County Historical Society; "Food Factory," *Harper's Weekly*, 57 (June 14, 1913), 15; *Wonders of Niagara;* Hurd, "Color Display," 24. The Natural Food Company had its own advertising department. See Cahn, *Out of the Cracker Barrel*, 216–17.

9. "Niagara Falls, the City," *National Magazine* 19 (October 1903), 129.

10. Niagara Falls Chamber of Commerce, *Niagara Falls, the Greatest Electric and Power City of the World* (Niagara Falls, N.Y., 1897), 62. The renowned engineers Clemons Herschel and G. W. G. Ferris, designer of the Ferris Wheel, subscribed to the same prediction. See Clemons Herschel, "Niagara Mill Sites, Water Connections, and Turbines," *Cassier's Magazine* 8 (July 1895), 249–50; Ferris's predictions are in William T. Love, *Model City: The New Manufacturing Center of America* (Buffalo, N.Y.: Niagara Power and Development Company, n.d. [1901]), 5.

11. "Niagara Falls, the City," 129; *Niagara Falls Gazette*, December 14 and 18, 1900.

12. See William H. Wilson, *The City Beautiful Movement* (Baltimore: Johns Hopkins University Press, 1989), 78–86.

13. Some of the more striking headlines in the *Niagara Falls Gazette*, include "Typhoid Fever Is Our Scourge" (March 15, 1900); and "Phew! What Makes the Horrible Stench!" (May 28, 1901).

14. Budgett Meakin, *Model Factories and Villages: Ideal Conditions of Labor and Housing* (1905; reprint, Garland Publishing, 1985), 67, 19–37. See also Daniel Rodgers, *The Work Ethic in Industrial America, 1850–1920* (Chicago: University of Chicago Press, 1978), 34; Daniel Nelson, *Managers and Workers: Origins of the New Factory System, in the United States, 1880–1920* (Madison: University of Wisconsin Press, 1975), 3–31. The problem of industrial fire, along with a promising solution to the problem, is the

subject of an article by Edward Atkinson, "Slow-Burning Construction," *Century Magazine* 37 (February 1889), 566–79.

15. Frederik Atherton Fernald, *The Index Guide to Buffalo and Niagara Falls* (Buffalo: Frederik A. Fernald, 1910), 172.

16. See John R. Stilgoe, *Metropolitan Corridor: Railroads and the American Scene* (New Haven: Yale University Press, 1983), 78.

17. See Robert A. Woods, "The Human Touch in Industry," *Munsey's Magazine* 29 (June 1903), 321–28; Meakin, *Model Factories*, 20–30 and passim; and Paul Monroe, "Possibilities of the Present Industrial System," *American Journal of Sociology* 3 (May 1898), 729–53. See also Nelson, *Managers and Workers*, 22–28, 101–21.

18. Edgar W. Work, "Trouble in the Cash Register Works," *Independent* 53 (June 13, 1901), 1371, 1371–73; "A Deplorable Strike," *The Nation* 73 (July 4, 1901), 6–7. See also Monroe, "Possibilities of the Present Industrial System," 739–53.

19. *Niagara Falls Gazette*, December 14, 1900; March 23 and August 31, 1901. See also E. T. Williams, *Niagara: Queen of Wonders* (Niagara Falls, N.Y., 1916), 104–5.

20. "Niagara Falls as Baker and Waiter," *World's Work* 3 (April 1902), 2017; *Niagara Falls Gazette*, April 16, 1901; December 14 and 22, 1900.

21. *Niagara Falls Gazette*, January 22, 1901; *Shredded Wheat Dishes, together with a Treatise on the Food Problem, with a Description of the Finest, Cleanest, Most Hygienic Food Factory* (Niagara Falls, N.Y.: Natural Food Company, 1910), 3.

22. *Niagara Falls Gazette*, January 2, 1901; April 16 and 22, 1901; February 14, 1901; January 2, 1902.

23. Letter in *Buffalo Express* reprinted in *Niagara Falls Gazette*, December 17, 1900; *Wonders of Niagara Falls*.

24. *Niagara Falls Gazette*, January 22, 1901; December 15, 1900.

25. Early sanitariums offered water cures, pure diets, fresh air, exercise, and instruction in the art of living. At Battle Creek, Michigan, John Harvey Kellogg expanded the sanitorium into a "University of Health." See James Whorton, *Crusaders for Fitness: The History of American Health Reformers* (Princeton: Princeton University Press, 1982), 78, 204; Harvey Green, *Fit for Life*, 65–66, 132–35.

26. *Niagara Falls Gazette*, December 14 and 22, 1900; March 11, 1901; April 16 and 22, 1901. According to Meakin, industrialists who lived on the factory grounds promoted a sound atmosphere for their enterprise. Meakin, *Model Factories*, 24–25.

27. *Niagara Falls Gazette*, April 22, 1901. Processed food companies began running cooking schools at the turn of the century to ease resistance to precooked, manufactured food. See Laura Shapiro, *Perfection Salad: Women and Cooking at the Turn of the Century* (New York: Henry Holt, 1986), 80–168.

28. *History of the Oread Collegiate Institute, Worcester, 1849–1881*, ed. Martha Burt Wright (New Haven, Conn.: Tuttle, Morchrome & Taylor Co., 1905), 450. See Shapiro, *Perfection Salad*, 4–17, 139–43.

29. *Wonders of Niagara Falls*.

30. *Niagara Falls Gazette*, December 14, 1900; *Shredded Wheat Dishes*, 3; Williams, *Niagara: Queen of Wonders*, 104. See also "Natural Food Company" and "Shredded Wheat Company" postcards and advertising cards in the *Collection of Advertising History* and in the Local History Room of the Niagara Falls Public Library.

31. Meakin, *Model Factories*, 77–78. For background on the architecture of the American Renaissance, see Richard Guy Wilson, *American Renaissance, Eighteen Seventy-Six to Nineteen Seventeen* (Seattle: University of Washington Press, 1979).

32. See Cheryl Barton, "Institutional and Corporate Landscapes," in *American Landscape Architecture: Designers and Places*, ed. William H. Tishler (Washington, D.C.: Preservation Press, 1989), 151.

33. Shredded Wheat Company advertisement, *Town and Country*, May 10, 1915, in *Collection of American Advertising*, Smithsonian Institution. Katherine C. Grier, *Comforts and Culture: People, Parlors, and Upholstery, 1850–1930* (Amherst: University of Massachusetts Press, 1988), 30, 20, 19–58.

34. *Happy Way to Health.*

35. *Niagara Falls Gazette*, May 16, 1901, and August 29, 1901; "Niagara Falls as Baker and Waiter," 2017.

36. Quotation from *Wonders of Niagara Falls*. See also Upton Sinclair, *The Jungle* (New York, 1906). For background on the muckrakers and the attempt to safeguard the purity of food, see Robert Crunden, *Ministers of Reform: The Progressives' Achievements in American Civilization, 1889–1920* (Chicago: University of Illinois Press, 1984), 162–74; Susan Strasser, *Satisfaction Guaranteed: The Making of the American Mass Market* (New York: Pantheon Books, 1989), 255–60.

37. *Literary Digest*, General Electric advertisement in Cecelia Tichi, *Shifting Gears: Technology, Literature, Culture in Modernist America* (Chapel Hill: University of North Carolina Press, 1987), 83.

38. Samuel Vyle, "The Advent of the Shredded Wheat Biscuit," *Chamber's Journal* 77 (January 27, 1900), 129–30; *Vital Question*, 106; "Niagara Falls as Baker and Waiter," 2017.

39. *Triscuit, the Electric Baked Food;* Strasser, *Satisfaction Guaranteed*, 55.

40. "Niagara Falls as Baker and Waiter," 2017; "Niagara Falls, the City," 129–32; Nels August Begtson and Donee Griffith, *The Wheat Industry, for Use in the Schools* (New York, 1915), 174–76; and Meakin, *Model Factories*, 77, 96, and passim.

41. *Niagara Falls of Today: Domestic and Industrial* (Niagara Falls, N.Y.: Board of Trade, 1907); *Niagara Falls Gazette*, May 16, 1901; Meakin, *Model Factories*, 107.

42. *A Food Factory: Shredded Wheat and Niagara's Oldest Power Plant* (Niagara Falls, N.Y.: Shredded Wheat Company, 1914); *Niagara Falls Gazette*, July 16, 1901.

43. "A Food Factory"; Meakin, *Model Factories*, 143–44; *Happy Way to Health.*

44. *Vital Question*, 111; Meakin, *Model Factories*, 203. See also Rodgers, *Work Ethic in Industrial America*, 102, 94–124.

45. Meakin, *Model Factories*, 77–78, 89, 96; Barton, "Institutional and Corporate Landscapes," 150.

46. Meakin, *Model Factories*, 245–46.

47. *Happy Way to Health.*

48. Quoted in Cahn, *Out of the Cracker Barrel*, 214.

49. *Niagara Falls Gazette*, December 22, 1900.

50. Meakin, *Model Factories*, 164.

51. *Niagara Falls Gazette*, December 14, 1900; August 31, 1901.

52. *Niagara Falls Gazette*, December 14, 1901; "Niagara Falls, the City," 129; *Niagara Falls of Today.*

53. "Niagara Falls, the City," 129–32; *Niagara Falls Gazette*, September 27, 1901.

54. *Niagara Falls Gazette*, August 29, 1901; postcard, "Niagara Falls," Vertical File, in Buffalo and Erie County Historical Society, Buffalo, New York.

55. *Happy Way to Health*. The health reformer and systematizer Horace Fletcher professed to be "charmed beyond description and gratified beyond expression with all

the details of organization. The atmosphere is redolent of mutual welfare in the true sense." See Natural Food Company advertisement, clipping, December 24, 1908, in "Shredded Wheat Company" folder, *Collection of Advertising History.*

56. "Niagara Falls, the City," 129.

Epilogue

1. "Over the Falls in a Barrel," *Literary Digest* 23 (November 9, 1901), 558.

2. John L. Harper and J. A. Johnson, "Hydroelectric Development at Niagara Falls," *Journal of the American Institute of Electrical Engineers* 40 (July 1921), 563, 561.

3. See Thomas V. Welch, "Report of the Superintendent," in *Sixth Annual Report of the Reservation Commissioners of the State Reservation at Niagara, from October, 1888 to September 30, 1889* (Albany, N.Y.: J. B. Lyon, 1890), 21, and J. Horace McFarland, testimony, Secretary of War, in *Hearings Upon Applications for Permits for the Diversion of Water from Niagara River . . . before the Secretary of War at Niagara Falls, N.Y., July 12, 1906* (Washington, D.C., 1906), 13.

4. In addition, a regrettable experiment in the planting of nonindigenous shrubs succeeded only in disfiguring the reservation islands. See John Chamberlain, "Native Plants at Niagara Falls," *Garden and Forest* 9 (July 1, 1896), 268.

5. Some of the more sensational articles in the *Niagara Falls Gazette* included "Hot Report of Supt. Welch on 'Scandalous' Condition of Affairs in This City" (September 9, 1901); "Reservation Police May Conduct a Raid" (September 28, 1901).

6. Charles Mason Dow, *The State Reservation at Niagara: A History* (Albany, N.Y., 1914), 189, 188–91.

7. John M. Clarke, "The Menace to Niagara," *Popular Science Monthly* 66 (April 1905), 496.

8. Dow, *State Reservation*, 195. Dow was president of the commissioners of the New York State Reservation at Niagara Falls from 1903 to 1914. For an analysis of the factors that made Queen Victoria Park so different from the New York State Reservation. See Gail Edith H. Evans, "Storm over Niagara: A Study of the Interplay of Cultural Values, Resource Politics, and Environmental Policy in an International Setting, 1670s–1950" (Ph.D. diss., University of California at Santa Barbara, 1991).

9. Dow, *State Reservation*, 112.

10. See the *Annual Report of the Reservation Commissioners* for each year during this period. See especially Andrew H. Green to Hon. Walter Q. Gresham, Secretary of State, October 17, 1894, in *Twelfth Annual Report of the Commissioners of the State Reservation at Niagara, from October 1, 1894 to September 30, 1895* (Albany, N.Y., 1896), 49–50; see also Dow, *State Reservation*, 117–23; Evans, "Storm over Niagara," 329–31.

11. Robert M. Crunden, *Ministers of Reform: The Progressives' Achievement in American Civilization, 1889–1920* (Chicago: University of Illinois Press, 1984), ix, 3–16; Robert H. Weibe, *The Search for Order, 1877–1920* (New York: Hill & Wang, 1967), 111–32.

12. Evans, "Storm over Niagara," 360–62.

13. William H. Wilson, *The City Beautiful Movement* (Baltimore: Johns Hopkins University Press, 1989), 50–52. See also Peter Schmitt, *Back to Nature: The Arcadian Myth in Urban America* (Baltimore: Johns Hopkins University Press, 1990), 30, 15–31.

14. For surveys of the muckrakers, see Herbert Shapiro, ed., *The Muckrakers and American Society* (Boston: D. C. Heath, 1968); Louis Filler, *The Muckrakers* (University Park: Pennsylvania State University Press, 1976); Arthur and Lila Weinberg, *The Muckrakers: The Era in Journalism That Moved America to Reform* (New York: G. P. Putnam, 1964), 242–44.

15. "Niagara and the Plutocrats," *Review of Reviews* 33 (May 1906), 522; "The Waste of Niagara," *The Independent* 58 (March 16, 1905), 620; "Niagara Be Damned," *Collier's*, February 17, 1906 cover; Gilson Willets, "The Rape of Niagara," *Leslie's Weekly* 102 (March 1, 1906), 209–10.

16. Alton Dean Adams, "The Destruction of Niagara Falls," *Cassier's Magazine* 27 (March 1905), 413; Clarke, "The Menace to Niagara," 497 (note 7 above); "Vandalism at Niagara Falls," *Scientific American* 92 (April 15, 1905), 298.

17. J. Horace McFarland, "Shall We Make a Coal-Pile of Niagara," *Ladies' Home Journal* 22 (September 1905), 19, 20.

18. Ibid., 19.

19. Ibid., 20.

20. Edward Bok to Horace McFarland, April 19, 1906, in U.S. Congress, House Committee on Rivers and Harbors, *Preservation of Niagara Falls (H.R. 18024), Hearings*, 59th Cong., 1st sess., April 1906, 161. See also Edward Bok, *The Americanization of Edward Bok* (New York: Scribner's, 1920), 352–55.

21. U.S. Congress, *Preservation of Niagara Falls, Message from the President of the United States Transmitting the Report of the American Members of the International Waterways Commission*, 59th Cong., 1st sess., March 1906, S. Doc. 242, 11, 10; "Public—No. 367, An Act for the Control and Regulation of the Waters of Niagara River, for the Preservation of Niagara Falls and for Other Purposes," U.S. Congress, *Preservation of Niagara Falls (H.R. 18024), Hearings*, 324–25.

22. Clemons Herschel, testimony, U.S. Congress, *Preservation of Niagara Falls (H.R. 18024), Hearings*, 135–41; Francis V. Greene, *Niagara Falls in 1907* (Niagara Falls, Ont., 1907), 47. The majority of those who testified at the hearings represented power and manufacturing interests.

23. Herschel testimony, *Preservation of Niagara Falls, Hearings*, 139; John Lyell Harper, *The Suicide of the Falls* (Niagara Falls, N.Y.: Niagara Falls Power Company, 1917); Harper and Johnson, "Hydroelectric Development at Niagara Falls," 564.

24. Peter A. Porter, *Niagara, an Aboriginal Center of Trade* (Niagara Falls, N.Y., 1906), 73–74, 3; Peter A. Porter, "The Niagara Region in History," *Cassier's Magazine* 8 (July 1895), 384.

25. Francis Stetson testimony in *Hearings before the Secretary of War, July 12, 1906*, 24.

26. Weinberg and Weinberg, *The Muckrakers*, 242–44.

27. Francis Stetson testimony in *Hearings before the Secretary of War, July 12, 1906*, 22–23.

28. Ibid., 25, 23.

29. Roderick Nash, *Wilderness and the American Mind*, 3d ed. (New Haven: Yale University Press, 1982), 134–40.

30. Edward G. Acheson and Arthur V. Davis, testimony, *Preservation of Niagara Falls (H.R. 18024), Hearings*, 215–17, 217–19; General Electric Company, "The Industrial Value of Niagara Falls," in ibid., 291–97.

31. "Public—No. 367," in *Preservation of Niagara Falls Hearings*, 324–25; Dow, *State Reservation*, 138. See also Edward T. Williams, "Harnessing Niagara and Tunnelling Catskills," *National Magazine* 41 (October 1914), 41–44.

32. Richard G. Skerrett, "Two Million Horse Power from the Niagara River," *Scientific American* 117 (December 29, 1917), 489; *Niagara Power: What Nature Has Provided, Man Should Utilize* (Niagara Falls, N.Y.: Thomson-Porter Cataract Co., n.d.); Peter A. Porter is quoted in "Power from the Lower Niagara," in *Illustrated Buffalo Express*, August 8, 1915.

33. *Niagara Falls Junior: A 2,000,000 Horsepower Development* (Niagara Falls, N.Y.: Thomson-Porter Cataract Co., 1916).

34. Thomas H. Norton, "Niagara on Tap," *Popular Science Monthly* 88 (February 1916), 179; *The Sun*, October 10, 1915. Undetectable waterwheels on scaffolds behind the cataract would harness 30 to 40 percent of Niagara's power when the water was turned on for tourists. See Thomas H. Norton, "Niagara on Tap," *Literary Digest* 52 (April 8, 1916), 964.

35. Norton, "Niagara on Tap," 181. *The Sun*, October 10, 1915.

36. *The Sun*, October 10, 1915.

37. "Niagara Falls as It Isn't, But May Be," *Herald American*, World Magazine Section, November 7, 1915.

38. Ibid.

39. William Joseph Showalter, "Niagara at the Battlefront," *National Geographic* 31 (May 1917), 413.

40. Ibid., 413–16. See also Skerrett, "Two Million Horse Power from the Niagara River," 489.

41. "Home Life in Buffalo," n.d., newspaper clipping in "Niagara Power" Vertical File, Buffalo and Erie County Historical Society.

42. "Memo Sheet 12, Pan-American Bureau of Publicity," in Pan-American Exposition—Tickets, Invitations, Vertical File, Buffalo and Erie County Historical Society.

43. "Buffalo Electric Show, October 16–25, 1919" (Buffalo, N.Y., 1919) (program), in "Exhibitions" Vertical File, Buffalo and Erie County Historical Society; Elbert Hubbard, *Power; or, The Story of Niagara Falls* (East Aurora, N.Y.: The Roycrofters, 1914), 27 and passim.

44. "Niagara's Industrial Beauty," *Literary Digest* 45 (December 7, 1912), 1060; "Niagara Already Spoiled," *Literary Digest* 56 (March 23, 1918), 24.

45. Clemons Herschel, quoted in Edward Dean Adams, *Niagara Power: History of the Niagara Falls Power Company, 1886–1918* (Niagara Falls, N.Y., 1927), 2:362–63.

46. Samuel Wyer, *Niagara Falls: Its Power Possibilities and Preservation* (Washington, D.C.: Smithsonian, 1925), 5.

47. William Cahn, *Out of the Cracker Barrel* (New York: Simon & Schuster, 1969), 217, 220.

Index